The
TEACHERS' STANDARDS
in PRIMARY SCHOOLS

SAGE was founded in 1965 by Sara Miller McCune to support the dissemination of usable knowledge by publishing innovative and high-quality research and teaching content. Today, we publish over 900 journals, including those of more than 400 learned societies, more than 800 new books per year, and a growing range of library products including archives, data, case studies, reports, and video. SAGE remains majority-owned by our founder, and after Sara's lifetime will become owned by a charitable trust that secures our continued independence.

Los Angeles | London | New Delhi | Singapore | Washington DC | Melbourne

The TEACHERS' STANDARDS *in* PRIMARY SCHOOLS

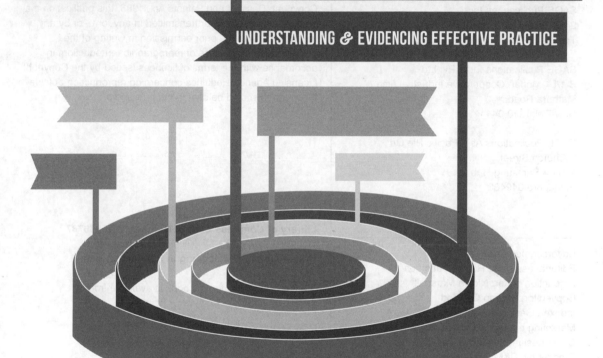

UNDERSTANDING & EVIDENCING EFFECTIVE PRACTICE

JOY CARROLL & GENEA N. ALEXANDER

Los Angeles | London | New Delhi
Singapore | Washington DC | Melbourne

Los Angeles | London | New Delhi
Singapore | Washington DC | Melbourne

SAGE Publications Ltd
1 Oliver's Yard
55 City Road
London EC1Y 1SP

SAGE Publications Inc.
2455 Teller Road
Thousand Oaks, California 91320

SAGE Publications India Pvt Ltd
B 1/I 1 Mohan Cooperative Industrial Area
Mathura Road
New Delhi 110 044

SAGE Publications Asia-Pacific Pte Ltd
3 Church Street
#10-04 Samsung Hub
Singapore 049483

Editor: James Clark
Editorial assistant: Robert Patterson
Production editor: Nicola Marshall
Copyeditor: Sharon Cawood
Indexer: Gary Kirby
Marketing manager: Dilhara Attygalle
Cover designer: Naomi Robinson
Typeset by: C&M Digitals (P) Ltd, Chennai, India
Printed and bound in Great Britain by Ashford
Colour Press Ltd

Library of Congress Control Number: 2015946787

British Library Cataloguing in Publication data

A catalogue record for this book is available from
the British Library

ISBN 978-1-4739-0695-2
ISBN 978-1-4739-0696-9 (pbk)

At SAGE we take sustainability seriously. Most of our products are printed in the UK using FSC papers and boards.
When we print overseas we ensure sustainable papers are used as measured by the PREPS grading system.
We undertake an annual audit to monitor our sustainability.

Joy Carroll would like to thank Matthew, Nicola and Ellie, who have been influential in making this book a reality. Their values and traits of belief, honesty and trust, were there in childhood and are present in every effective teacher. Forever my rocks.

Genea Nicole Alexander would like to dedicate this book to Stella, Trevor and Jon, who, combined, represent the supportive, nurturing past and who have helped to shape the person I am today. To Kennedy Tai, representative of the present, my greatest achievement, unwavering source of inspiration and hope and a future 'mover and shaker'.

CONTENTS

ABOUT THE AUTHORS

 **Joy Carroll** is a senior lecturer in Primary Initial Teacher Training (ITT) at the University of Worcester. She teaches on the undergraduate and post-graduate courses and is Partnership Placement Manager. Before moving into ITE she worked as a teacher and Assistant Headteacher in primary schools in London, Hereford, Worcester and Stafford and was the Manager of a private Nursery School. Following this, Joy worked as an Advisor within the area of School Workforce in a Local Authority, working closely with schools on deployment of support staff. She is currently working on doctoral research into how schools and universities work collaboratively to support ITE.

 **Genea Nicole Alexander** is the PGCE Primary Course Leader at the University of Worcester. As a Senior Lecturer in Primary Initial Teacher Training (ITT), she has developed a keen drive to support adult learners to become the best they can be, as child educators. As part of a dedicated team, she has worked with both undergraduate and post-graduate trainees in her specialist areas of primary music, languages and professional and pedagogical practice. Genea has an active role in the management, supervision and support of trainee teachers and impact-focussed, is dedicated to promoting the best outcomes for all: pupils, trainee teachers and school partners alike. Prior to her career in ITT, she worked as a primary teacher, in age phases spanning nursery to year 6 and completed her MA in education, with a music specialism. She continues to research actively, as an academic.

ACKNOWLEDGEMENTS

This book would not have been possible without the inspiration and enthusiasm of the next generation of teachers at the University of Worecester who gave Joy Carroll the idea that such a book was needed.

Joy Carroll would like to thank the amazing colleagues she has worked with in schools who have been influential in shaping her vision and views of education. Finally, many thanks to Susan Mercer for her encouragement and for always being there.

Genea Nicole Alexander would like to thank the teachers and academics with whom she has had the pleasure of working for their expert advice; for modelling excellent pedagogical practice; their invaluable professional guidance and continual inspiration. Specific thanks to Richard Hunter, Joe Purnell, Paul Smith, Judy Bridges, Sarah Gillett and Dr. Scott Buckler.

INTRODUCTION

'And what is the use of a book', thought Alice, 'without pictures or conversation?' (Carroll, 1865, p. 17)

Alice was a learner. She had clear views and opinions on various topics and worked within the boundaries of rules, logic and order. She was educated and inquisitive; she had formed her own philosophies, yet sought answers to questions with curiosity and determination and it seems wholly suitable for us to make reference to these characteristics when setting the scene for this book and considering the role of the newly qualified teacher (NQT), embarking on a journey of their own and seeking ways forward in practice.

The Teachers' Standards in Primary Schools: Understanding and Evidencing Effective Practice is an essential companion for all primary trainee teachers, newly and recently qualified teachers and school mentors. With regard to Alice's musing concerning the perceived use of a book (Carroll, 1865), our intention is for this book to be just that: useful. It is not intended to be read in isolation, from cover to cover, unless this is your preferred style. Conversely, this text is recommended as an invaluable tool to be used in conjunction with professional dialogues, engagement with the many activities, models and ideas suggested within the book and a dedication, on the part of the reader, to participate in professional development, in order to impact positively on the children within their care.

The book provides practical guidance on ways in which the Teachers' Standards (DfE, 2013a), which were revised in 2012 and adapted in July 2013, can be evidenced. It supports current government legislation, whilst recognising the future possibilities of educational development and the flexibility to offer transferable advice, support and ideas in the event of subsequent adaptations. This is achieved through excellent coverage of the key aspects that make up the foundations of effective practice. This essential handbook provides a current, up-to-date view and sets the Teachers' Standards in a national context, providing background, theory and practice, in order for readers to gain a holistic understanding of the meaning of each standard and ways in which supporting evidence can be found.

The Teachers' Standards: what are they and to whom do they apply?

The Teachers' Standards were introduced following the recommendations in the reports of the 'Independent Review of Teachers' Standards', chaired by Sally Coates, in order to set a clear baseline of expectations for the professional practice and con-duct of teachers (DfE, 2013a). The standards define the minimum level of practice expected of trainees and teachers and are used to assess all trainees working towards QTS and those completing a statutory induction period. They are also used to assess the performance of all teachers with QTS and may be used to assess the performance of teachers who are subject to these regulations and who hold qualified teacher learn-ing and skills (QTLS) status.

Why do trainee teachers, newly and recently qualified teachers and mentors need this book?

The over-arching aim of this book is to break down each of the Teachers' Standards into their sub-sets and provide useful guidance and support in evidencing each crucial ele-ment, drawing on theory and examples from practice. The chapters aim to de-mystify the Teachers' Standards and help readers to both know and understand them, allowing them to underpin effective practice and gain confidence in the provision of relevant evidence.

The book is useful to anyone engaging with the Teachers' Standards and can be used as a practical pedagogical tool in ensuring effective learning and teaching. It will offer background and contextual information and discuss how the standards are embedded in effective practice during the different stages of a teacher's career. There will be significant links between the standards, showing how they are inter-related and why this is of paramount importance when seeking evidence in daily practice. In addition, reference will be made to short reflections and advice, embedded in chapters, from professionals in the field of education.

Breaking it down

For ease of reference, we have included several key features in each chapter, which aim to orientate the reader. A brief overview of each feature is outlined below.

What's this all about?

This section is situated at the beginning of each chapter and aims to help the reader to understand how the standard can be applied to classroom practice and why this standard is important to teachers. It provides a rationale for the chapter whilst considering the key issues within the standard.

How can this be demonstrated?

This is the scope of the standard and further breaks down the different aspects of the standard into tangible, practical aspects of practice.

Chapter overview

As the title suggests, this provides an outline to the chapter and draws on theory to set the scene for the breakdown of each standard. It provides an opportunity to consider the synthesis of theory and practice.

Taking it apart and putting it back together

These sections commence the breakdown of each standard into sub-sets. Each sub-set is explored in detail and then considers opportunities from both theory and daily practice in finding evidence to meet the standards, as fully as possible.

Top Tips

Each chapter contains many tips to aid success, including useful ideas to try out.

Practice examples

Each chapter contains many fictional examples of practice, which add context to each of the standard sub-sets. The practice examples aid the reader in visualising how evidence may be collected in order to support the Teachers' Standards and are useful in the provision of ideas. It should be noted that all practice examples are fictitious.

Key questions

Each chapter contains thought-provoking questions with which teachers can engage, to support their developing practice.

Possible sources of evidence

A useful summary list of places where evidence may be acquired is provided at the end of each chapter. This provides a springboard for teachers wishing to seek evidence to link to their own practice.

Chapter summary

Each chapter will conclude with a revision of the key elements of the chapter and the learning opportunities within, thus supporting and encouraging active critical reflection.

What's your modus operandi?

The book is written with flexibility in mind. There is no requirement to read the text in one sitting, from cover to cover. Whilst there are helpful links and recurrent themes throughout the book, the chapters have been written in a way that allows the reader to engage with them at different points, according to identified professional development needs. The many activities and ideas can be engaged with at the leisure of the reader and each chapter provides significant opportunities for further exploration and reflection. Above all, this book aims to help teachers in developing an understanding of the Teachers' Standards and in knowing how to locate strong supporting evidence.

'Would you tell me, please, which way I ought to go from here?'

'That depends a good deal on where you want to get to,' said the Cat.

'I don't much care where –,' said Alice.

'Then it doesn't matter which way you go,' said the Cat.

'– so long as I get *somewhere*,' Alice added as an explanation.

'Oh, you're sure to do that,' said the Cat, 'if you only walk long enough.' (Carroll, 1865, p. 62)

However you choose to engage with the book and whichever way you walk on your journey, we hope that you find it a useful source of support and a key tool in helping you on your road to the successful completion of NQT induction and beyond.

THE TEACHERS' STANDARDS QUICK REFERENCE TOOL

Preamble

Teachers make the education of their pupils their first concern and are accountable for achieving the highest possible standards in work and conduct. Teachers act with honesty and integrity; have strong subject knowledge, keep their knowledge and skills as teachers up to date and are self-critical; forge positive professional relationships; and work with parents in the best interests of their pupils.

Part One: Teaching

A teacher must:

1. Set high expectations which inspire, motivate and challenge pupils:

- establish a safe and stimulating environment for pupils, rooted in mutual respect
- set goals that stretch and challenge pupils of all backgrounds, abilities and dispositions
- demonstrate consistently the positive attitudes, values and behaviour which are expected of pupils.

2. Promote good progress and outcomes by pupils:

- be accountable for pupils' attainment, progress and outcomes
- be aware of pupils' capabilities and their prior knowledge, and plan teaching to build on these
- guide pupils to reflect on the progress they have made and their emerging needs
- demonstrate knowledge and understanding of how pupils learn and how this impacts on teaching
- encourage pupils to take a responsible and conscientious attitude to their own work and study.

3. Demonstrate good subject and curriculum knowledge:

- have a secure knowledge of the relevant subject(s) and curriculum areas, foster and maintain pupils' interest in the subject, and address misunderstandings
- demonstrate a critical understanding of developments in the subject and curriculum areas, and promote the value of scholarship
- demonstrate an understanding of and take responsibility for promoting high standards of literacy, articulacy and the correct use of standard English, whatever the teacher's specialist subject
- if teaching early reading, demonstrate a clear understanding of systematic synthetic phonics
- if teaching early mathematics, demonstrate a clear understanding of appropriate teaching strategies.

(Continued)

(Continued)

4. Plan and teach well-structured lessons:

- impart knowledge and develop understanding through effective use of lesson time
- promote a love of learning and children's intellectual curiosity
- set homework and plan other out-of-class activities to consolidate and extend the knowledge and understanding pupils have acquired
- reflect systematically on the effectiveness of lessons and approaches to teaching
- contribute to the design and provision of an engaging curriculum within the relevant subject area(s).

5. Adapt teaching to respond to the strengths and needs of all pupils:

- know when and how to differentiate appropriately, using approaches which enable pupils to be taught effectively
- have a secure understanding of how a range of factors can inhibit pupils' ability to learn, and how best to overcome these
- demonstrate an awareness of the physical, social and intellectual development of children, and know how to adapt teaching to support pupils' education at different stages of development
- have a clear understanding of the needs of all pupils, including those with special educational needs; those of high ability; those with English as an additional language; those with disabilities; and be able to use and evaluate distinctive teaching approaches to engage and support them.

6. Make accurate and productive use of assessment:

- know and understand how to assess the relevant subject and curriculum areas, including statutory assessment requirements
- make use of formative and summative assessment to secure pupils' progress
- use relevant data to monitor progress, set targets, and plan subsequent lessons
- give pupils regular feedback, both orally and through accurate marking, and encourage pupils to respond to the feedback.

7. Manage behaviour effectively to ensure a good and safe learning environment:

- have clear rules and routines for behaviour in classrooms, and take responsibility for promoting good and courteous behaviour both in classrooms and around the school, in accordance with the school's behaviour policy

(Continued)

(Continued)

- have high expectations of behaviour, and establish a framework for discipline with a range of strategies, using praise, sanctions and rewards consistently and fairly
- manage classes effectively, using approaches which are appropriate to pupils' needs in order to involve and motivate them
- maintain good relationships with pupils, exercise appropriate authority, and act decisively when necessary.

8. Fulfil wider professional responsibilities:

- make a positive contribution to the wider life and ethos of the school
- develop effective professional relationships with colleagues, knowing how and when to draw on advice and specialist support
- deploy support staff effectively
- take responsibility for improving teaching through appropriate professional development, responding to advice and feedback from colleagues
- communicate effectively with parents with regard to pupils' achievements and well-being.

Part Two: Personal and professional conduct

A teacher is expected to demonstrate consistently high standards of personal and professional conduct. The following statements define the behaviour and attitudes which set the required standard for conduct throughout a teacher's career.

Teachers uphold public trust in the profession and maintain high standards of ethics and behaviour, within and outside school, by:

- treating pupils with dignity, building relationships rooted in mutual respect, and at all times observing proper boundaries appropriate to a teacher's professional position
- having regard for the need to safeguard pupils' well-being, in accordance with statutory provisions
- showing tolerance of and respect for the rights of others
- not undermining fundamental British values, including democracy, the rule of law, individual liberty and mutual respect, and tolerance of those with different faiths and beliefs
- ensuring that personal beliefs are not expressed in ways which exploit pupils' vulnerability or might lead them to break the law.

(Continued)

(Continued)

Teachers must have proper and professional regard for the ethos, policies and practices of the school in which they teach, and maintain high standards in their own attendance and punctuality.

Teachers must have an understanding of, and always act within, the statutory frameworks which set out their professional duties and responsibilities.

Source: Teachers' Standards (DfE, 2013a)

CHAPTER 1

SET HIGH EXPECTATIONS WHICH INSPIRE, MOTIVATE AND CHALLENGE PUPILS

Teachers' Standard 1 – Set high expectations which inspire, motivate and challenge pupils:

1a Establish a safe and stimulating environment for pupils, rooted in mutual respect

1b Set goals that stretch and challenge pupils of all backgrounds, abilities and dispositions

1c Demonstrate consistently the positive attitudes, values and behaviour which are expected of pupils.

What is this all about?

Having high expectations and instilling high expectations are significant traits of the astute professional teacher. By demonstrating fair and positive behaviours, pupils can learn to develop behaviour for learning. A positive classroom ethos can result in more successful and meaningful learning experiences for pupils, with minimum disruption to learning. By establishing a safe and stimulating environment in which pupils feel secure, are clear about agreed rules and are encouraged to learn, successful outcomes can be facilitated and the overall learning experience can become more enjoyable and positive. Similarly, an inclusive, child-centred philosophy that seeks to provide outstanding opportunities for the pupils in your care, is an essential teacher quality. It is critical to ensure that these opportunities are bespoke and tailored to challenge individuals, to ensure the best outcomes for all.

How can this be demonstrated?

Teachers' Standard 1 encompasses the values an effective teacher should hold in successful practice. It starts with how you envision your classroom environment to be exciting, engaging and calm. What stems from this vision is the consideration of how these qualities can be achieved and how this impacts on learning and pupil progress.

In daily practice, consistency, such as the development of regular routines, is essential in order to promote habitually positive behaviours and an environment in which pupils wish to learn and be successful. In addition, challenging pupils to exceed their potential is a pre-requisite to ensuring outstanding pupil progress. These goals may be achieved through excellent behaviour management; clear systems for rewards and sanctions; attention to detail with classroom display; excellent, thoroughly considered questioning; and promotion of pupil autonomy. These are many examples of good practice and key ingredients in promoting successful learning experiences, to which we will return in subsequent chapters. Of course, learning from other professionals is a superb way of deciding on what works for you as a teacher and whilst there will be excellent examples of highly effective practice within your individual setting, let us not forget that the world of the internet can yield inspiring results, from educational websites to sharing forums. As an effective professional, it is your responsibility to engage with and implement good practice, in order to impact positively on and engage the pupils you teach.

Chapter overview

How much effort do you put into inspiring, motivating and challenging pupils? How high a priority do you place on this element of your developing practice?

Nottingham (2013) considers the desire to achieve as being essential to the outcome: 'how much effort someone puts into a task is equal to how much they *want* to achieve it multiplied by how much they expect to achieve it (p. 12).'

When considering the above citation, do so from dual perspectives: that of the *teacher* and that of the *learner*. From the standpoint of the effective teacher, the fact that you are taking the time to engage in professional development by reading this book, is the first step on the path to effective practice. Have high expectations for your own personal and professional capabilities. Now take the perspective of the learner and ask yourself the following question: *How do you instil, in your pupils, positivity, respect and the motivation to succeed and exceed expectation?* If you have some answers to this question, you are part-way to achieving and evidencing successful practice.

In this chapter, we intend to explore the following key themes:

- Ways in which teachers can encourage pupils to engage in and display positive behaviours *for* learning, grounded in mutual respect and perseverance to succeed.
- Ways in which the stimulating classroom environment can be used as a 'tool' for learning, whilst we explore how this can be created. In addition, we discuss how to challenge *all* pupils in daily practice and develop an understanding of ways in which hearing 'the pupil voice' can be explored and used to good effect, in the classroom.
- How teachers and pupils can work as a team in order to promote positive attitudes, values and behaviour.

Having considered a rationale for the standard, the chapter will provide exemplars of effective practice that the reader could consider adapting for personal use, in order to develop further. Integrating theory with practice, the chapter will go on to explore the background and nature of inclusive education and ways in which teachers can ensure that they are meeting the needs of and challenging pupils of all backgrounds, abilities and dispositions. In the chapter, there will be opportunities for the application and practice of acquired skills, knowledge and understanding, through the engagement of key questions and practical, relevant ideas. Finally, there will be sections on how and where to find sources of evidence and helpful resources.

Taking it apart and putting it back together

In the sections that follow, we will unpick the standard sub-sets and explore them in greater depth. Each section will be underpinned by theory and evidence from practice, with clear guidance on how to evidence the standard in your own practice.

1a: Establish a safe and stimulating environment for pupils, rooted in mutual respect

Safeguarding

Pupil safety and well-being should be paramount in any primary setting. Pupils not only need to feel safe, but it is the responsibility of the teacher and other adults working with pupils to ensure their safety, in the role of *loco parentis*. Each setting will have a safeguarding policy and it is the responsibility of adults working with children to be familiar with this, in addition to implementing practice guidelines. Getting to know your pupils well is an integral part of the safeguarding process and becoming familiar with potential indicators that threaten the safety or well-being of children is crucial. Engagement in whole-school safeguarding training is essential, in addition to demonstrating a clear understanding of school safeguarding procedures, such as what to do in the event of a pupil disclosure, or knowing the roles and responsibilities of designated senior teachers from whom you can draw support and guidance. Do not wait until an issue presents itself: be proactive in exploring school policy and national initiatives and guidance as a priority, in your role as a teacher. For further information and guidance, visit: www.gov.uk/childrens-services/safeguarding-children and *The Bristol Guide* (University of Bristol, 2014).

Environmental factors

What is meant by 'environment'? The environment is multi-faceted and like the encircling layers of our solar system, it is the affecting surroundings in which pupils learn. On a small scale, environment could mean the learning space that immediately surrounds the pupil(s), for example equipment, chair, desk, peers. On a medium scale, this could be the classroom. On a larger scale, it could be the whole school. On a colossal scale, this could be the stimulating world in which we live, outside of the school environment (see Figure 1.1).

Thus, meeting this standard requires the teacher to consider both the physical environment in which planned learning is occurring, other potential learning environments in which pupils can learn and the people within those environments, or the *social* environment, that may have an impact on learning. As Adams (2011, p. 6) suggests: 'The physical layout of the room has a major positive influence on children's behaviour if set out carefully.'

The immediate physical environment

One of the most exciting moments for any teacher is the design of their classroom environment. Careful attention to detail must be considered if pupils are to feel

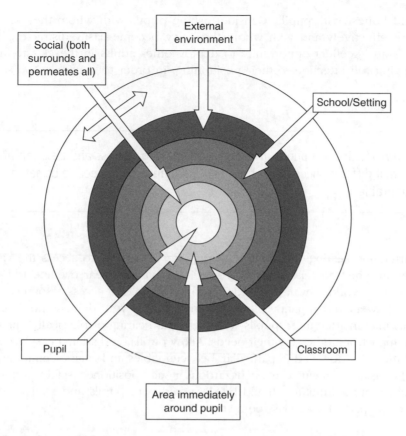

Figure 1.1 Environmental factors

stimulated, secure and motivated to learn. Let us examine some of the key features of the immediate physical environment and ways in which teachers can demonstrate that they are meeting Teachers' Standard 1a. We will do this through the use of an acronym and consideration of the teacher's role being to *F.O.S.T.E.R.* learning through the physical environment:

Furniture

How and where furniture is placed in the classroom is essential to smooth and successful daily practice. Pupil seating is integral to the effective running of the classroom and whilst there exist many schools of thought relating to this area, it is often down to the personal preferences of the class teacher and of course, the individual needs of the pupils. *To sit with friends, or not to sit with friends?* This is the question. Use your professional judgement when considering this question and be open and honest with pupils. Consider asking pupils with whom they know they will work effectively and with whom they may become easily distracted. This, of course, is an excellent opportunity to deploy other adults in the classroom effectively, giving full attention to their positioning, in order to maximise the scope for support.

> ⚲ *Top Tip*: Involve pupils in the decision-making process and be adaptable to their differing needs, over time. Seating plans do not need to be set in stone: be adaptable.

When arranging seating, ensure that all pupils will be able to access the variety of resources around the classroom. This may be having a clear eye-line towards the board, or any 'working walls', in addition to being able to access resources, such as personal drawers and apparatus, as appropriate. Know your pupils (and their needs) well. This may include those pupils who are sight, hearing or physically impaired, as this will impact on addressing their needs. Allow pupils (and adults) easy access to all areas of the classroom and in particular, between tables and chairs. Think 'safety' and assess the risks: furniture can be hazardous if not positioned safely and securely. Movement around furniture should be discussed with pupils and adults within the classroom, as part of your classroom ethos.

Opportunities

Provide a variety of learning opportunities in the classroom for pupils to access independently. This may be, for example, a reading corner or an interactive display. Identify clear rules for their usage and encourage pupils to be a part of the rule making. This instils a sense of joint ownership and encourages pupils to respect their classroom environment. This will be explored in subsequent chapters. Ensure that the classroom is inviting and encourages curiosity and thinking. An easy way of engaging pupils is through the use of effective display and easily accessible, clearly labelled resources (use images and text). In addition, it may be prudent to consider a designated area for 'time out'. This may be an area that pupils choose to use in order to steady their emotions, or work through a problem, should they require it, or an area that could be used by teachers to promote positive behaviours. In addition, 'circle time' could be used to enhance self-discipline, self-esteem and positive relationships (Mosley, 1996).

Senses

Engage pupils in a variety of ways and provide autonomous opportunities for interaction with the classroom environment. Here are some simple ways in which this can be achieved:

- *Visuals*: Ensure that there is plenty to look at, including a celebration of pupil work and information to support learning.
- *Audio*: Set up an interactive listening station or use 'sound buttons' as part of visual displays. Encourage pupils to record their own voices and include these in displays. Try playing calm, beat-free music during learning activities (but please be aware of differing pupil preferences with regard to this).
- *Kinaesthetics*: Allow pupils to access a variety of items to touch and feel as part of displays. This may be something as simple as 3D shapes or different textured papers. Think creatively. Ask questions of pupils or invite pupil questions.
- *Aroma*: Ensure that the classroom has an inviting aroma, or perhaps include an 'aroma station' as a stimulus for writing.
- *Taste*: Try using 'taste' as a stimulus for creativity, writing or understanding contrasting cultures.

When considering all of the above, it is important to be acutely aware of pupil allergies and specific needs and triggers to emotional or physical responses. These triggers could include any of the above.

Top Tip: Invite all pupils to take a wrapped sweet (please ensure that you have notified parents/carers ahead of this and that you are aware of potential allergies). Ask them to place the wrapped sweet in the centre of a blank piece of paper. Individually, or supported by an adult, invite pupils to look at, smell and feel the wrapped sweet and to record their responses to it around the sweet wrapper, on the paper (either in words or pictures). Invite pupils to slowly unwrap the sweet and repeat the exercise, but this time ask them to record their response to the 'unwrapping'. Finally, encourage pupils first to taste the sweet, record their responses and then eat the sweet. Explore the sweet-tasting journey in words and use this as a stimulus for creative writing, such as poetry, descriptive work or art.

Technology

Technologically Enhanced Learning (TEL) is now a staple in the primary classroom and can add real value and meaning to a learning experience. However, when providing pupils with technology, such as laptops, tablets or interactive boards, ensure that the rationale for their use maximises the potential of both pupil learning and the resource.

> *Top Tip*: The clue is all in the name: use the interactive board for interaction ... and record the date and intended outcomes in beautifully modelled handwriting on a board on which you can write with a pen. This means that the interactive board isn't being over-used, pupils are not relying on the harsh light of a screen for hours of information relay and teachers are modelling good practice in handwriting for pupils to mimic. Simple.

Ethos

A positive classroom ethos is the key to success. A teacher may have the best displays and most interactive resources in the school, but without a mutually respectful, positive, inclusive classroom ethos, grounded in support, challenge and partnership, the impact is lost. A healthy classroom ethos encourages positivity and sharing, has zero tolerance for unacceptable behaviours and provides security for the pupils within, ensuring that there are clear boundaries and high expectations for behaviour, collaboration and learning. Involve pupils in all aspects of classroom rule design and remind them of this when things don't go according to plan.

Resources

Ensure that all resources are clearly labelled (with images and words, or try 'sound buttons') and accessible. Orientate pupils and encourage respect for resources and independent access. This will minimise demands on your time during classroom activities and encourage pupil independence. Provide resources that are necessary, such as rulers and sharpened pencils; inspiring, such as objects and images to spark discussion; and supportive, such as pencil grips for pupils who have challenges in controlling their fine motor skills. Above all, ensure that pupils know where the resources are, know that they are to be respected and shared and that they can be accessed independently.

A moment of inspiration:

The Magic Classroom by Chris Mullane

This room is like no other, there is magic in the air.

It seems kind of disorganised, and there's colour everywhere.

There are beanbags, cushions, couches, some dividers and a screen.

And over on the other side, some tables can be seen.

Over there beside the window, the sun is shining bright.

But near the inside wall we see there is a lot less light.

In the background there is music for those who learn by sound.

And earmuffs are here for those who are the other way round.

On every wall there are pictures, each one a story tells;

There are also touchy feely things and even pens with smells.

How anyone could use this room I haven't got a notion.

It seems more like a recipe for some kind of magic potion.

Perhaps this room is magic and will cast a special spell,

So that everyone who enters here will learn so very well.

Be they tactile, auditory, or visual kinaesthetic.

An impulsive or a global or a reflective analytic.

No longer need they feel a sense of great frustration when

Concentrating, processing, and retaining information. (Cited in Prashnig, 1998, p. 50)

The wider physical environment

The wider physical environment could encompass the school, the parents or carers, the community, the media and beyond. As a teacher, it is rather challenging to exercise control over all of these external factors, however let us consider ways in which a seemingly impossible task can become a reality.

The school

A classroom is a small part of a larger picture and it is essential that a whole-school ethos is reflected in the school environment as a whole, as well as permeating through-out individual classrooms. Ensure that your classroom ethos matches whole-school values and refer pupils to these signposts throughout the school. Be part of a team that encourages positive behaviours and has consistent high expectations for behaviour, attitudes and learning.

The community

Place good practice at the centre of the community. Invite external speakers into your classroom and share pupil achievements with the local community. Advertise collaborative partnerships and ensure that inclusivity and school values are well advertised and embedded within the community. This can be achieved through the advertising of community–school events; collegiate school groups, such as parent teacher associations (PTA); regular correspondence via newsletter, letter or year-group booklets; and positive telephone calls home to discuss pupil achievements. There are a myriad of ways in which parents, carers and the local community can be involved in school life and contribute to a shared positive impact on pupil development.

The social environment

Whether classroom-based, or external, the social environment has the potential to impact significantly on pupil progress and well-being. Encouraging positive social interactions within the classroom environment may also impact on both the wider school and external environments. Hansen (2011) asserts that 'creating a positive ethos permeates all activities and areas of the curriculum' (p. 233) and goes on to propose that there are many opportunities in which positive social interactions can be embedded, such as Personal, Social and Health Education (PSHE). We would argue, however, that the encouragement of positive social interactions and perhaps more specifically, what positive social interactions *look like* can be an integral part of daily practice, both inside the classroom and in other areas of the school. Examples of meeting this element of Teachers' Standard 1a could be simple classroom signage; rules and routines; use of talk partners; buddy systems; adult-led playground games and activities, etc. In short, pupils should be given opportunities to engage with a variety of models of positive social interaction, as part of daily school routines and perhaps, more importantly, be respected and guided to engage in them independently.

What is 'mutual respect' and how can you show you are achieving it?

Simplistically viewed, mutual respect in the primary classroom may be seen as respect for individual pupils by the adults and peers with whom they are working and by the individual pupils for the adults and peers with whom they are working. The use of the word 'adults' here is important, as it is essential that all adults working alongside pupils, whether in the classroom or in the dining hall, are afforded the same level of respect as the teacher (and indeed, afford the same level of respect to the pupils). Pupils insist on fairness and why shouldn't they? However, pupil perceptions of what is and isn't fair can sometimes be influenced by emotions, peers or simply poor or under-developed consideration or understanding. A role of the successful teacher is to nurture effective communication in all aspects of school life. Respect should be earned by all parties and it is through effective communication that this, in part way, can be achieved. Encourage pupils to communicate their feelings in a calm manner and provide useful classroom tools to facilitate this process, such as a 'time-out' area for cooling down, or written/verbal support for pupils in response to work. Show pupils you value them, their efforts and achievements through positive reinforcement, regular praise and bespoke support. Listen to and observe their needs and show them that you are interested in them, as individuals. With this in mind, we asked a child aged 10 to answer the following question:

In what ways could your teacher show that (s)he respects you?

The child replied:

She smiles at you; she's kind to you and puts nice comments in your work, like 'Well Done!' You've really shown how good you can be.' She likes talking to you and her voice is quite soft, for example not shouting or being serious. Then you reply and you listen to each other when you are talking. It also shows her respect because if you show her you can be respectful, she'll be respectful back. (Kennedy, aged 10)

 Top Tip: Listen to the voice of the child.

 ### Practice examples – Teachers' Standard 1a

STELLA

Stella noticed that a child in her class had been inattentive in lessons and confrontational in the playground. The child had not demonstrated these character traits previously and Stella grew concerned about the child's well-being. Although Stella was unsure that this was not simply a phase and a natural part of maturation, she decided to report the changes in behaviour to the designated senior teacher within her setting.

(Continued)

(Continued)

Stella ensured that the designated senior teacher recorded the disclosure and with their clear guidance and support, kept a close eye on the child and noted any changes, confidentially.

JUDE

Jude's classroom was an Aladdin's Cave. As soon as you entered the room, the senses were stimulated by a variety of sounds, aromas, sights and curios ... areas of calm and areas of stimulus ... interactive displays and clearly labelled resources. Jude had devised clear rules for independence within his classroom, including expectations for behaviour and procedures to follow when work was completed. This guidance was created *with* and *for* pupils and showcased a whole-class understanding of and respect for the classroom environment.

 In relation to Teachers' Standard 1a and your own practice, consider the following key questions:

- Consider the design and layout of your classroom. How will you maximise the potential of this space to support effective learning and positive behaviours?
- Have you conducted a risk assessment of the classroom environment?
- How can you engage parents/carers and the local community in school life?
- What values do you wish to instil in your pupils?
- Are you clear about safeguarding procedures in your setting?
- What does 'mutual respect' mean to you and how could you communicate a shared understanding with your pupils?
- How well do you know your pupils? What are their interests? Needs? Triggers?

Possible sources of evidence for Teachers' Standard 1a:

- Your classroom environment and any additional environments to which you have contributed;
- Taking a look at social educational forums for great classroom ideas and developing your own plans;
- Planning: 'showing how you know' your pupils and their developing needs;
- Having your classroom values, developed with pupils, clearly displayed and understood by pupils;
- Pupil behaviours/interactions that will exemplify your classroom ethos;

(Continued)

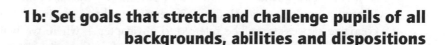

(Continued)

- Pupil/teacher two-way feedback that show how you support and nurture pupil development and how they respond to this;
- Parental/carer or community events/interactions and communications.

1b: Set goals that stretch and challenge pupils of all backgrounds, abilities and dispositions

Inspired by a former colleague at Robin Hood Primary Academy, Birmingham, throughout this book we will refer repeatedly to the following, slightly adapted mantra: *Engage pupils. If they've got it, move them on.* In short, if pupils have a *secure* understanding of a concept, idea or application, they should be challenged. This idea is far from new in the world of education, but the revised Teachers' Standards have ensured that challenge for all pupils is at the forefront of good teaching and a focus on the needs of the individual is an essential aspect of effective practice.

When discussing the idea of pupil challenge with trainee teachers, in *all* lessons for *all* pupils, several key questions emerge:

- How do I plan for it?
- What does it look like?
- Isn't it just more work in case they finish sooner than I'd hoped?

As a starting point, we will first consider the place of what is known by teachers as 'Bloom's Taxonomy' (Bloom et al., 1956) and subsequently examine the above questions in greater depth.

Bloom's Taxonomy

In the 1940s, a group of researchers sought to classify educational objectives. As Forehand (2012) states:

'Their intent was to develop a method of classification for thinking behaviors that were believed to be important in the processes of learning. Eventually, this framework became a taxonomy of three domains:

The cognitive – knowledge-based domain…
The affective – attitudinal-based domain… and
The psychomotor – skills-based domain…'

Forehand (2012) goes on to describe the hierarchical levels within the domains as often depicted as a 'stairway', a hierarchy of lower-level to higher-level thought: 'The lowest three levels are: knowledge, comprehension, and application. The highest three levels are: analysis, synthesis, and evaluation' (Orey, 2012, p. 41–42). The taxonomy has also been described as 'a framework for classifying statements of what we expect or intend students to learn as a result of instruction' (Krathwohl, 2002, p. 212).

This system of classification was known as 'Bloom's Taxonomy' (Bloom et al., 1956). Since then, several revised taxonomies have been created (Dave, 1970; Harrow, 1972; Anderson and Krathwohl, 2001) and adaptations are used in a variety of ways within educational settings. Anderson and Krathwohl's (2001) matrix of levels of knowledge, which offered a two-dimensional, cross-referencing grid to combine the subject matter and the cognitive processes, will be referred to in Chapter 4, where we will examine what could be considered as an interpretation of the taxonomy in practice. Bloom's Taxonomy (Bloom et al., 1956), in its most simplistic form, considered the lower to higher order strands as knowledge, comprehension, application, analysis, synthesis and evaluation and these were displayed as a pyramid, with knowledge at the base and evaluation at the peak.

Pupils working at the higher end of the pyramid are demonstrating higher order skills and knowledge, whilst those working at the lower end need to develop the higher order skills and knowledge in order to progress further. This, of course, has implications for objective design and planned questions, if pupils are to be challenged successfully.

💡 *Top Tip*: Use Bloom's Taxonomy (Bloom et al., 1956) as a tool for the creation of learning objectives. Consider the verbs used within the taxonomy, for example: *To create a still life image.* In addition, plan questions and challenging tasks to promote a variety of thinking, such as: *How have you created your still life image? Evaluate a partner's still-life image.*

Now that we have considered using Bloom's Taxonomy as a tool, we will return once more to the key questions identified earlier, in relation to pupil challenge in *all* lessons for *all* pupils.

Challenge: How do I plan for it and what does it look like?

Planning for challenge should be embedded in excellent practice, not simply added onto a lesson plan. That said, the identification of challenge for groups of pupils or individuals should be observed in lesson planning. Below is a simple step-by-step guide to planning for challenge:

1. Consider the intended outcomes for each group of pupils or individuals within your class.
2. Plan activities and questions that facilitate pupils achieving the intended outcomes (the creation of 'success criteria' can support this).
3. Consider activities and questions that could help pupils progress to the next level and ways in which pupils may be able to engage with these, independently.

Thus, planning for challenge could be as easy as 1, 2, 3. The exemplar lesson in Figure 1.2 identifies ways in which pupils can be challenged and this, of course, can be adapted to suit your individual planning style and the age of your pupils.

Planning for challenge will depend on the individuals within your setting and factors such as pupil age, experience, capabilities, confidence, etc. What is important is that you consider ways of guiding pupils to engage in challenges autonomously, so that they view them in a positive way. Lower ability groups may simply move on to the tasks of higher ability groups, if applicable and purposeful, although consolidating learning through questioning is a good transition from intended outcomes to challenging outcomes. This also allows the teacher to assess pupil progress in a systematic way.

> *Top Tip*: Try hiding colour-coded, differentiated teacher challenges around the classroom and allow pupils autonomous access to these, once they have achieved the intended outcomes. Add an element of competition and rewards for completed challenges. Above all, ensure that all pupils have access to a challenge, in line with their needs and reiterate this 'fairness' to pupils. Oh and make it fun but purposeful.

David Didau, as cited by Beere (2012), presented a continuum model, devised to assist pupils in understanding different stages in their learning and ways in which they could aspire to achieve the next stage. Building on Bloom et al. (1956), the continuum shows simplistic progression from a starting point through to higher-order thinking and articulation of a particular objective. An adaptation of this model is shown in Figure 1.3.

By using a similar model and displaying this prominently, pupils can independently identify their own next steps and engage in autonomous challenge. Support cards could be used with younger pupils, in addition to adult support, with clear visual imagery in place of words. For older pupils, an element of peer support and as identified previously, competition can be implemented to engage pupils more thoroughly in the journey to greater success.

Maths focus: Problem solving (Linked to topic)			Term: Summer 1, Y4

Targets:
I can solve two-step problems involving all operations
I can multiply a one-digit number by a two-digit number

Prior learning: *Project to help the school with the bills (2nd of two-part lesson). One digit multiplied by two-digit number taught discretely last week but now need to ensure they can apply the skills to a real-life problem*
Resources: *Electricity activities*
TA: Introduction: Work with LA pupils on targets
Main: Support PP pupils
Plenary: Any child-specific support required
Target pupils: Pupil Premium: X, Y & Z

Intended outcomes	Review	Key learning and activities	Plenary
Pupils will apply their knowledge and understanding of multiplication and logical problem solving in a real-life context related to our topic	2–3 minutes Look at yesterday's targets: pupils reply to marking and complete developmental tasks	30–40 minutes **Main teaching** Introduce the problem: the school electricity bill is too high! The challenge by the end of the lesson is to have helped the school finance manager to reduce the bill. Introduce the table of items that we spend the most money on each day. Remind children of W and kW. *What does this show us? How can we calculate the total amount of electricity used for each item?* Look at lights usage, as the example. *If electricity costs 8p per kW, how are we going to work out how much electricity that item has used?* Paired-talk. Discuss multiplication method. *Who can remind me how to set out the multiplication?* Children to scribe on whiteboards and show	5 minutes **Activity** Suggestions on how to reduce the bill and how much money it will save Refer to targets and prove it
See activities linked to outcomes	**Mental/Oral**	**Got it? Move on to group activities:** MA: to calculate the costs of other items HA: to calculate the costs of other items (with time difference and W conversions LA: to calculate the cost of other items in base 10 **Not yet?** Children identified through questioning and support – teacher support	**Reflection questions** *How would you suggest we solve the problem?* *Do you agree? Why?* *How could we calculate...?* *How much money would it save if...?*
	5 minutes 8 times tables. Two are right, two are wrong and two could be either. Children to discuss possibilities and solve on whiteboards. 'Pounce and bounce' questioning *Do all multiples of 8 end in an even number?*	**Challenge.** MA: *How much money would we save if....?* HA: To reduce the daily bill to less than £5 by reducing the length of time items are on for Reasoning skills and logical methods **Interventions:** TA to work with X, Y & Z (intervention tasks and questions provided to TA) **Ultimate challenge!** Using your suggestions to reduce the daily bill, what would you now estimate the yearly bill will be?	**Next steps:** Relate to data handling Money

Hinge question to ensure that children are all confident with calculations:

How much did it cost to run a lawn mower for 2 hours?

T

Figure 1.2 Examples of ways in which pupils can be challenged

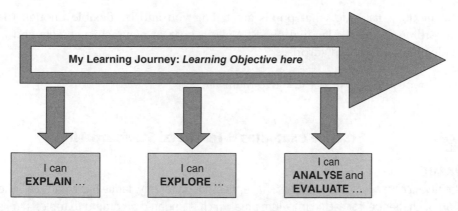

Figure 1.3 An adaptation of Didau's continuum (Beere, 2012)

Isn't it just a little more work, in case they finish sooner than I'd hoped?

Absolutely not. *Extension* activities are not the same as *challenge* activities. Extension activities may only consolidate existing knowledge and skills, unless an element of challenge is built in. Extension and challenge activities should always relate to the learning objectives and build on existing achievements in order to promote pupil progress. As identified previously, it is important to note that challenge can occur in a variety of ways and does not necessarily need to be an activity.

Seven sensational ways of challenging:

1. A range of questions: ask pupils questions that challenge thinking and insist on deeper answers. Try using a simple questioning tool, such as *hinge point questions* (Beard, 2011). According to Beard (2011), hinge point questions provide the opportunity to take a lesson in a variety of directions and can aid teachers in identifying pupil needs, thus allowing them to adapt accordingly. By assessing for this purpose, a teacher can make a striking impact on learning by delivering tailored teaching to each individual student (Beard, 2011).
2. Engaging activities: ensure that you are designing activities that will engage pupils and encourage them to strive for success. Know what they enjoy and what turns them on to learning.
3. Independent exploration: allow pupils to explore further, perhaps using texts or designing enquiry questions.
4. Technology-enhanced learning: ask pupils to use technology to extend their learning – they're pretty good at it, independently.
5. Involve pupils in the process: ensure that they are clear about their learning goals and next steps to make extra progress.
6. Plan for choice: pupils engage more thoroughly if there is an element of choice. Allow pupils to choose their challenges and possibly design them for peers.

7. Be flexible: listen to what pupils are telling you and be flexible enough to act according to their individual needs. Make a note of new achievements and individual successes (and surprises).

Engage pupils. If they've got it, move them on.

Practice examples – Teachers' Standard 1b

JAMIE
Jamie encourages pupils to access challenges independently. Jamie has created a 'little bag of challenge' for each curriculum area which is updated according to topics. Pupils are encouraged to access challenges once they have completed at least one challenge designed for specific lessons. Challenges are written in child-friendly language and images are used to support the text. For pupils with difficulties in reading, Jamie has teamed them with a 'reading buddy', who can help with occasional reading, if required.

ALICE
Like all good teachers, Alice embraces the needs of all individuals within her class. Alice has designed a low-level wall display on which are displayed the images of her pupils. Pupils are encouraged to add post-it notes to their images during each school day. Green post-it notes indicate their successes and pupils are encouraged to draw or write their achievements. Red post-it notes indicate challenges. Jessica builds in time after lunch and towards the end of the school day to address individual pupil needs and ensures that all pupils have been involved in one-to-one discussions by the end of each school week. Alice keeps a record of these discussions in a notebook and pupils feel empowered to solve problems independently and strive for success. On occasions, Alice invites parents/carers to share in these learning discussions with the pupils first thing in the morning or after school.

 In relation to Teachers' Standard 1b and your own practice, consider the following key questions:

- What is your definition of challenge and in what ways do you apply it in daily lesson planning?
- How do you know that you know your pupils and their differing needs and how does this impact on your daily practice?
- What strategies do you employ in order to ensure challenge for all?

(Continued)

(Continued)

Possible sources of evidence for Teachers' Standard 1b:

- Feedback from pupils;
- Subject expectations for prior and subsequent year groups;
- Assessment data;
- Planning;
- Whole-school data sets;
- Pupil progress data.

1c: Demonstrate consistently the positive attitudes, values and behaviour which are expected of pupils

A teacher is a role model. As outlined in the Teachers' Standards Part Two (DfE, 2013a): 'Teachers uphold public trust in the profession and maintain high standards of ethics and behaviour, within and outside school.'

In short, you need to demonstrate the high standards of attitudes, values and behaviours that are also expected of the pupils in your care. Whilst a positive ethos can be fostered within the classroom setting, this is often challenging to evidence, as it is something that teachers 'just do'. As professionals, teachers model positive behaviours in their daily practice, so where can evidence be found to support this?

Pupil behaviours

You can learn a great deal about a teacher's values and standards simply by walking into a classroom. How pupils conduct themselves, how they engage with learning, how they interact with others and perhaps more pertinently, how the teacher interacts with the pupils, are all evidence of this Teachers' Standard 1c – and all of this without observing teaching or talking to anyone! We will discuss behaviour in greater depth in subsequent chapters, however it would be useful to consider these few simple steps:

- Consistently encourage appropriate, positive behaviours that encourage learning, at all times.
- Have clear expectations for behaviour and communicate these clearly to pupils. Ensure that pupils understand why these are the expectations and help them to be successful in displaying these by sharing good examples and modelling.
- Smile and be approachable.
- Deal with inappropriate behaviours with speed and appropriate gravitas.

- Bring it back to the learning.
- Use positive reinforcement.

As Beadle (2010, p. 9) argues: 'Sweat the small stuff and the big stuff don't happen.'
   Ensure that you are clear about rules, routines and expectations and never, ever, say one thing and do another. The rules must apply and pupils must be clear about why they are in place and how they impact on them, as individuals, on others around them and on their learning. As Beadle (2010) suggests, never lower your expectations and you are more likely to achieve success in promoting positive behaviour for learning. In short, don't let it slide for particular individuals or in particular lessons; be fair to the pupils and true to yourself.

Reward and sanction systems

Pupil rewards should be celebrated and this should be on display for all to see and have pride of place in your classroom. Draw regular attention to positive behaviours and attitudes and promote a positive classroom ethos at all times. Ensure that classroom rules have been developed *with* and *for* the pupils and have these clearly displayed and accessible to all.

Class and whole-school values

Ensure that class values align with school values and that all pupils are aware of them. Use valuable discussion time as a medium through which agreements can be made with pupils and refer to these values often. Hearing the pupil voice is essential and it is important that values and expectations are discussed *with* them, rather than imparted *to* them. Above all, ensure that pupils understand what they mean and how to demonstrate them and have clear sanctions in place for those who do not adhere to the agreed class rules.

Attendance and punctuality

This is a class non-negotiable. Ensure that you are doing everything to promote the value of high levels of attendance and punctuality with pupils and parents/carers. Encourage pupils to start the day early by engaging them in independent opportunities that motivate them at the start of the school day. Allow an element of choice and collegiate working. If this is applicable in your setting, consider working alongside colleagues within your phase and allow pupils to move freely between classrooms and to work with friends and other adults, if they prefer. This is one way in which you can maximise the potential for a positive start to the school day. Praise pupils who have regular, good attendance and punctuality and encourage pupils with incentives and rewards. Beere (2012, p. 42) suggests that:

It is a basic tenet of neuroscience that learning is an emotional experience. Nothing is more important than you and the aura you project in the classroom. This includes your relationship with the students and your belief in yourself as a great teacher.

Believing in your ability to teach, to engage pupils in learning and to be a good role model is a tall order but an essential quality of the effective teacher. Be mindful of the fact that this is what you are trained to do and know that how you present yourself in the classroom should exude a confidence and be grounded in high expectations and positive values.

 Practice examples – Teachers' Standard 1c

TAI
Tai has a display in the classroom of a life-size teacher and pupil, created with pupils. Tai has encouraged pupils to identify the key qualities, behaviours and values they expect each to hold and allows pupils to interact with the display and record their ideas on strips of paper that can be stuck to the display, around the teacher and the pupil. The display is referred to regularly and used as a positive reinforcement tool. Pupils refer to the display with one another and it has served as a particularly useful tool during break and dinner times, when challenging behaviours may occur outside of the classroom setting.

TREVOR
Trevor demonstrates that he values all individuals within his class by having 'Why I'm Great!' profiles at each pupil's desk. The profile includes an image of the pupil and positive comments about the pupil, regarding values, behaviours and qualities identified by other pupils in the class. Pupils are encouraged to reflect on the class values when constructing profiles. Copies of the profiles have gone home to parents/carers and Trevor has a personal teacher profile displayed next to the board.

 In relation to Teachers' Standard 1c and your own practice, consider the following key questions:

- How could you *show* that you have high standards for attitudes, values and behaviour in your setting?
- What do you do to promote your own positive attitudes, values and behaviours and how do pupils know you are doing this?

(Continued)

(Continued)

- In what ways could you engage parents/carers in this process?
- If we were to visit your setting, what would we see, in relation to Teachers' Standard 1c?

Possible sources of evidence for Teachers' Standard 1c:

- Pupil learning journals;
- Displays;
- Pupil behaviours;
- Positive reinforcement strategies;
- School policies directly linked to classroom practice;
- Pupils engaged in learning and interacting with others in positive ways;
- Clear processes for when things go wrong that pupils recognise and are able to access independently, in order to seek solutions;
- Peer mediators: try setting up a class system that trains pupils to act as intermediaries when difficulties arise, in order to seek solutions to problems.

Chapter summary

Consider your setting and the environment in which pupils learn each day. How can you maximise the potential for pupil learning, support and challenge by considering environmental factors? Question the stimuli around your classroom and develop these with the pupils. Show that pupils are valued and respected and orientate pupils regarding a display of mutual respect and value for others. Give pupils the confidence to aim high and ensure that learning goals stretch them whilst being attainable. Praise pupils regularly for their achievements. Display consistently the behaviours, attitudes and values that you expect from your pupils and guide them, sensitively, to understand the impact of this on them, as individuals, adhering to the safeguarding policies of the school. Seek to maximise opportunities for pupils and showcase these at every opportunity. Be proud of your pupils and their achievements and show this in your facial expressions, body language and through positive comments and help them to understand how they can be the best they can be – and be a good role model for this yourself.

CHAPTER 2

PROMOTE GOOD PROGRESS AND OUTCOMES BY PUPILS

Teachers' Standard 2 – Promote good progress and outcomes by pupils:

2a Be accountable for attainment, progress and outcomes of the pupils

2b Plan teaching to build on pupils' capabilities and prior knowledge

2c Guide pupils to reflect on the progress they have made and their emerging needs

2d Demonstrate knowledge and understanding of how pupils learn and how this impacts on teaching

2e Encourage pupils to take a responsible and conscientious attitude to their own work and study.

What is this all about?

Supporting pupils to achieve the best they possibly can through planning, teaching, monitoring and assessing is a key principle of this standard. It requires the teacher to be proactive and take responsibility for the continuing development of each child. It is through knowing the children in the class that the effective teacher will be able to recognise a child's needs, track their development and plan the next steps of learning to enable the pupils to improve and develop. Through having good knowledge of how children learn, the teacher will understand the importance of supporting pupils to become autonomous, confident learners.

How can this be demonstrated?

There are many ways in which you will be able to draw on evidence to support this standard. First of all, getting to know your pupils is critical and over time you will develop an understanding of their interests and needs which you can show through your planning. Assessment records could be used to show evidence of the impact of interventions or strategies you have implemented. Feedback to pupils will also provide valuable evidence of progress, including marking, target setting and of course a pupil's response to feedback. Consider how you use peer assessment and what opportunities you include to support pupils to demonstrate their understanding. Through providing occasions for a pupil to explain something to another person, you can gather valuable information because if they have understood a point then they will be able to explain it, in their own words, to others. Other more formal evidence could be used, such as test or SATs results or the EYFS profile data. Additionally, you must consider how you will show an understanding of pedagogies, which may be through the way that you have organised your classroom or the learning and teaching activities you have planned. Why have you decided to do it in this way? How does it draw on some of the learning theories you place value on?

Chapter overview

When you decided to take up a career as a primary school teacher, you displayed a commitment and genuine interest in children and wanted to support them as they grow and develop. You are naturally interested in helping children to achieve and this can be a very rewarding part of your role as you experience their achievements. Teachers are in a very privileged position in which they are role models, influential in a child's life and possibly someone that the child will remember for the rest of their life. As a teacher, you are fortunate in being able to share a pupil's progress and scaffold their learning until they are ready to be independent. Vygotsky's theories placed emphasis on the importance of learning through being supported, which he termed the Zone of Proximal Development (ZPD). Vygotsky suggested that progress occurs when a more knowledgeable other supports the learning until the learner can do it on their own (Cooper, 2014). This chapter will examine how the teacher can take responsibility for pupil progress whilst also raising awareness of the importance of peer support and paired working as ways of showing evidence of progression. There are four major strands that we will return to throughout this chapter. These strands are:

- Accountability for pupil progress;
- Knowing the learners and demonstrating this through both planning and teaching to ensure the pupils' needs are met and they make progress;
- Creating a positive learning environment which supports pupils to become independent and reflective in their learning;
- Understanding learning theories and knowing not only what you need to do but also why you do it in this way.

Discussion of Teachers' Standard 2 will include the synthesis of theory and practice to give concrete examples for you to consider. Further references and resources are included as a means of additional sources to draw on. The greatest times within your classroom will be those when a pupil has shown an improvement and moved forward in their learning. Your role is to assume ownership and take responsibility for making sure each and every pupil makes progress. This can seem a daunting task, but when you see the progress made it will be one of the most memorable and rewarding times for you.

Taking it apart and putting it back together

As we explore each sub-set, we will consider what the standard looks like in practice and how you can evidence the whole standard. It is important to remember that the sub-sets do not sit in isolation and whilst evidencing one sub-set you may also be able to link to another sub-set and to other standards.

2a: Be accountable for attainment, progress and outcomes of the pupils

Teachers understand how they are accountable for attainment, progress and outcomes and they take responsibility for this. This will be through carrying out a range of both formal and informal procedures for monitoring progress and assessing teaching and learning.

Accountability

Being a teacher is a responsible profession in which you are accountable. This may seem quite a scary thought at first when you consider that not only are you accountable to your head teacher and governors but also to the parents of the children you teach and of course, to the children themselves. Ewans (2014) points out how the profession is also accountable to the public, whilst Cullingford (2010, p. 77) goes on to suggest that 'implications of accountability are pervasive'. Yet, being a professional in the public domain need not be a threatening experience and through your daily practice you will be able to demonstrate how you have assumed responsibility. As a professional, you are dedicated to helping children achieve their best, you have regard for the school's policies and procedures and will be committed to the school ethos. You will come to know your class better than anyone else and will collect a lot of information about each child. This may be from your own observations as well as from parents, colleagues and the children. The ways in which you have gathered this evidence will provide valuable examples of how you have been proactive and responsible for collecting data that will help you to plan for all children to achieve their potential. Being organised and keeping well-structured records of children's achievements will be essential and this can provide evidence of your accountability.

Attainment

We have highlighted the teacher's commitment to the learner but also need to recognise the significance of the pupil's commitment to learning (Hayes, 2009). Attainment, quite simply, means to achieve a goal that you have set yourself. Pupils need to be involved in their target setting if they are to reach a goal and they need to fully understand how to achieve it. The teacher has a key role here and can demonstrate how they have supported pupil progress through the strategies used to set and share targets with pupils. Initially, you will have used a method of assessment to identify what the child knows and what they need to do to improve. This may have been a writing activity, a practical activity or a discussion with pupils. Discussions with pupils will stimulate their interest in their own learning and can be used to promote a desire to want to improve. Teachers need to have high expectations for every pupil in their care. How you encourage pupils to remain focused on their targets is equally important – for example, are the targets displayed in the classroom or are they put in the front of a book? Identifying the next steps in learning can be tricky for pupils and the teacher can break down learning into manageable steps to ensure there is attainment at each level. The curriculum frameworks can be used as a guide for finding out how to move a pupil on, as can discussions with subject coordinators. Throughout the teaching activity, you can draw on the ways you have encouraged pupils to reflect on their progress towards meeting their target through such questions as, 'Which part of your target do you think you feel confident about?' Your comments to the pupil on their achievement can be used as further evidence of how you have supported learning and helped the pupil to recognise what they have done well and what they need to do next.

Progress and outcomes

We will focus on three key aspects – individual pupil progress, pace of progress and pupil confidence – to consider how to improve opportunities for all pupils.

Individual pupil progress

First, teachers need to ensure that every child is progressing well. This is not an easy task with a class of 30 pupils and different strategies will be deployed in order to achieve this. Early in their teaching career, teachers realise that they cannot possibly give every child in their class the same attention at the same time. Whilst teachers work with a group, other groups will be working independently, but that does not mean children cannot all make progress. Consider how teachers organise learning to enable independent learners to move forward and make progress. This may be through the activities that have been planned, through specific targets set or through the resources used. By having a clear focus on a child's progress, teachers are able to identify and explain the techniques used to measure the progress. This is likely to include frequent checks using formative methods of assessment, such as questioning, observation and feedback to pupils. Valid evidence can include the way a pupil's progress has been accelerated through the use of catch-up or intervention programmes. In this way, evidence can be used to demonstrate how planning around the needs of each child has been considered, with a clear indication of the expectation that all learners should achieve high standards.

Pace of progress

An effective teacher can maintain a good pace in the classroom. It is like driving a car: go too slow and you may not get there, but if you speed along you may miss an essential signpost. At any stage of learning, the speed at which pupils are learning has to be appropriate and this will ensure a good pace is maintained. The suggestion is that if the lesson starts slowly and lasts for a long time at this pace, then children will become restless and lose concentration. If the pace is too fast, then children may become frustrated as they will not have enough time to absorb the information. So let's be clear that pace does not refer to speediness. Through the timings on the planning, teachers will be able to show how they ensure an activity does not last too long or that, equally, it is not over too quickly. This can be further evidenced through planning to show how the overview of the lesson has been shared, so that pupils have a sense of what is expected of them within the time frame.

Pupil confidence

The last point to consider is about building a pupil's confidence. A saying that is very pertinent is the phrase, 'You don't know until you have had a go!' but having a go can be difficult for someone who is not self-assured. A teacher's role is to deploy strategies, such as using peer support to promote engagement and to encourage children to have a go. It may be suggested that it is hard to measure a child's confidence, but it is possible to capture changes that are observed in how pupils work and behave, which may suggest a more confident grasp of a concept. Another way this can be evidenced is through considering the tone of voice and the encouraging words used, which may be all a child needs to try something out and to be successful. This involves taking a risk and the way a positive learning environment is created is worth considering, such as how teachers model learning. Modelling can provide an effective strategy as it engages the pupil cognitively. The teacher first models the task, the child performs the task at their own pace and then the task is reviewed: 'Modelling increases the perception that a task is achievable and it is important for a teacher to demonstrate that mistakes and errors are not only inevitable when learning, but they are also opportunities' (Robins, 2012, p. 125). Through observing how the teacher is thinking, the child is able to imitate the learning behaviour and this can be very powerful. The idea is based on the social constructivism learning theory. Vygotsky (1962, 1978) and Bruner (1986) are accredited with developing the social constructivist theory, in which language and social interaction are vital tools in supporting a child to construct knowledge and understanding (see Cooper, 2014).

> *Top Tip*: Being organised and having a good, brisk start to the lesson will help to secure a good pace. Remember that pace and depth of learning are both integral parts of progress. Effective questioning will help you to identify who has 'got it' and who may need to further consolidate understanding.

 Practice examples – Teachers' Standard 2a

EVIE

Evie uses a range of formative assessment methods with her Year 5 class to identify what the pupils know. On her planning, she includes a range of differentiated questions which she will use with specific targeted pupils to encourage deeper

(Continued)

(Continued)

thinking and offer an opportunity for pupils to demonstrate their understanding. In her daily practice, she shows evidence of pupil learning. Evie also monitors achievements through keeping assessment records to track progress over time.

CHARLIE

Charlie is a teacher in the early years. He uses and encourages others to use an app on the ipad to capture and record pupil progress. This enables Charlie to track progress and use the observation notes to create a report on the progress of each pupil. This information is used to help Charlie with planning for future lessons to ensure he is building on what the pupils already know.

 In relation to Teachers' Standard 2a and your own practice, consider the following key questions:

- How do you know what motivates your pupils?
- What do you do to ensure a good pace is maintained throughout the lesson?
- What documents do you use to identify next steps in learning?
- Where have the pupils come from and where will you take them on their learning journey?
- What records are you expected to keep as part of the school policy and what personal records do you keep of pupil progress?

Possible sources of evidence for Teachers' Standard 2a:

- Assessment records, both formal (tests) and informal (formative feedback);
- Feedback from pupils, including pupils' comments on meeting their targets;
- Observation notes;
- Pupil progress and teacher tracking records;
- Performance management reviews;
- Records from pupil progress meetings;
- Intervention and catch-up programmes – evidence of actions and impact;
- IEP reviews;
- Book scrutiny, marking;
- Planning (gap analysis and interpretation of data);
- EYFS profile data.

2b: Plan teaching to build on pupils' capabilities and prior knowledge

This sub-set is about how teachers can maximise potential through knowing what learning has already taken place and helping pupils to build on this with new knowledge. Research suggests that learning continues to develop mainly from prior knowledge as this helps the learner to understand new content and make connections between this and what they already know (Daniels, 1993). It is necessary for the teacher to know this because if the pupil's knowledge is actually full of misconceptions, then this can cause a negative effect on learning as it affects how the learner sees new information. When you correct a misconception, you are supporting the pupil to make progress. An effective way to find out about prior knowledge is to start the lesson with a review of learning as this will activate a child's thinking process about what they know and understand. Consistency in checking understanding will help you to develop a clear idea about what pupils know, rather than having a misconception continue. You may consider drawing on work that has been marked or on a previous test result, which will give an indication of what the child knew at that time, but there also needs to be consistent checks, through discussion with the child, to ensure that the concept is fully understood. Tracking progress daily through the use of formative assessment strategies and maintaining records will support you to make a confident judgement about pupil progress.

In your teaching, there will be times when you will ask the children to apply what they know to a new concept, such as when spelling and applying what they know about phonemes to a new word. The learning theories of Jean Piaget state how children make sense of their world by accessing their prior knowledge and adding new information to create a schema or mental map: 'Schemata are like templates developed from previous experience, into information that can be organised. They mean that people do not have to reinterpret the world every time they encounter it' (Jordan et al., 2008, p. 43).

When teachers employ strategies to support pupils to develop their schema, they are encouraging cognitive development as they ask questions and pose comments for pupils to reflect on. This process helps a pupil to take ownership of their ideas and to make connections in their learning. At the same time, teachers need to be mindful that they are not imposing their ideas on the children because this does not allow the children to internalise concepts and make their own knowledge (Jordan et al., 2008).

A further way of finding out about children's prior knowledge is to look at school systems. It is a good idea to ask about the system your school has for passing information on from one teacher to the next; some schools will hold a meeting specifically for this purpose or there may be more informal ways for teachers to meet and discuss the needs and interests of pupils. This will give you valuable information about individual pupils who are going to be in your class.

Top Tip: The pupils in your class will not be coming into your class with a blank slate. They will have a wealth of knowledge already. Find out as much as you can about the pupils, from colleagues and parents, before the start of term. Continue to build on this by getting to know them through observation, questioning and discussion.

Practice examples – Teachers' Standard 2b

LOIS

Lois plans a science lesson with her Year 2 class. This is the first lesson of a series of six lessons on plants and growing. She has used the data from the previous teacher to identify where the pupils are in their learning but she realises that the last lesson on plants was some time ago. Lois is keen to find out what the children can still remember and understand and she has set up a couple of activities to assess their knowledge. First of all, Lois starts the lesson by asking the children to draw a mind map of everything they know about plants. This enables the pupils to record their understanding in a supportive climate where there is no right or wrong. It gives Lois a lot of information about each child's awareness of plants. Lois then gets the children working in pairs to explain their mind map to their partner. This offers a further opportunity for her to check prior knowledge and record any misconceptions. At the end of the lesson, Lois asks probing questions to address some of the misconceptions she has heard. She uses the assessments to plan for the next lesson, thus building on the children's prior knowledge.

JACK

In Jack's class, he has a mixed age group of 24 Year 3 and Year 4 pupils. The class has been working on multiplication problems and this is the third lesson. Jack has used his assessments from the last lesson to identify the level of understanding of each pupil. As well as marking work, he used the observations he had made and the TA's records of assessment of the group she was working with. On Jack's planning, he was able to demonstrate how he has taken into account prior learning and his annotations show how he has made this judgement. He has modified one of the planned activities for this lesson to ensure greater challenge for a specific group of children who he had assessed as having a confident grasp of the concepts.

In relation to Teachers' Standard 2b and your own practice, consider the following key questions:

- How will you track and record what a pupil knows to ensure you can confidently claim they have made progress?
- What opportunities do you include in your lessons for pupils to demonstrate prior knowledge?
- How do you organise learning within the classroom to enable pupils to share their prior learning with each other?
- How do you link lessons to ensure there is both continuity and progression from one lesson to the next?

Possible sources of evidence for Teachers' Standard 2b:

- Formative assessment strategies;
- Lesson plans to show key questions, differentiated activities, interventions;
- Notes from observations;
- Target setting;
- IEPs, annotated;
- Notes on observations;
- Tracking of information from the previous teacher and evidence of how you have used this information;
- EYFS profile;
- Records of how you have worked with other professionals, such as the behaviour support team, an educational psychologist, etc.

2c: Guide pupils to reflect on the progress they have made and their emerging needs

To meet this sub-set, there needs to be a firm grasp of the concepts, ideas and principles of reflective practice. This includes an understanding of how to support pupils to engage in their own learning and the impact of this. To do this, teachers need to demonstrate, through their practice, that they employ a range of strategies which support pupils to recognise their achievements and to be able to say what they need to do next to improve their work.

Reflection

'The content of reflection is largely what we know already. It is often a process of re-organising knowledge and emotional orientations in order to achieve further insights' (Moon, 2004, p. 82). A key to successful learning, for all learners, is the ability to be able to reflect on experiences and to consciously consider their relevance. As an effective teacher, you will support pupils to be reflective. The concept of reflection has been much debated and Moon (ibid. p. 80) suggests that 'reflection, as a process, seems to lie somewhere around the notion of learning and thinking'. The idea is that learning happens as a consequence of reflection. In the classroom, this becomes very significant as teachers support learners to engage in a process of analysis and evaluation of learning. To do this, you need to develop a good understanding of what reflection means to you. As a teacher, you may be naturally reflective and as we all reflect in different ways and at different times, it is not something that is necessarily easy to teach. However, we can provide opportunities, through activities and strategies within our teaching, to support pupils to reflect in their own way. As McVittie (2012, p. 11) points out, 'reflection is concerned with the process and not the product and many theorists put the process at the centre of their research by considering levels of reflection'. An important model when referring to levels of reflection is Bloom's Taxonomy, developed in 1956. This is still used widely in today's classrooms to encourage pupils to think more deeply (Hayes, 2009). The model, consisting of six categories, can be used to support the teacher in asking questions that require more demanding and complex thinking from the pupils. The categories move from knowledge, comprehension, application, analysis and synthesis though, finally, to evaluation. Questions based on the higher-order thinking skills can be used by a teacher to encourage pupils to reflect on their learning. In your planning, you can evidence how you have considered which questions you will be using to target specific children. The teacher can assess the use of 'application' by providing a new context, 'in which the student has to restructure a problem, work out how best to respond and thereby demonstrate transfer' (Moseley et al., 2005: 49). Bloom's Taxonomy is discussed further in Chapter 1 of this book. Whilst being mindful of the levels of reflection, another key part of a teacher's role is to develop ways to engage pupils in the reflective process. This is considered next.

Involving pupils in their learning

How teachers involve pupils in their learning is a critical part of the planning stage. It does not just happen and it takes time to develop a climate of trust and respect in which all learners feel they can contribute in the classroom. A positive learning environment helps pupils to realise that all contributions are valued and that active engagement is indeed expected. Pupils are not passive in the learning process but they participate and are involved in making decisions, in problem solving and in asking and answering questions. This can be achieved through including opportunities for peer and self assessment as ways for pupils to identify areas of success and for further development. Sharing the learning objective in child-friendly language will support pupils to understand their progress towards meeting this, as well as to consider what questions they may have about the learning and to identify the standard they are aiming for. During marking and feedback, effective use can be made of talk and discussion between teacher and pupil and between pupils. Not only does this reinforce the teacher's expectation that the pupil needs to engage and their contribution is valued, but it can also be a great way to boost a pupil's confidence. At the end of a unit of work, it is valuable to enable pupils to comment on their ideas about their progress. An example of this can be given after a Design and Technology unit of work in which pupils make a vehicle. After completion of the model, pupils can be asked to record what they liked about the model, what the challenges were in making it and what they might change. Opportunities can be created throughout the lesson for pupils to share examples of their work and explain what they have done well and what their next step will be to further improve their work. What is evident through these examples is that reflection is part of the learning process, not a bolt on. It is part of effective classroom practice which teachers consider an essential part of teaching and learning.

Involvement and ownership

There is a joint responsibility for teachers and learners to take an active role, to each 'do their bit' to ensure progress is made. The experience in the classroom should be one that *engages, empowers* and *enhances* learning. Engagement can encourage and facilitate collaborative and active learning. Active learning is a crucial part of any lesson and it is suggested that there is increased neural connectivity and enhanced learning as the brain makes greater connections when there is active learning. This is because a child is engaged in constructing their own knowledge. The key features of an effective lesson include interaction and active learning. Pupils are not passive in their learning but in control. The whole experience can give a sense of empowerment to pupils.

The most significant improvement in learning occurs when pupils take ownership of their own learning. This can be very motivating, for example the use of a computer programme can act as a focal point for group work, data collection and interpretation. It removes the manual element from work so that pupils can access higher levels of intellectual engagement. Rather than spending a large part of the lesson drawing a graph, this can be done quickly using a computer programme, hence children spend more time engaged in the higher order scientific thinking skills of reflection and analysis.

Finally, reflection should enhance learning. The role of the teacher is to plan opportunities for reflection that focus on extending learning and provide opportunities that may previously not have been possible, ensuring a meaningful context for learning and progress.

> *Top Tip*: It can be helpful to create a list of the different strategies that you will use to enable pupils to reflect on their learning. Identify when and how you can include these to ensure a range of different ideas are included and whether your focus will be on the whole class or on a specific focus group.

Practice examples – Teachers' Standard 2c

ELAINE

In Elaine's school, there is a strong emphasis on engaging pupils in their learning. All staff demonstrate commitment to this through following the whole-school policy and holding staff meetings on the progress of whole-school initiatives. In Elaine's Year 6 class, one of the initiatives she has employed is the use of paired peer feedback. Following an English lesson based on descriptive writing, she organised the pupils into pairs and they read through and then commented on each other's work. Elaine gave each pair a set of criteria on which to base their judgements, i.e. have they used adjectives in the writing? The pupils were able to suggest to each other what they had done well and make comments on how to further develop their writing. Elaine was able to demonstrate this standard through her evaluation of the activity.

MARC

In Marc's Year 1 class, the children are used to reflecting on their own work and the work of others. An example Marc provided to demonstrate this was in a dance lesson. At certain points in the lesson, children shared their dance sequence and others commented on what they thought the pupil had done well and what they could have done to further improve. The pupil who was performing also had the opportunity to say what they liked about their performance. Marc was able to demonstrate how he had provided these opportunities for pupils to reflect on their learning and progress, through his lesson plans.

In relation to Teachers' Standard 2c and your own practice, consider the following key questions:

- How do you engage pupils in dialogue about their learning and progress?
- What opportunities do you provide for pupils to use self or peer assessment tasks and activities to support them in developing reflective skills?
- When do you support learners in making judgements about their progress towards meeting the learning objectives?
- How do you ensure pupils know what they have achieved and work out what they need to do next to improve?

Possible sources of evidence for Teachers' Standard 2c:

- Lesson observations/evaluations;
- Self and peer assessment opportunities;
- Responses to marking and feedback;
- Class environments promoting space for reflection;
- Planning to show activities/strategies which encourage reflection;
- Formative assessment, marking with pupils using target setting/success criteria.

2d: Demonstrate knowledge and understanding of how pupils learn and how this impacts on teaching

How pupils learn

An understanding of how pupils learn is integral to teaching, enabling activities to be planned which are appropriate to the age and stage of pupils. These activities should provide enough challenge but should not be so demanding that they disengage pupils. There are many different psychological theories to explain how children learn and the main ones used in classrooms are behaviourist theories and cognitive theories (Pritchard, 2014). The term 'behaviourism' is based on the understanding that behaviour can be measured, trained and changed. This involves actions that are observable and central to this educational theory is an understanding that the teacher controls the learning (Cooper, 2014). Cognitive theories, on the other hand, are concerned with learning being an active process involving thinking and memory. Jean Piaget was amongst the theorists who developed this theory. Other influential theorists include

Vygotsky, whose central concept emphasised the value of learning taking place through social interaction. In early years settings, the philosophy of Reggio Emilia may be influential in recognising the value of children following their interests and the role of the teacher as a facilitator. The purpose of this chapter is to raise awareness of some of the different learning theories and to consider how these approaches influence classroom practice. The practice examples below will further illustrate this.

Your own values will influence the decisions you make in the classroom – for example, if you place importance on children using language and questions to challenge each other's thinking, you may draw on the theories of social constructivism in your teaching. When teachers use an enquiry-based approach, they do so because they place importance on children being active enquirers, who create personal and shared meanings. As you consider this example, think about how this approach supports learners to have a positive disposition to learning through their active engagement, asking questions and how it supports children who are motivated. The approach you use will impact on the culture and ethos within the classroom. Developing a secure understanding of learning theories is not only relevant but essential, because as a teacher you are a role model and the pupils in your class will be influenced by your behaviour and will consider this as a platform for how they should behave. The theoretical underpinning helps teachers to interpret some of the learning situations they are faced with, although, as Jacques and Hyland (2007) highlight, it is sometimes difficult for inexperienced teachers to assimilate theory and practice. Experience will help with making connections, as will an ability to consider different theories.

Age and stage

Pupils are at the heart of every classroom and this has to be the starting point for the choices you make about what teaching and learning will look like within the classroom. To meet this standard, you will need to demonstrate that the strategies and activities you have chosen are appropriate for the pupils. This means carefully considering the age and stage of the children. Although you may be teaching a class of Year 2 children, you will know that they are at different levels, socially and academically. How you plan for the child who is performing at a level which is three years below his or her peers will be different to your planning for the others. You may plan for the child to use different resources or have additional adult intervention. This planning may include shorter tasks or activities that require more of a hands-on, kinaesthetic approach where play will be important and for this you may draw on theories that recognise the value of play. Equally, if you have a class of children who are mostly active learners, who enjoy interacting with each other, then your teaching methods will reflect this. You may use more of a social learning theory in which you provide opportunities where pupils can talk to each other and use this as a way of creating new knowledge. On one occasion a teacher in a Year 1 class was observed and during this lesson the children sat for 40 minutes.

The teacher wondered why the children were restless, distracted and uninterested in the lesson. The age of the children impacts greatly on the methods you decide to use and an effective teacher will understand how to engage learners. You will be able to evidence this through your planning and justify why you have chosen to use a specific approach: 'It is the interplay of theory and practical application that leads to understanding. Only daily contact with children in a range of learning situations can help here' (Jacques and Hyland, 2007, p. 88).

 Top Tip: It is not good enough simply to know how to teach without considering why you do what you do and what the impact of this will be. Ultimately, it will be the needs of the pupils that will determine the approach that you use and this will vary for each class that you teach. Theories stay the same but each class you teach will be different.

Practice examples – Teachers' Standard 2d

MARIA

Throughout the last two years of teaching in an early years setting, Maria has become familiar with the expectations of teaching this age group. In particular, she has drawn on the philosophy of the Reggio Emilia approach to inform her practice. She has evidenced how she has arranged the classroom environment to take account of the needs of young learners to enable them to experience an emergent curriculum, based on their interests and needs. Exploration and discovery are at the core of Maria's teaching and she demonstrates this through the environment, through her planning and through the activities the children engage in.

JESS

As a teacher in a Year 1 class, Jess used the data from the EYFS profile to inform her about the new class she would be teaching. As evidence of how pupils learn, she submitted a reflective account from a meeting she had with the Reception year teacher when discussing the EYFS profile and specific children. In her reflections, she noted the stage the children were working at and how she would be managing the transition into a Year 1 class to support the children to settle into a new curriculum. This included using social constructivism as a philosophy to create situations in which pupils could talk to construct learning together.

In relation to Teachers' Standard 2d and your own practice, consider the following key questions:

- How will you ensure the tasks set provide an appropriate challenge? What data can be used to inform your judgement?
- With a range of different learning styles and abilities in the class, how can you ensure all pupils can access the curriculum?
- To what extent are the main learning theories evident in your classroom practice?

Possible sources of evidence for Teachers' Standard 2d:

- Planning to show differentiation for pupils with EAL/SEN or with different learning styles;
- Professional development opportunities/staff training;
- Reflective accounts/evaluations;
- Evidence of modifying lessons in response to pupils' needs through observations/ formative assessment strategies;
- Feedback from lesson observations.

2e: Encourage pupils to take a responsible and conscientious attitude to their own work and study

The role of a teacher is complex and ever changing in response to the needs of pupils and in an effort to develop confident, self-assured individuals. Earlier in this chapter, we discussed Vygotsky's Zone of Proximal Development (ZPD) as a scaffold for learning and now we move on to discuss strategies that will help pupils to be independent in their learning. However, this does not mean they are left to sink or swim. The ZPD may be used as a strategy for building independence; as Cooper (2014) notes, the pupil can draw on the support of a 'slightly more able other' who may be another pupil, rather than an adult. The teacher still has a crucial role to play in developing independence because, as the teacher and pupil talk through the challenges and ideas, pupils are able to clarify their thinking, explain ideas and use higher-order thinking skills. As Pritchard (2014) writes, 'The teacher has the role of stimulating dialogue and maintaining its momentum' (p. 26). (See Figure 2.1.)

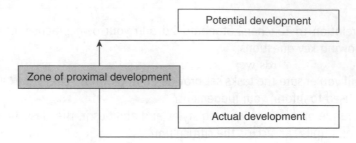

Figure 2.1   Vygotsky's Zone of Proximal Development (Jacques and Hyland, 2007)

What makes an independent learner?

An independent learner is motivated, enjoys mental challenges and is resilient as they strive to reach their aims and targets. They use their minds effectively and develop a certain mindset. Based on empirical research, Dweck (2012) proposed the idea of mindsets being either fixed or growth. In a fixed mindset, learners find it hard to 'have a go', as opposed to those with a growth mindset where the learner has a 'can do' attitude. This is significant for teachers as Dweck (ibid.) discovered that teachers alongside parents are influential in how a child's mindset develops. A growth mindset generates a love of learning and through providing the right experiences in the classroom a teacher can enable pupils to see themselves as life-long learners.

The encouragement of metacognition, encouraging pupils to think about their learning, enables a learner to become responsible for their own learning. Effective methods of supporting metacognition include modelling reflection in your practice and developing opportunities for pupils to reflect on their own skills and understanding. According to James et al. (2007, p. 99), a characteristic of metacognition is the ability to be 'aware of your learning process so that you can self-regulate, i.e. plan what to do next and evaluate and revise strategies'.

This suggests that a learner needs to be willing not to give up and to keep trying. This takes confidence and the way that you organise the learning environment can help to create a positive climate in which pupils feel safe, trusted and can speak freely, knowing their contribution is valued. There are many examples from practice that will help you to evidence this standard, including how you encourage pupils to ask and answer questions, explain their thinking to others, share new ideas and make decisions about their learning. When are pupils supported to develop their own ideas and do they share these with others beyond their own classmates? A Year 4/5 class recently visited the local university to share ideas with trainee teachers on how a good geography lesson should look. The pupils shared lesson plans they had written, including ideas for activities and then taught the trainee teachers. At the end of their presentation, they asked for feedback. Evidence of their resilience and independence shone through during the feedback as they valued comments that would help them to refine and further improve their activities. They were not looking for praise but looked to the trainees for thoughts on how to make their ideas even better. External rewards were not the motivator; rather, the desire to succeed, the intrinsic motivation, was the reason they were so enthusiastic about their learning.

However, Jacques and Hyland (2007) highlight a significant point – this level of autonomy does not just happen: 'During the early stages of learning a new task or topic, learners need plenty of encouragement to succeed. Later, completion of the task itself and the associated satisfaction derived from it may be all the motivation that is needed' (p. 79). As you consider evidence to meet this standard, think about where on the line of continuum your pupils are towards becoming more autonomous. Independence in the classroom can be fostered through providing opportunities for pupils to keep trying and not to give up. In the classroom, modelling can be effective. As Robins (2012, p. 125) explains: 'Modelling increases the perception that a task is achievable and it is important for a teacher to demonstrate that mistakes and errors are not only inevitable when learning, but they are also opportunities.' Pupils need to experience difficulties and challenges in order to build up the tenacity to keep trying. In your practice, try to put enough challenge into an activity to ensure the pupil is engaged, but this should not be so difficult that it causes frustration for the learner. It is all too easy to do a task for a child or to over support them, but by doing this you rob the pupil of a rich learning opportunity. Having the chance to carry on in the face of challenge will develop a resilient disposition. The kinds of activities you plan need to take account of a pupil's interests so that they can demonstrate concentration and involvement and can keep trying until they achieve their target. This means setting up an enabling environment, so that pupils can maintain a focus for extended periods of time and remain fully engaged. The selection of resources is also worth discussing as pupils need to be able to choose the best tools to work with. How accessible the equipment is will have a bearing on the amount of independence a pupil has. The layout of the classroom needs to facilitate easy access to materials, which need to be clearly labelled and well organised. Examples of how you organise the classroom, to facilitate independence, can be used as evidence of your role in encouraging pupils to make choices about their learning.

> *Top Tip*: Over the course of the week, ensure that each pupil has been able to work without the support of an adult. Be careful not to build an island around specific pupils so that they become too dependent on an adult. Clearly communicate the strategies which you expect to see pupils using before they approach an adult for help.

Practice examples – Teachers' Standard 2e

JODIE

Developing independent learners is at the centre of Jodie's values and philosophy. At the beginning of term, Jodie shares a range of strategies with the pupils so that they know what they can do if they get stuck with their work. There is a classroom display with a visual reminder for the pupils which Jodie has taken a photograph of as evidence of how she is supporting the pupils in her class to be more independent. She monitors the use of the strategies, through her observations and makes a record of those children who are using them with confidence, as well as those that may need to be reminded as they are less confident.

RAY

Through his planning, Ray demonstrates how he supports a lower ability group of pupils to develop greater independence and confidence in working on their own. He clearly records which group is supported by the teacher, by the TA and which group is working independently. Over the course of the week, it is easy to see that each group has been supported equally and that each group has worked independently.

 In relation to Teachers' Standard 2e and your own practice, consider the following key questions:

- How do you create opportunities within and outside of the classroom for pupils to become independent learners?
- What level of adult support do different groups receive within a lesson?
- How is the TA deployed? Does the same group always work with the TA?
- How do you show that all pupils have some time when they are supported and some time when they can work autonomously?
- Do pupils know what to do when they are 'stuck'?
- What strategies do pupils use to work through a problem without seeking the support of a teacher or TA?
- What strategies do you use to let pupils know that you cannot be interrupted when working with a target group?
- Do you have photographs of wall displays with strategies for independent working clearly shown?

(Continued)

(Continued)

Possible sources of evidence for Teachers' Standard 2e:

- Books/pupils' work;
- Observations;
- Pupils discussing their targets and suggesting improvements;
- Lesson evaluations.

Chapter summary

This chapter has explored the teacher's role in supporting pupils to achieve the best they can. Attention has been drawn to the ability of the teacher to plan opportunities to ensure pupils can generate their own ideas, take risks, find ways of working out challenges and feel confident in working out their own ways to problem solve. An effective teacher will find ways to meet individual children's interests and provide teaching and learning activities which inspire, motivate and engage pupils to enhance the learning experience. By planning for pupil autonomy, a teacher is able to promote a love of learning. Effective learning is not about completing a task; it is about understanding the process of working out a challenge and the sense of achievement when you have struggled and then found the answer for yourself. This can lead to a feeling of confidence and independence. You may have memories, from when you were at school, of a time when you struggled over a concept – perhaps a word you struggled to read or a spelling that you could not get right. The sense of satisfaction and growth in self-esteem when you mastered this challenge and made progress, form a memory that will stay with you forever. The achievement of self-efficacy and enjoyment of learning is something every effective teacher wants for their pupils.

CHAPTER 3

DEMONSTRATE GOOD SUBJECT AND CURRICULUM KNOWLEDGE

Teachers' Standard 3 – Demonstrate good subject and curriculum knowledge:

3a Have a secure knowledge of the relevant subject(s) and curriculum areas, foster and maintain pupils' interest in the subject, and address misunderstandings

3b Demonstrate a critical understanding of developments in the subject and curriculum areas, and promote the value of scholarship

3c Demonstrate an understanding of and take responsibility for promoting high standards of literacy, articulacy and the correct use of standard English, whatever the teacher's specialist subject

3d If teaching early reading, demonstrate a clear understanding of systematic synthetic phonics

3e If teaching early mathematics, demonstrate a clear understanding of appropriate teaching strategies.

What is this all about?

Developing secure subject knowledge in all aspects of the National Curriculum (DfE, 2013b), appropriate to the age range of pupils within your setting, is an integral part of teacher development and improvement. As professionals, teachers are expected to stay current with new initiatives and subject knowledge and this requires teachers engaging in scholarship, as good practice. It is with a thorough grounding in subject knowledge that teachers are able to plan engaging learning tasks for pupils and to maximise opportunities for progress.

How can this be demonstrated?

By engaging with teacher training programmes and practice in school settings, subject knowledge develops naturally. However, evidencing Teachers' Standard 3 requires the demonstration of a secure understanding of subjects, in addition to how they can be taught in ways that engage learners and ensure they make good progress. There are many ways in which a teacher can demonstrate this, including planning, teaching, pupil progress, to name but a few and it is essential that the developing teacher displays a commitment to regular development in this area, in order to be the best they can be for the pupils they teach. Staff development opportunities are often advertised, both internally and externally and you should choose to engage with any opportunities that arise to increase the value of impact on pupils. In addition, engaging in scholarly activity, such as wider reading, professional discussions with colleagues or registration on accredited courses, is a way in which subject knowledge can be deepened. An additional challenge of Teachers' Standard 3 is evidencing *how* you foster and maintain pupil interest in your teaching and their learning and achievement.

Chapter overview

As teachers, we are in the business of inspiring learners. As identified by Gilbert (Ryan, 2011), there are many ways in which this can be achieved, but it is that essential 'sparkle' that is required in order to demonstrate a dedication to teaching and to the pupils in your care:

> It means to 'breathe life into', inspiration. Not 'perspire' or 'expire' but 'inspire'. To take something inert and lifeless and make it live. Like god with clay when he made humans according to many religions. Only for teachers it is with 8-year-olds. With clay. And paints. And pens. And a sparkle in their eyes. (Ryan, 2011)

Inspirational teaching, underpinned by an expert knowledge and understanding of a subject and planned to engage pupils, paves the way for progress and inspirational, autonomous learning. With curriculum developments ever-changing, it is often challenging for busy teachers to stay up to date – one of the many spinning plates that must be kept aloft in the role of a teacher. Being an effective teacher, however, means seeking out opportunities and engaging with them in order to impact both on professional practice and pupil enjoyment, engagement and outcomes.

In this chapter, we will explore the following key themes:

- Ways in which teachers can develop subject knowledge and provide evidence of this;
- Teachers inspiring learners as a sense of duty;
- Engaging and re-engaging pupils in learning experiences;
- Developing critical approaches to education;
- The value of scholarship and its impact on pupils;
- Ways of evidencing and an understanding of systematic synthetic phonics in early reading and teaching strategies for early mathematics.

Having considered a rationale for the standard, the chapter will provide exemplars of effective practice that you may consider adapting for personal use, in order to further develop your own teaching. Integrating theory with practice, the chapter will go on to explore the background and nature of inclusive education and the ways in which teachers can ensure that they are meeting the needs of pupils and providing challenge, regardless of backgrounds, abilities and dispositions. In the chapter, there will be opportunities for the application and practice of acquired skills, knowledge and understanding, through the engagement of key questions and practical, relevant ideas. Finally, there will be sections on how and where to find sources of evidence and helpful resources.

Taking it apart and putting it back together

We will now examine ways in which teachers can evidence each of the sub-sets, by exploring each in detail and relating it to research and professional practice. We will identify ways in which teachers can locate evidence in order to support this standard.

3a: Have a secure knowledge of the relevant subject(s) and curriculum areas, foster and maintain pupils' interest in the subject, and address misunderstandings

Secure subject knowledge and addressing misunderstandings

OK, so you have engaged thoroughly with all aspects of your training and experiences in school and you think you know your subjects. But how can you demonstrate this deep understanding when colleagues, parents, carers or – let's face it – inspectors walk into your classroom and you suddenly find yourself in a high-pressure situation and all eyes are on you? Simple. You've planned for this. In everyday learning situations, it is your responsibility to your pupils to 'show what you know' and to find ways of supporting them in their developing understanding. Pupils think that teachers are the font of all knowledge and there is nothing wrong with that, except that we are not. Keeping the dream alive, however, is a powerful tool in reassuring pupils that great learning can be achieved through hard work and dedication. It can act as an invisible motivator and the teacher becomes an effective role model for learning. In reality, what effective teachers demonstrate is a thorough subject knowledge that is grounded in facts, an understanding of progressive stages and the ability to communicate this to pupils in ways in which they can access learning.

Primary teachers have the added pressure of staying current with all subjects. As teachers, there is the expectation that we are well-versed in all aspects of every curriculum subject, regardless of our specialisms and subject preferences. Whilst training and school experience seek to deepen this knowledge and understanding, to be an effective teacher you need to examine the opportunities around you in order to capitalise on this. So, where can they be found? In order to answer this question, we will examine the environment in which a teacher operates.

Use what you know

Reflect on your learning and development and refer back to training notes and supportive subject-specific resources. Draw on the experiences you have had in your setting. How does this link to your existing knowledge and contribute to your understanding? Draw on the National Curriculum (DfE, 2013b) and unpick the meaning of the subject content objectives. Attempt problems yourself and record the stages you go through in order to make progress. What difficulties or potential questions arise?

💡 *Top Tip*: Try mind-mapping a subject or topic and identify all that you know about the subject, including any questions that could be raised. Linking this to curriculum objectives, use this as a basis for your own subject development and planning for pupils.

Colleagues and subject leaders

In schools, people are resources. Draw on the expertise of colleagues with greater experience and in particular those who hold a subject responsibility. Often, subject leaders construct whole-school planning and have an excellent understanding of how this relates to age phases and curriculum requirements. Never be afraid to ask questions – this can be viewed in a positive light and as proactive professional conduct. A positive school ethos is one which embraces teacher development and collegiate working.

Resources

Most settings have great libraries and within them, a variety of non-fiction texts to help support pupil understanding on a range of topics. Teachers can use them, too! Professional subscriptions to journals, some of which may be funded by school, are another resource. In addition, the internet can provide some excellent resources to support subjects (e.g. www.tes.co.uk/teaching-resources) and there are a wealth of teacher forums and social and professional networking sites, of which you can become a part. In the modern age of technologically enhanced learning, it is inexcusable to be ill prepared for a lesson when a world of information is – literally – at your fingertips.

Research

Research-informed practice is a pre-requisite to reflective, effective teaching. Later in this chapter, we will explore ways in which a teacher can maximise research opportunities and use these for the benefit of their own professional development and the development of their pupils.

So, now that I know it, how can I show it?

Below, are some simple ways in which you can demonstrate your excellent subject knowledge:

- *Planning*: A lesson plan can show how well you understand a subject by the way in which you pitch activities; the intended learning outcomes identified for groups of learners and individuals; the age and stage for which you have planned; activities that provide challenge and support; lesson structure; opportunities for autonomous learning; identification of assessment opportunities; key questions; innovative ways of using (and supporting) other adults; and pre-empting pupil misconceptions.
- *Teaching*: If you understand your subject, it radiates from you when you are teaching. Confidence will be greater and explanations and support, clearer. The ways in which you teach and the activities you design and implement will demonstrate your subject knowledge effectively and how you address questions and misconceptions (with sensitivity) will exemplify your knowledge.
- *Impact*: If your pupils are learning *and* making progress, your teaching, grounded in thorough and up-to-date subject knowledge, is having an impact on learners. This impact can be seen in pupil engagement, in work, questions, participation, for example.

Very often, teacher passion for a subject can be infectious and learners cannot help but get caught up in the magic of an engaging, well-planned lesson. Keep in mind – it is not about what you do but how this can impact on learning and progress.

- *Dissemination and collegiate working*: This could be through classroom or school displays, such as 'working walls' or sharing at team or staff meetings. Showing your subject knowledge and the developing subject knowledge of pupils through dissemination is an easy way to evidence this part of the standard. Showcase this knowledge and show pupils that their developing knowledge is valued.

Foster and maintain pupils' interest

How can pupil interest be defined and how can you spot it? If pupils are interested in something, their behaviour, attitude to learning and engagement with a task are affected. Pupils may show that they are more motivated to learn if the subject holds a particular interest for them and they may seek out challenge, independently. Conversely, pupils may display undesirable behaviours or 'switch off' if they are not interested in a task or subject. In turn, they may lack the motivation to complete a task and disengage from the process. Consequently, developing knowledge of ways in which pupil interest can be a tool to support learning, is crucial, as is a recognition of ways in which pupils can be motivated and engaged in order to foster and maintain interest.

'If the optimal conditions are provided, the learner will achieve their potential' (Buckler and Castle, 2014, p. 221). Achieving and indeed *exceeding*, learner potential, as identified by Buckler and Castle (2014), is a principal aim of a teacher. The 'optimal conditions' described here could include a wide range of factors, such as environmental, physical and psychological, but by engaging pupils in learning experiences, opportunities for achievement can be exploited. In Chapter 1, we discussed ways in which pupils can be engaged, however maintaining pupil interest is crucial if learning and progress are to be achieved. On motivation, Buckler and Castle (2014) propose: 'Although teachers can influence motivation, it is not something we can "give": it is something teachers can facilitate within each learner to ensure they utilize their inherent energy and direct this into an educational activity' (p. 237).

They go on to suggest that:

> One way to achieve such a potential is through ensuring that the learner has a sense of autonomy and choice in their learning, that they understand their skills (or know how to develop them), also that they can work with others, both peers and teachers: in other words, the three components of self-determination theory. (p. 237)

Providing pupils with autonomous learning opportunities as a motivational tool to hold or spark pupil interest, is one way in which a teacher can evidence this sub-set.

In addition, the provision of support and signposts to aid learning are essential tools in increasing pupil independence and can preclude barriers to learning and 'I can't' statements from learners.

Nottingham (2013) reminds us that 'how much effort someone puts into a task is equal to how much they *want* to achieve it multiplied by how much they expect to achieve it' (p. 12). He goes on to state: 'To believe they can succeed, children need to feel that they can influence outcomes' (p. 13).

Successful outcomes can be achieved, then, if pupils are motivated to learn *and keep on* learning. There exist, of course, many definitions of motivation (Chandler and Connell, 1987; Hayamizu, 1997; Ryan and Deci, 2000) and these are worthy of independent research, but the element of maintenance of interest and pupils exhibiting a dedication to a learning experience are essential considerations in demonstrating Teachers' Standard 3a. In Chinese martial arts terminology, pupil dedication could be considered as 'kung fu' or 'skill achieved through hard work'. This relates to Nottingham's (2013) model of: *effort = desire x expectation*. Engagement and maintenance of pupil interest are exemplified through the amount of effort a child places on a task or learning experience, their motivation for perseverance and their high expectations for and self-belief in the achievement of successful outcomes. In short, pupil interest can be observed by ways in which they engage with a task, but a swift response and action are essential at the moment of disengagement, in order to further maintain interest and increase motivation. This may mean using positive reinforcement in order to encourage pupil self-belief or simply enthusing about the task and the satisfaction of achievement.

The ways in which you teach and your pupils learn and progress will provide additional evidence for this standard. Show that you know your pupils exceptionally well and use this knowledge to better provide meaningful experiences for pupils. Above all, show that you know what matters to them, in addition to their *intrinsic* and *extrinsic* motivators (Ryan and Deci, 2000). Summarised, *extrinsic* motivators may be described as being motivated to do something in order to avoid a punishment or perhaps to gain some type of reward. In context, this may be a pupil engaging in a task simply to earn a sticker. *Intrinsic* motivators come from within; the reward being simply an inherent desire to achieve something without the external motivation of a reward or punishment. Linking back to previous discussions relating to fostering pupil interest, if this is to be maintained, children need to be engaged and motivated in order to continue to be interested. Put simply, what happens if the sticker chart is full? Where is the motivation? Thus, *intrinsic* motivators have the potential for engagement longevity. Smith (2010) suggests that, in order to engage pupils, teachers should 'be unpredictable' (p. 14) at times, in order to keep pupils focused and interested, but balance this with clear routines and an environment in which pupils feel secure. To foster and maintain pupil interest, you need to engage your pupils from the start. Ryan (2011) explains this by using the following metaphor: 'Learning from Clinton Cards: The entrance to Clinton Cards is the most important space in the store. It seeks to hook you in so that you feel compelled to make purchases' (p. 27).

By learning from the ways in which products are displayed in a store front and applying this to education, perhaps our 'entrances' could be our classrooms or introductions to lessons and the 'purchases' could be pupil motivation and investment in time to engage with learning.

Practice examples – Teachers' Standard 3a

BEN

When Ben introduces a new topic to pupils, he begins by asking them to communicate or record all of the questions they have about a topic. These questions are recorded on post-it notes on a mini working wall for that subject and as each question is answered and all pupils show their understanding, the pupils tear it from the board and shout the answer in unison, moving it to the 'We've got it!' section of the board.

MACKENZIE

Mackenzie is research-active. Recently, she has been asked to lead in teaching primary languages and whilst she has some linguistic capabilities and training on languages methodology and pedagogy, she has decided to develop her subject knowledge further by enrolling on a language course. Mackenzie aims to build on her linguistic capabilities through interaction with colleagues on the course, in addition to developing her understanding of language acquisition by engaging in wider reading and examining case studies in school settings. Mackenzie has written an 'impact plan' in order to consider fully the impact of her development on the pupils and staff in her setting.

In relation to Teachers' Standard 3a and your own practice, consider the following key questions:

- How do you stay current with regard to subject knowledge?
- Explore professional development opportunities in your setting. In what ways can you develop further?
- When pupils have questions about a particular topic, how do you handle these in a way that supports pupils, sensitively?

(Continued)

(Continued)

- How do you engage pupils?
- What strategies do you employ to maintain pupil interest?

Possible sources of evidence for Teachers' Standard 3a:

- Colleagues;
- The setting: take a look at the resources around you;
- Observing *and* reflecting on great practice;
- Your pupils: how well do you know them and their interest? What engages them? How well do you plan to include these 'motivators' in your lessons?

3b: Demonstrate a critical understanding of developments in the subject and curriculum areas, and promote the value of scholarship

Being aware of current subject and curriculum developments is an obvious essential attribute of an effective teacher, but having the confidence to take a critical view of these and then communicate this critical view or have it impact on practice, is a step further. As Wilson (2009) stresses, standing back from practice is necessary in order to develop a deepened understanding of the implications of your practice and ways in which it can be developed further: 'in order to understand why things happen in the way they do, this necessitates standing back and taking time to deliberate more explicitly about practice' (p. 3).

In order to achieve this, first let us examine what it means to be critical and then the ways in which you can address this standard within your setting and beyond, in order to develop your professional practice.

The critical teacher

Systematic and rigorous critical reflection, as defined by Ghaye and Ghaye (1998, p. 9), should be a part of regular practice for the primary teacher:

> Teaching is value-laden practice. Values help teachers to make decisions on how to proceed. Evidence helps teachers make wise and principled decisions. Confident and competent

teaching requires teachers to reflect systematically and rigorously on evidence derived from practice. Reflective teaching and learning then is evidence-based.

By collecting and analysing evidence of successes and areas for development, a teacher can move forward with confidence and competence, secure in the knowledge that they have done all that they can to succeed for the pupils with whom they are working.

Brookfield (1995, p. 15) perhaps one of the most notable theorists on critical reflection, argues: 'Good teaching = whatever helps students learn. Best teaching is critically reflective – constant scrutiny of assumptions about teaching/conditions fostering learning.'

On Brookfield's argument, Miller (2010, p. 15) considers:

The goal of the critically reflective teacher, for Brookfield, is to garner an increased awareness of his or her teaching from as many different vantage points as possible. To this end, Brookfield proposes four lenses that can be engaged by teachers in a process of critical reflection: (1) the autobiographical, (2) the students' eyes, (3) our colleagues' experiences, and (4) theoretical literature. These lenses correlate to processes of self-reflection, student feedback, peer assessment, and engagements with scholarly literature. Cogitating on these processes provides the foundation for good teaching and the means to become an excellent teacher.

Considering Brookfield's (1995) four lenses and using Miller's (2010) approach to defining each lens, we will now relate these lenses to the classroom environment and explore where and how these 'vantage points' can aid critical reflection, by simplifying the meaning of each:

1. The autobiographical: Critically reflect on your own experiences as a learner and a teacher and use these to inform good practice.
2. The students' eyes: Using information gained from questioning, peer assessments, responses to marking and pupil progress, consider, critically, how the learning could have been improved for individuals and use this information to impact on future planning and teaching.
3. Our colleagues' experiences: Learn from others and listen to advice. Take suggestions for areas for development as a platform on which you can build better learning experiences for pupils.
4. Theoretical literature: Be research-active. Interact, critically, with the literature and use it to inform your own opinions, pedagogical philosophies and research-informed practice.

Critical reflection deserves a chapter in its own right and the importance of learning about this aspect of professional practice and the ways in which it can impact on your own, cannot be understated.

> Top Tip: Engage in *critical* wider reading regarding critical reflection. Interact with research and use it to (a) inform your own pedagogical philosophies and (b) impact on practice. Begin to view the word 'critical' as a positive element of practice.

Classroom critical

Being critically reflective, as discussed, is part of the role of a teacher. This may start, at classroom level, by being critically reflective with regard to your teaching and planning and how this impacts directly on pupils. A step-by-step guide to being classroom critical may facilitate this process:

Reflect on each lesson. Ask yourself the following questions:

> *Did your pupils learn what was intended?*
> *How do you know? (Evidence)*
> *What could you have done differently to facilitate learning and progress?*
> *How will this impact on future practice?*

These questions and perhaps more importantly, the answers, could be recorded as annotations on a lesson plan, as part of a lesson evaluation or simply in a notebook. Use these critical reflections to inform future practice and to improve the learning experience for your pupils.

Workplace critical

Within educational settings, there exists a vast array of policies, plans and procedures, all of which are open to scrutiny and review by members of staff. Whilst you will have read school policies, you may have a particular viewpoint, perhaps informed by theory or experience, that may impact on the way in which these documents are presented. In some cases, the senior leadership team, or subject leaders, may welcome constructive, sensitively approached reflective, critical comments and suggestions, if these have the potential to improve and impact positively.

In addition, there should be many opportunities for you to engage in observation of good practice in your setting, whether during a formal teaching and learning observation involving a member of the teaching team, or a learning walk. Both opportunities provide excellent openings in which to engage in critical dialogue with colleagues. That is not to say that you *criticise* colleagues, but rather that you discuss anything with which you were previously unfamiliar or about which questions were raised, or simply discuss pupil impact, from a productively critical stance. However, it is important to note that, as Wilson (2009) points out:

> Becoming a teacher involves more than just being 'told what to do', developing skills or mimicking other teachers. Therefore, reflecting *on* and *in* classrooms is an important part of being a teacher and is the essence of researching practice. (p. 15)

Beyond the workplace critical

This is where your role as teacher-researcher comes to the forefront. Being research-active is vital if you are to remain at the vanguard of education and teach with authority. Sotto (1994) considered teaching *as* learning and the impact that this can have on pupils. Discussing the importance of teacher clarity, Sotto suggested the following attributes as essential:

1. Having a thorough knowledge of one's subject

2. The ability to see to the heart of a topic

3. The ability to see the matter from a learner's perspective, and

4. The ability to explain the matter simply. (Sotto, 1994, p. 18)

Whilst points 2 and 4 may be down to the individual teacher's personal skills, research-informed practice can pave the way to successful outcomes in all of these areas. With this in mind, the following are some simple ways in which you can engage actively and critically with research.

Wider reading

Know what is current and stay up to date with educational change. An easy way to do this is through educational forums or weekly publications, where educational developments are presented, analysed critically and shared. In addition, consider the range of pedagogical theorists and texts with which you engaged during training.

Explore:

1. How do these theories shape your own view of pedagogy?

2. In what ways do you use this knowledge and understanding to impact on the *improvement* of your lessons?

3. What don't you agree with and what evidence can you present to form a counter-argument?

The above questions are simply a scaffold on which to hang your own ideas and opinions. Dedicated teachers not only engage with educational issues, debates and developments but begin to develop their own evidence-based theories. Thus, teachers also become researchers and theorists. Believe in yourself and your developing abilities as a teacher. You have valid opinions that can be supported by evidence of your own experiences and practice. Share these and use them to develop further.

Classroom-based research

If you wish to explore a particular element of pedagogical practice, consider engaging with small-scale research within your own setting. Actually, teachers do this on a daily basis: teachers use what the evidence tells them in order to adapt practice and improve learning experiences. However, to use a phrase coined by a colleague, it is prudent to remember that 'the only way is ethics' (#TOWIE)! The design of more scientifically and ethically sound research can occur within your setting and by gathering data pertaining to areas of interest or school improvement. It is essential to engage, periodically, in data-gathering exercises that have the potential to impact, with immediacy, on pupil progress and feed into whole-school data. Alternatively, you may wish to present an 'impact study' of a particular child or children in your class. For example, you may have a child who has exhibited difficulties in grasping numerical concepts who has suddenly achieved success in this area. By engaging in critical reflection and wider reading pertaining to this topic, an impact study of this child may lead to future innovations, adaptations to practice and impact beyond your own classroom.

Alternative setting research

As teachers, it is very easy to become submerged within the confines of your setting, particularly as a newly qualified teacher. It is important for teachers to develop an understanding of successful practice in other settings in order that it may inform improvements in their own. Moreover, it is important to share good practice and think 'beyond the classroom', if teachers are to impact more widely, to the potential benefit of children everywhere.

What kind of teacher are you? Do you sit back and let the learning happen or do you become actively and reflectively involved, demonstrating an improvement and impact focus and contribute to educational theory by evidencing your own practice? In the words of the poet, O'Shaunessy (1874), are you 'a mover and shaker'?

(Continued)

(Continued)

We are the music makers,

And we are the dreamers of dreams,

Wandering by lone sea-breakers

And sitting by desolate streams;

World-losers and world-forsakers,

On whom the pale moon gleams:

Yet we are the movers and shakers

Of the world for ever, it seems. (O'Shaunessy, 1874, p. 308)

 Top Tip: Actively seek out opportunities to collaborate with other settings and devise best practice scenarios. Share those things that work well and those that don't and work as a team in order to develop excellence in education. Be 'a mover and shaker'.

 ### Practice examples – Teachers' Standard 3b

CHRISSIE

Chrissie has made links with other local primary schools and has formed a 'hub' for developing excellent practice within the early years. Early years representatives from all settings meet on a monthly basis in order to share successes and engage with current developments relating to early years practice. Chrissie ensures that she disseminates this to other members of staff within her setting and has documented evidence of the impact on her own practice and the practice of her pupils.

RHIANNON

Rhiannon is a Year 6 teacher. In order to better facilitate the transition for her pupils into Year 7, she has forged links with local secondary schools and throughout the

(Continued)

(Continued)

academic year, schools meet to discuss curriculum content, educational developments and ways to better improve the transition between phases. All teachers involved in this union have benefitted from increased subject knowledge beyond their phase of expertise and have used this to improve the experience of pupils in their care.

 In relation to Teachers' Standard 3b and your own practice, consider the following key questions:

- When was the last time you engaged with a journal or educational text?
- In what ways could you develop your own research practice?
- How do you stay current, with regard to your own subject knowledge?
- In what ways can you evidence your own critical reflection and the impact of this on your own practice?

Possible sources of evidence for Teachers' Standard 3b:

- Feedback from pupils;
- Pedagogical journals and texts and publications, such as the *Times Educational Supplement* (how will you use these to demonstrate that theory impacts on practice?);
- Local settings (what can you learn?);
- Colleagues and collegiate commentary/working;
- Social media and education forums (how could you use these?);
- Records of your own professional development;
- Pupil progress data analysis and action;
- Annotations on lesson plans and adaptations to subsequent lessons.

3c: Demonstrate an understanding of and take responsibility for promoting high standards of literacy, articulacy and the correct use of standard English, whatever the teacher's specialist subject

As identified previously, a teacher is a role model and thus, a teacher is required to articulate the highest standards of literacy and standard English, in every aspect of their working life. On reflection, this is an obvious trait of a professional teacher, as the subsequent fictitious scenario demonstrates:

Miss X was a teacher of Year 2 pupils in an inner-city school. Miss X had graduated from university with a first-class honours degree in primary teaching and was extremely dedicated to her chosen profession. One day, in a rush to send out the weekly class newsletter, Miss X neglected to proofread and edit the content thoroughly and the letter went home to parents/carers. Unfortunately, in her haste, Miss X had neglected to spot several spelling errors in the letter content and was horrified when her head teacher approached her on Monday morning, indicating that several parents/carers had complained about the quality of Miss X's literacy skills and expressed their concerns regarding Miss X educating their children. Whilst Miss X issued a written apology to parents/carers with her usual, high standard of literacy, the damage had been done and parents/carers had lost confidence in her abilities as a literate educator. In turn, this reflected poorly on the school.

💡 *Top Tip*: Check every worksheet, letter, display, comment and word, carefully. It is vital that you demonstrate the highest standards of literacy in all aspects of your profession and act as the best form of role model, in this regard.

Bennett (1996) writes about teachers being role models to the children with whom they work:

If we want our children to possess the traits of character we most admire, we need to teach them what those traits are and why they deserve both admiration and allegiance. Children must learn to identify the forms and content of those traits. (p. 11)

These words have significant value and the essence of their meaning is grounded in Teachers' Standard 3c. It is your responsibility to model effective literacy skills in every aspect of your practice and this is non-negotiable. No matter what learning difficulties you may experience, the fact that you have gained your teaching qualification is a testament to the fact that you are able to demonstrate these skills effectively. We will begin by considering how these high standards can be demonstrated in everyday practice, before considering how difficulties can be overcome for teachers with learning disabilities, such as dyslexia.

High standards of literacy in everyday practice

Teacher checklist:

- Prepare texts well in advance of lessons.
- Ensure that all spelling, grammar and punctuation on displays, flipcharts, in marking, letters, worksheets, homework and the board are accurate and without errors.

- When writing with and in front of pupils, have the confidence and professionalism to use a dictionary to check any unfamiliar words or words which you have difficulty spelling, rather than guessing and making errors. Better still, involve pupils in this good practice of checking spelling.
- Ensure that other adults working with pupils in your class are provided with grammatically accurate text with which to work and check that their own standards in literacy are high and without error. If you have any doubts about this, it must be addressed, as you will be accountable.
- Where minor errors occur, discuss these with pupils. Do not simply ignore the errors and 'pretend' that they aren't there.
- When speaking to pupils, ensure that you are demonstrating the highest standards of oracy and grammatically correct speech. Encourage pupils to do the same and teach them the rules.

In demonstrating Teachers' Standard 3c, you are exercising the necessary professionalism and rigour that is expected of a qualified teacher and sufficient time should be devoted to this essential element of practice.

Teachers with learning disabilities: dyslexia

As a teacher, having a learning disability, such as dyslexia, has the potential to help you better understand the needs of the pupils with whom you work. Haigh (2001, p. 6), for example, identifies 'the empathy they have with children who have differing learning needs'. That is not to say that teaching (and learning) with dyslexia isn't a challenging task, but those who have chosen to rise to this extensive challenge and pursue a career in teaching, already display a commitment to self-improvement and a willingness to address their individual needs. When working as a teacher with dyslexia, it is important to engage in rigorous checking of the written word; to identify local support networks within your area; and to have a self-belief that you can offer the same high quality education to pupils as non-dyslexics. Above all, be transparent and display a commitment to working *with* dyslexia rather than it being a barrier to your success.

Further advice and support for those teachers requiring it (at the time of print) is available from: The British Dyslexia Association, Unit 8, Bracknell Beeches, Old Bracknell Lane, Bracknell, RG12 7BW. Helpline: 0333 405 4555; email: helpline@bda-dyslexia.org.uk; website: www.bdadyslexia.org.uk/.

3d: If teaching early reading, demonstrate a clear understanding of systematic synthetic phonics

Whilst Ofsted (2012) focuses on systematic synthetic phonics excellence as an approach to teaching phonics in the early years, developments in this area have moved away from a standardised model of teaching, offering the teacher of phonics flexibility in their teaching style. The four-part model of revisit and review; teach; practise; and apply (DfES, 2007) is, however, favoured by many teachers and research has shown that this model of teaching can be effective, when combined with other activities, in supporting early reading (Whitehead, 2010; DfES, 2007, in Glazzard and Stokoe, 2013).

Systematic synthetic phonics is based on the assumption that simple decoding is all that is required in reading and teaches the sounds of individual letters and the 44 phonemes (Whitehead, 2010: 140). However, it has been suggested by Glazzard and Stokoe (2013) that:

> unless children learnt to apply the learning from their phonics lessons to reading and writing, teaching of phonics will not be effective … This is because the quality of teaching is judged by its impact on pupils' learning … Consequently, as much effort needs to go into teaching children how to apply their phonic knowledge and skills as is put into the teaching of phonics. (p. 76)

As a teacher of early reading, classroom strategies in settings may differ, with some settings demonstrating a structured, daily approach to phonics 'lessons', whilst others embed phonics more flexibly in daily activity. However, in order to meet Teachers' Standard 3d, you will be required to demonstrate that your understanding is thorough and your articulation of phonemes during teaching is without error.

It is important to be aware of the different views on phonics. Glazzard and Stokoe (2013) state: 'The effective teaching of synthetic phonics necessitates a systematic approach where there is a clear teaching sequence to enable children to build on their prior learning' (p. 64), although Whitehead (2010) has suggested that 'overdependence on a daily literacy and phonics session tends to downgrade the inside and outdoors areas as prime sites for literacy learning and discoveries' (p. 149).

Whatever the strategies employed within your setting, ensure that you are well planned and well versed in pronunciation and demonstration of systematic synthetic phonics. Wider, up-to-date reading in this area is essential, in order to build on your initial teacher training and school experiences. It may be prudent to maximise the learning opportunities within other learning areas and to plan for developmental phonics as part of free-flow pupil exploration and play. These activities could be adult-guided or independent and involve both the written graphemes and audio-support devices, such as sound recorders, computers or tablets. Glazzard and Stokoe (2013) suggest that teachers need to be aware that children might not automatically apply their phonic knowledge and skills in their independent reading and writing outside the phonics lesson and aware of the importance of developing a print-rich environment in order to facilitate development in early reading.

Top Tip: In your teaching and planning, show what you know and highlight what your pupils know. Support what they don't and apply and challenge what they do.

 Practice examples – Teachers' Standard 3d

ROXANNE

Roxanne has built in phonics activities in all free-flow areas of her learning environment – both inside and out. She has printed and displayed name labels for classroom and outdoor items and each label includes a sound button. The sound buttons demonstrate how to say the word and how the word can be broken down into its separate components. Roxanne has encouraged pupils to make the recordings and when a pupil is seen engaging with the sound buttons and using these to aid learning they are given a reward.

ANTHONY

Anthony is committed to maximising the potential for learning in the outdoor learning area. He has created large, laminated sound cards for outdoor use and encourages pupils to engage with these in order to form words. Sometimes guided by an adult and sometimes independently, pupils are encouraged to write their words on an outdoor board, followed by their initials and rewarded for their efforts. This learning tool provides evidence of what pupils are able to do, which informs the planning of future activities.

 In relation to Teachers' Standard 3d and your own practice, consider the following key questions:

- Where can phonics learning occur in your setting?
- In what other ways do you support early reading?
- How do you assess individual pupil progress in daily practice?
- What opportunities do you give pupils to apply their knowledge and understanding and how do you assess this?

(Continued)

(Continued)

Possible sources of evidence for Teachers' Standard 3d:

- Displays;
- Resources and activities;
- Learning areas;
- Planning;
- Regular observation and assessment monitoring and data;
- Accuracy in teaching;
- Celebration of pupil successes;
- Pupil progress.

3e: If teaching early mathematics, demonstrate a clear understanding of appropriate teaching strategies

When planning for early mathematics, it is essential to build a bridge between early mathematical experiences with which the children have previously engaged and the school or nursery setting. Unless children have already had formal schooling experiences, perhaps by being part of a pre-school, their encounters of mathematics will have been real-life interactions, through thought, experience and play. Tucker (2010) suggests: 'Frequently, when young children begin formal schooling, they lose interest and confidence in their mathematical abilities, often because their experience of mathematics has gone from the meaningful to the abstract very quickly' (p. 8).

How early mathematics is taught, then, will require a thorough examination of this transition process in order to better serve the pupils in our care.

 Top Tip: Make time to observe great practice. If you have the opportunity, visit other settings and engage in professional dialogues regarding best practice.

Clements and Sarama (2014) consider 'learning trajectories' as being a way forward in the effective teaching of mathematics. Linking theory to practice, learning trajectories have three significant parts to them: a specific mathematical goal; a path along which children develop to reach that goal; and a set of instructional activities that help children move along that path. In essence, the three elements ensure that teachers have a secure understanding of mathematics, of the way that children think and learn about mathematics and of what can help them learn it better (Clements and Samara, 2014, p. ix).

In an independent review of mathematics teaching in early years settings and primary schools (Williams, 2008), it was recommended that teachers need to embrace more fully the mathematical learning that occurs outside of the school or pre-school setting. In addition, it was recommended that early years practitioners should:

> have the opportunity to continually develop their knowledge and their understanding of effective pedagogy in supporting young children's mathematical development. That must include a clear grasp of children's understanding of mathematical concepts ... and appropriate ways of developing a learning environment that facilitates learning about these things through play. It also involves building knowledge of how to engage with children and extend the way in which their play helps them become familiar and confident with mathematics as part of their everyday world and experience. (2008, p. 40)

The key messages here are concerned with how teachers embrace continuing professional development opportunities that display an impact on pupil learning and ways in which pupils learn. Pedagogy, grounded in theory and forming the basis of effective teaching and consequently, learning, signposts excellent mathematical teaching. Cotton (2010) considers learner misconceptions as a starting point for developing effective teaching strategies. One way in which you can develop your teaching strategy repertoire is by identifying potential pupil misconceptions and exploring how to assist pupils in developing their knowledge, skills and understanding. In a report published by Ofsted (2011), it was shown that practical activities are of crucial importance for 3–7-year-olds, coupled with plenty of opportunities for developing an understanding of mathematical language and ensuring pupils fully master each stage before the next steps are introduced. This, of course, has huge implications for teaching and learning. In all cases, a thorough understanding of mathematics, the curriculum and related pedagogy is essential in evidencing Teachers' Standard 3e. You will be required to demonstrate your understanding through your teaching, planning and assessment and your recognition of those factors that aid pupil development in mathematics. You will be expected to show your knowledge of how pupils can be supported and challenged in all areas of early mathematics and to provide excellent opportunities to do so, both in and beyond the classroom. Close home–school links are essential in outstanding provision, as this allows pupils to be well supported in their mathematical development in all aspects of their life. Tucker (2010) supports this: 'One of the most powerful, self-motivating contexts for mathematics in the home and daycare settings is play, and thus it can provide a meaningful link with school' (p. 5).

By making mathematics meaningful through the provision of effective, cross-curricular learning opportunities, both in your setting and extended to the home environment, through exceptional communication and home–school liaison, you will support mathematical learning. Ensure that you take time to observe excellent, up-to-date practice and engage in wider reading in order to further improve your own practice. Evaluate the effectiveness of your teaching and pupil learning and adapt subsequent inputs accordingly. The incorporation of a variety of teaching strategies that embrace a variety of learning approaches is essential, if learning is to be successful and inclusive for all.

> *Top Tip*: Make the most of early years resources in supporting early mathematical development. Engage pupils in mathematical songs, stories and role play; provide resources to prompt mathematical thinking; encourage kinaesthetic learning experiences, such as drawing numbers in the sand. Make early mathematics exploration and learning fun, in order to pave the way for life-long mathematical learning.

Practice examples – Teachers' Standard 3e

BAILEY

Bailey has made a set of 'maths bugs'. The idea behind the bugs is to provide additional support for pupils requiring further assistance with mathematical understanding. Bailey has instilled within his Reception class a sense of mutual support and sensitivity and maths bugs are centred on pupil-to-pupil support. If a child is having difficulty with mathematics, at any time, they are able to collect a maths bug from a bag and share it with a 'maths buddy'. It is the responsibility of the maths buddy to help support the child. If an understanding is reached, the bug is placed on a display and the child who had initially requested the bug has the opportunity to 'show off' their understanding to other pupils. The supportive pupil gains a reward. Where understanding is still insecure, the bug can be placed on the 'teacher time' display for one-to-one support.

JOLIE

Jolie has introduced the topic of 'Goldilocks and the Three Bears' in her foundation stage setting. Prior to introducing the story, Jolie created a mind map of all of the mathematics that could be learned through the story, such as numbers, counting and size. Linking with other areas of the Early Years Foundation Stage (EYFS) curriculum, Jolie transformed her classroom and outdoor learning area into a Goldilocks themed setting in which she presented a wide variety of guided and independent mathematical learning opportunities for pupils. Pupils were immersed in rich mathematical exploratory activities, which acted as motivators, developed skills, knowledge and understanding and sparked pupil curiosity.

In relation to Teachers' Standard 3e and your own practice, consider the following key questions:

- How do pupils develop mathematical knowledge, skills and understanding in your setting?
- What informs the design of your teaching strategies?
- How do you assess individual pupil progress in daily practice?
- How do you measure the impact of your teaching on pupil progress?

Possible sources of evidence for Teachers' Standard 3e:

- The learning environment;
- Resources and activities;
- Teaching;
- Planning and activity design;
- Regular observation and assessment monitoring and data;
- Pupil progress.

Chapter summary

Stay up to date with initiatives and curriculum developments. Pre-empt pupil misconceptions and build time into your lessons to address these. Listen to your pupils and know what sparks their interest and enthusiasm. Vary the learning experiences you provide and allow an element of pupil choice. Challenge your thinking by engaging with literature and research and engage in small-scale research of your own in order to impact further on the pupils you teach. Be a good role model for learning and hard work and share your findings and educational interests with your pupils. Consider your setting and the environment in which pupils learn each day. How can you maximise the potential for pupil learning in early reading and mathematics? Demonstrate a good understanding of early mathematics teaching and systematic synthetic phonics teaching strategies and vary your approaches to these, adapting to the needs of individuals. Exhibit high standards of literacy and oracy at all times and demand the same of your pupils.

CHAPTER 4

PLAN AND TEACH WELL-STRUCTURED LESSONS

Teachers' Standard 4 – Plan and teach well-structured lessons:

4a Impart knowledge and develop understanding through effective use of lesson time

4b Promote a love of learning and children's intellectual curiosity

4c Set homework and plan other out-of-class activities to consolidate and extend the knowledge and understanding pupils have acquired

4d Reflect systematically on the effectiveness of lessons and approaches to teaching

4e Contribute to the design and provision of an engaging curriculum within the relevant subject area(s).

What is this all about?

Planning for exceptional learning experiences that ensure progress for all, is intrinsic to becoming a successful teacher. In addition, planning for high quality teaching that embraces the intended learning outcomes, considers the needs of all learners and actively engages pupils in learning (and progressing) is essential. A significant part of effective planning and teaching is due consideration for the way in which individual lessons are structured, to ensure that the key themes are addressed.

How can this be demonstrated?

Whether you are a trainee teacher on practice in a school or a newly qualified teacher (NQT) working in school, there are numerous opportunities to meet this standard in daily practice. Teachers' Standard 4 encompasses the very essence of what it means to be a successful primary practitioner and more specifically, a developed understanding of the importance of planning within a cycle of professional practice is vital. Through liaising with mentors, year group partners and other key staff within the setting, the 'ingredients' for a successful, well-structured lesson can be acquired, in addition to a thorough understanding of pedagogy. Furthermore, there are many opportunities for development in this area outside of the school environment, such as websites, teacher forums, professional networking, to name but a few, all of which have the potential to facilitate the development of high quality lesson planning and as a result, pave the way to outstanding teaching and perhaps more importantly, outstanding learning.

Chapter overview

The most important purpose of teaching is to raise pupils' achievement. Inspectors consider the planning and implementation of learning activities across the whole of the school's curriculum, together with teachers' marking, assessment and feedback to pupils. They evaluate activities both within and outside the classroom. They also evaluate teachers' support and intervention strategies and the impact that teaching has on the promotion of pupils' spiritual, moral, social and cultural development. (Ofsted, 2014, p. 2)

Ofsted (2014) considers pupil achievement, in addition to their spiritual, moral, social and cultural development, as the essence of effective teaching and learning. Whilst there are no specific requirements for planning design and teaching strategies, both are conducive to effective learning and as such, are often examined thoroughly on inspection. The key principle, therefore, is that the learning, development and attainment of individual pupils are quintessential to the planning and implementa-tion processes and it is through thorough planning, including, amongst other things, good subject knowledge and the creation of bespoke learning opportunities and carefully structured and well-paced, engaging implementation, that this can be achieved.

Effective planning for effective learning and teaching are the stepping stones to successful practice. Thoroughly considered and well executed, a comprehensive understanding of these crucial elements of the role of a teacher, are fundamental in the development of pupil achievement, in addition to a recognition of the 'inter-connectedness' between planning and assessment as a means to promoting effective learning (Robinson et al., 2013). In addition, development of the self-confidence to plan exciting and fulfilling learning opportunities, which will, ultimately, impact on both your practice and the successes of the learners you teach, is an essential attrib-ute of the successful practitioner. As Castle and Buckler (2009, p. 49) propose: 'Self-confidence is that elusive, magical ingredient that gives us supremacy over our thoughts, actions and, ultimately, our performance.'

In this chapter, we intend to help you develop greater self-confidence by consider-ing strategies for effective lesson planning, with a focus on pupil engagement and the development of a 'love for learning', encompassing:

- An outline of the core elements of effective long-term, medium-term and short-term planning;
- A consideration of securing pupil progress and engagement;
- An exploration of 'what makes learning happen';
- A review of current research examples of good practice;
- The development of self-reflection as a tool for improving practice, in order to strive to become an 'outstanding' practitioner.

In the chapter, there will be opportunities for the application and practice of acquired skills, knowledge and understanding, through the engagement of key questions and practical, relevant ideas. Finally, there will be sections on how and where to find sources of evidence and helpful resources.

Taking it apart and putting it back together

So, let's start the task of straightening out what you need to do to evidence the standard. To do this, we will separate out each sub-set to explore the detail and then we will consider some of the opportunities you will have in your daily prac-tice, that will support you in finding evidence from your practice, to meet the standards.

4a: Impart knowledge and develop understanding through effective use of lesson time

This is the 'teaching', the implementation of all that has been planned. The somewhat traditional view of the teacher in the role of the 'sage on the stage' has been replaced with the teacher as a facilitator of learning. Often referred to as 'chalk and talk', it is widely considered that, whilst effective teaching *for learning* must take place, it is the interaction between learner *and* teacher and learner *and* learner that can lead to success, coupled with the learner's understanding of what is being taught and their engagement with the activities through which they are learning. It is through the effective use of lesson time that this can, in part, be achieved. As Beere (2012, p. 10) suggests: 'The relationships you have with your students are the most important aspects of setting up your learning environment.'

In the jigsaw puzzle that is learning, the vital connections between teacher and learner, within a learning environment that is both accessible to and understood by the learner, are crucial when considering pupil progress. As a teacher, well-developed subject knowledge provides the foundations for effective teaching, but it is the ability to be able to communicate this knowledge in a way that is *accessible to all* that can often present the most challenges. If we were to view the inter-play between teacher, learner and learning, we may consider this as represented diagrammatically, as in Figure 4.1.

As each element inter-relates, with the end 'product' being developed understanding, thorough consideration should be given to these inter-connected areas in order to facilitate the learning process and promote success for the learner. The 'impart knowledge'

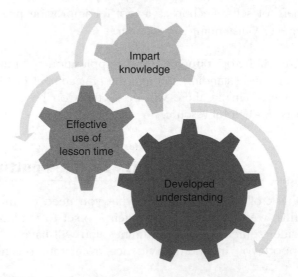

Figure 4.1 Inter-connecting learning and teaching

(teaching) and 'effective use of lesson time' (structure, activities, pace and so on) elements work in harmony in order to develop the understanding of the learner. Exploring the concept that learning is a process, not an outcome (Nottingham, 2013), the role of the teacher as 'process facilitator' could be considered, with the pupil being central to and actively, rather than passively, involved in the process (Dale, 1969).

Learning throughout the lesson: coverage, structure, pace and transition

It is essential that your lesson is well timed, with good pace and smooth transitions between activities. Talk is OK, isn't it? Your classroom should be a busy, productive hive of activity with well-paced tasks that allow pupils the maximum opportunities to progress. Pace does not simply relate to timing, but also to how engaged pupils are with the content. In addition, a well-paced lesson ensures that there is timely support for those pupils for whom this is a concern and for those who are secure, opportunities to move on quickly. In short and as suggested in previous chapters: *if they've got it, move them on!* and this should be guided but independent. Good planning and classroom routines will ensure that these transitions are smooth and focused, with little disruption to other learners.

In addition, all activities will need to ensure good coverage of intended learning outcomes by the end of a lesson and it is essential that regular reflections occur throughout, in order to maximise the potential of this. Do not wait until the end of the lesson to discover that coverage, learning and pupil progress are not as planned; be proactive and in control at all times. More frequently referred to as *mini-plenaries*, these reflective pit stops can be whole-class, small group, paired or independent and should all focus on the end goal for individuals, resulting in progress for all. Trainee teachers often ask for clarification regarding what a mini-plenary should 'look like'. Mini-plenaries can be varied and are very much dependent on the content of the lesson and the variety of pupils within it. Mini-plenaries should, however, be focused on the learning objective (or objectives) and the success criteria and always about making improvements and checking that pupils are on the right track to success. Some examples are given below, but this is not an exhaustive list:

- *A 'stop, look, listen' reflective task:* Pupils are asked to cease working and engage in listening to good practice and practice where elements could be improved. This may be the sharing of pupil work and class discussion on elements that meet the objectives (and success criteria) and next steps. These activities should be short and focused, as there is a danger of disruption to flow and disengagement of pupils, so ensure that they are beneficial for all. Ensure that, if you stop all pupils, that it will be beneficial to all pupils – if not, stop specific groups of pupils only.
- *Key questions:* Questions could be circulated prior to the activities, shared by an adult working with a group of pupils or presented on the board in written or audio format.

Similarly, pupils could be involved in devising their own questions for peer or independent reflection and improvement. Whilst it is considered good practice to question pupils throughout a lesson, there is no requirement to take the whole-class approach. Mini-plenaries can occur for different pupils, at different times, depending on their needs.

- *Focused activity:* Groups of pupils may be asked to engage in an activity that enhances their work and supports progress. This may be using an inverse method of calculation in mathematics in order to check answers, for example.

> *Top Tip:* Allow groups working independently to engage in their own mini-plenary by having it prepared beforehand, on the table. For younger learners, a quick interaction to support this will allow you to focus on other groups, thus differentiating your mini-plenaries and supporting the needs of all learners.

Teacher as 'chameleon': adapting to pupil needs

A thoroughly planned lesson will account for the needs of all learners and it is essential that you are ready for those 'off-script' moments for which you hadn't planned. A well-designed lesson will ensure that you have provided bespoke activities for groups of learners and pre-empted pupil questions (and prepared answers). An effective lesson takes account of these potential adaptations and is flexible enough to accommodate them.

Whilst lessons should work within a pre-considered structure, it is essential to consider that this structure must be fluid enough to adapt, should the needs of the learners require it. In addition, learner needs should be planned for throughout, from the start of the lesson to the plenary and all of the parts in between.

Varied start to a lesson

Whilst they have an important place, there is no requirement for a whole-class introduction in which all pupils are engaged in the same activity. In fact, many teachers fall into the trap of a whole-class introduction when, for some learners, this may not be required. A short, whole-class introduction to orientate the learner can lead into a selection of tailor-made, differentiated introductory activities in which all adults in the classroom are engaged in supporting specific learners. Of course, all of this is pre-planned, discussed with all adults involved, with clear outcomes for pupils.

A common criticism of lesson introductions is pupil (and adult) inactivity. I return once more to: *If they've got it, move them on!* This could be a challenge or the next activity. Similarly, if they haven't got it, record this and ensure that you plan to return to it at a later date, providing exceptional levels of support for those pupils who require it.

Throughout the lesson

All activities should be planned to account for the needs of all learners and whilst this may be, on occasion, by outcome, there should be sufficient opportunities to adapt and support learners to enable progress to be made. This part of the session may involve a flexible model to incorporate group work, free-flow activities or focus groups. It is essential that the activities engage all learners and encourage autonomous learning. Some teachers find this challenging to manage, but a thoroughly planned lesson and a sound classroom ethos can act as enablers.

> 💡 *Top Tip*: Plan for those pupils who may require further support; plan for those who will definitely require further support; plan additional, challenging learning opportunities for those who are likely to rise to any challenge and speed through the work; and plan for those who are working at the expected level but have the potential to be challenged further.

Mini-plenaries throughout the lesson are opportunities not to be missed and will ultimately lead to a greater chance of a successful outcome. They allow the teacher (and the learner) to reflect, adapt and ensure progression. Above all, encourage pupils to challenge themselves and provide opportunities for them to do so via autonomous access to learning materials.

End of a lesson

Plenaries provide the ultimate opportunity for pupils to recognise their own next steps. Key questions can guide pupils towards solutions to problems and the answers can provide the teacher with the information required to adapt teaching. Always leave time for a plenary, as it is an essential part of reflective learning for progression. Make it a meaningful experience for all learners and ensure that pupils are clear about their own next steps.

Top Tip: Whilst you may be working alongside one or two focus groups of learners during a lesson, it is essential to be aware of what is going on around the classroom, in order to check on the learning of others. Reiterate expectations for independent tasks and refer frequently to intended outcomes, providing independently accessible challenges for all groups. This will minimise demands on your attention, allowing you to focus on those learners who require you to adapt your teaching in order to meet the needs of individuals.

Practice examples – Teachers' Standard 4a

PATRICIA

Patricia is a dynamic teacher who engages pupils with her character. Patricia ensures that her classroom is engaging through excellent use of display, which she refers to during her lessons. Patricia's displays value pupil contributions and progress and she changes key words and topic-related information regularly. Her classroom is an exciting place to be and pupils value their learning environment.

JONNY

Jonny's pupils take responsibility for their own progress, guided by their teacher. At the end of each lesson, his pupils are encouraged to assess their own learning and record their own progress and understanding through a 'traffic light' reflection system. Red circles mean that they have not yet got it, amber circles mean that they are on the way to securing it and green circles mean that they have got it and are ready for their next challenge. Jonny responds to all pupil feedback during marking and provides appropriate GAP (Go And Practice) or Next Steps tasks, with which pupils engage with during early morning activities.

In relation to Teachers' Standard 4a and your own practice, consider the following key questions:

- In what ways can you plan to adapt to pupils needs, throughout a lesson?
- Which of the above activities have you tried in your context and which might you adapt to try?
- Can you create definitions for 'learning' and 'teaching'? How will these impact on your practice?

(Continued)

(Continued)

- Reflect on the activities that have been successful in your lessons. What made them effective?
- What questions do you plan when considering a lesson?
- How do you plan your explanations to pupils in order to secure learning?

Possible sources of evidence for Teachers' Standard 4a:

- Short-term planning examples;
- Teaching (and learning) resources;
- Feedback from pupils;
- Assessments and observations.

4b: Promote a love of learning and children's intellectual curiosity

'Miss! Who is going to make us sing?' (Alexander, 2011)

One of the greatest challenges of teaching is engaging the learner throughout the lesson. As highlighted in the words of an innocent child, the use of the verb 'make' indicates a reluctance to learn – a challenge faced by teachers every day. So, how can we, as effective educators, foster a love for learning that will, potentially, lead to pupil progress?

If pupils are to be motivated to excel as learners, then a love of learning must be omnipresent in the classroom; an integral part of classroom and whole-school ethos, planning, displays, values, teaching, activities, the list is endless. It is not simply a matter of planning for engaging activities; a devotion to learning, from the outset, should be core class business.

Pupils are naturally inquisitive and should be encouraged to be so. How you respond to pupil questions is equally as important – show that you value what they say and give their answers due consideration and time. Reward pupils for their efforts and encourage them to succeed on their individual learning journey.

Throughout your practice, it is essential to consider this fundamental aspect of teaching and to ensure that the learner is at the heart of all practice.

In the words of Beadle (2010, p. 64):

It's one thing to have passion, though it's another to be able to convey it credibly; to manifest it so that it is transmitted to your students and they wait in lines outside your lesson jumping up and down in a feverish state of excited anticipation, devising sweetly sung, musical couplets in your praise.

What makes learning happen?

Involvement *for* learning

> Effective teaching means becoming a reflective practitioner, and for that you need a theory of teaching. Using that theory, and your experience and knowledge of the content you are teaching, you can ponder how you are handling it and wonder how you might handle it more effectively. (Biggs, 2003, p. 13)

As Biggs proposes, reflective practice is underpinned by theory. It is a sound understanding of this that leads to more effective teaching (and learning). Dale (1969) considered the process of learning with specific regard to the learner being actively involved in that process. Dale argues that the active learner, engaged fully with the process, is more likely to 'remember' than the passive learner. Involving pupils in the learning process as fully as possible not only creates further opportunities for success, but also promotes autonomous learning. Autonomous learners rely on their understanding of a focus or an activity to be able to engage with it effectively, with little or no direction, thus taking a responsibility for their own learning. It is this sense of responsibility that can aid progression and pave the way to a deep-rooted love of learning, underpinned by a desire to understand and develop further.

When reflecting on education within an historical context, educational theorists throughout time, notably Dale (1969), Biggs (2003) and Nottingham (2013), have moved forward from the more traditional view that pupils learn passively: teachers engaging in 'chalk and talk' with pupils listening attentively. Biggs (2003) categorises approaches to learning as 'deep' and 'surface': 'Appropriate learning activities are referred to as comprising a deep approach to learning, and inappropriate activities as a surface approach. Good teaching supports the deep approach and discourages the surface' (p. 31).

Advancements in educational research have a renewed focus on the active role of the learner in the process of learning and consequently, it is the ways in which pupils can be encouraged to engage with the knowledge imparted in all stages of a lesson that we intend to discuss in the sections that follow, in order to facilitate a developed understanding. Nottingham (2013) suggests that learning is a process, not an outcome (p. 12) and thus, it is the stages one goes through that helps the learner achieve their goal. The role of the teacher, therefore, is to support the *process* in order to assist the pupil in achieving the desired outcome and to praise them regularly for doing so.

Engagement *for* learning

Each learner is unique and may have a wide variety of ways in which they acquire knowledge, skills and understanding, in addition to the ways they process the information with which they engage. Consequently, pupil engagement needs to be considered thoroughly in order to better ensure a successful learning experience for each pupil. The selection of activities and resources and the ways in which these are presented to pupils are essential considerations here, during all stages of a lesson. An engaging, well-paced introduction to a lesson may encourage pupil engagement, but subsequent activities will need to build on this and keep pupils engaged throughout. When pupils 'switch off', it is often then that learning and progress cease.

Pupil relationships can often aid engagement. Show them that you value their comments, efforts and work and reward them for this. It is often a challenge for teachers when teaching a topic that is deemed to be uninspiring and one of the professional attributes of a teacher is to present topics in ways that have the potential to engage pupils. Where this is not possible, try breaking up the lesson with short, focused activities in order to allow pupils to re-charge. Examples may include activities that encourage pupils to actively engage in 'thinking'. This may be an activity that is completely unrelated to the learning within a particular lesson, but provides pupils with breathing space, to allow them to re-focus. A popular choice is 'chatter topics' which, when used effectively, can be both a source of amusement for pupils and prompt meaningful discussion and promote pupil inquisitiveness. An example of a chatter topic is: *If a square didn't exist, what impact would that have on the world?* There are some excellent texts to support chatter topics and similar short, meaningful activities, such as Gilbert (2007), Keeling (2009), Emeny (2012) and Roberts (2012).

> Q *Top Tip*: Try to choose activities that allow for varied pupil interest and show that you know your pupils. Plan for an element of choice to encourage autonomous learning and stop groups of learners at various points throughout the lesson to reflect, re-energise and secure. Give them time to choose, explore and reflect but don't give them time to disengage.

 Practice examples – Teachers' Standard 4b

TAJ

Taj has developed an effective rewards system in order to motivate his pupils to learn. His pupils know that their efforts, correct or otherwise, will be rewarded and their progress is displayed clearly for all to see. Taj provides daily opportunities for

(Continued)

(Continued)

all pupils to access rewards and pupils are encouraged to praise and reward each other, by deciding on rewards in tandem with the class teacher.

GEORGIA

Georgia takes a pupil-centred approach to new topics. She commences by asking the pupils what they know and what they would like to know about a topic, which has the added benefit of acting as an assessment tool. Pupil enquiry questions are recorded on a prominently displayed area of the classroom and there are opportunities built into pupils' extra-curricular time that allow for the exploration of answers, such as additional homework tasks that pupils may choose to complete or independent access to online resources during break times.

 In relation to Teachers' Standard 4b and your own practice, consider the following key questions:

- What is your philosophy of learning and teaching?
- What have you learned about pedagogy from theory and how can you apply this knowledge to your own philosophy of learning and teaching?
- How do you engage pupils for effective learning within lessons?
- How do you deal with 'reluctant learners'?
- How can you develop your learning experiences to encourage a love of learning in all pupils?
- What are your strategies for promoting the engagement of pupils?

Possible sources of evidence for Teachers' Standard 4b:

- Feedback from pupils;
- Observation data;
- Classroom display;
- Extra-curricular tasks;
- Teaching;
- Pupil engagement in lessons.

4c: Set homework and plan other out-of-class activities to consolidate and extend the knowledge and understanding pupils have acquired

Beyond the classroom

If pupils engage with a topic, they are keen to seek out ways of improving their existing knowledge. Pupils should be provided with opportunities to expand on their learning independently, beyond the classroom. This standard stretches far beyond homework tasks, extending to school excursions and web-based forums, such as school blogs and interactive learning opportunities. Technology-enhanced learning is becoming a fundamental norm in schools and many pupils are eager to get involved with social networking and technology-based home–school projects. Many schools are providing opportunities for pupils to engage with such activities or are simply allowing pupils to explore technologies in non-timetabled time. Some schools have developed 'soft mornings', whereby pupils are permitted to arrive at school within a more flexible time frame along with their parents, or carers, if desired, to self-register and engage in cross-phase activities of their choice. Some schools are finding that this approach supports subsequent learning, in addition to building home–school links.

Teachers at the forward-thinking Hillstone Primary School, in Birmingham, have trialed a pilot of a homework scheme that encourages both autonomous and engaging learning and parental, or carer, involvement. The inclusive idea, which is grounded in Bloom's Taxonomy of educational objectives (Bloom et al., 1956) and excellent practice, builds on the provision of opportunity for choice within a specific topic or focus. In order to encourage pupils to engage with homework activities, teachers within the school produce regular, thematic homework grids for out-of-hours learning. Each grid provides opportunities for cross-curricular tasks to be completed by pupils within a set time frame and pupils are encouraged to engage with activities that they will enjoy, in addition to those that will challenge and extend their learning. The activities within the grid encourage home–school links, for example through discussion of topics with parents/carers or by engaging them in specific projects to support their child's learning. An example of this excellent practice, with the kind permission of Judy Bridges, a class teacher at Hillstone Primary School, is shown in Figure 4.2.

Early findings have highlighted the success of the intuitive project and the school is receiving positive feedback.

Long-term pupil projects can be planned to allow pupils to thoroughly explore a topic outside of the classroom. Competitions can be set up for pupil contributions to knowledge. External agencies and other adults, such as parents/carers or members of the local community, can be included in classroom projects, in addition to partnerships with other schools, both within the UK and abroad.

Development of higher order skills →

Bloom's Taxonomy Grid	Knowing	Understanding	Applying	Analysing	Creating	Evaluating
Verbal I enjoy reading, writing and speaking	Find out five fascinating facts about India	Re-tell a traditional Indian story	What are the 5Ks from the Sikh religion?	Write a diary pretending you are a child living in India	Create a tourist guide to encourage people to visit Barcelona	Discover which animals are sacred in India and reasons why
Mathematical I enjoy working with numbers and sequences	How far is it from Birmingham to New Delhi in India?	True or false: The River Ganges is the second longest river in the world	What are the populations of India, Spain and Henley-in-Arden?	Learn to count to 10 in an Indian language	Draw the Sikh symbol and investigate how many lines of symmetry it has	Research five number facts about The Taj Mahal
Visual/Spatial I enjoy painting and drawing	Draw the Spanish flag	Design a logo for Henley-in-Arden	Can you write your name in Hindi?	Copy one of Pablo Picasso's paintings or create your own in his style	Create a 3D Indian temple	Evaluate the work of Pablo Picasso and give your opinion on his paintings
Kinaesthetic I enjoy doing hands on activities, sports and dance	What sports are India and Spain well known for?	Re-enact a crucial moment for the Barcelona football team	Learn some simple 'Bollywood' moves to shares with the class	What do different 'Bollywood' moves represent?	Create a flamenco dance	If you could take three giant steps, where would you go and why?
Musical I enjoy making and listening to music	Watch a 'Bollywood' clip on the internet	Research traditional Indian instruments	Write your own song or rap to show what you have learnt about this topic	Listen to Spanish guitar music and write down your thoughts	Compose your own Spanish piece of music. What makes it Spanish?	Compare music from Spain and India. Which do you prefer and why?
Interpersonal I enjoy working with others	Find out what Henley-in-Arden is famous for	Bien hecho para la elaboración de lo que dice	Design your own flavour of ice cream to be sold at Henley's ice cream parlour	Try some Indian food. Do you like it?	Design and make your own sari	Debate whether or not you and your family agree with Spanish bull fighting
Intrapersonal I enjoy working by myself	Write down six Spanish speaking countries	Who was Gandhi?	Would you rather have two thousand rupees or two hundred euro?	Research a famous landmark in India or Spain	Design a henna tattoo pattern for your hands	Would you rather visit Spain or India? Why?

Figure 4.2 Three Giant Steps' homework grids (Bridges, 2014)

Practice examples – Teachers' Standard 4c

KEITH

Keith has set up a class blog on the school website. This is carefully monitored by staff in school and allows pupils to post information and links relevant to current classroom topics. The blog is referred to in lessons and for those pupils without available technology at home, opportunities are provided for independent access via a 'VIP Pass' during breaks and lunchtimes.

JACQUELINE

At the start of each half term, Jacqueline sets her pupils a long-term home–school project in which pupils can explore aspects of the curriculum through extended research and activities. For example, the pupils in Jacqueline's class were exploring thermal insulators. Pupils were asked to design and make a suitable outfit for explorers in cold climates. Where required, resources were available in school, although parental contributions were also requested. Jacqueline asked pupils to consider ecological elements of outfit design, as well as comfort and practicality. Pupils were asked to present their rationale for outfit design and engage in peer evaluation in relation to the objectives.

 In relation to Teachers' Standard 4c and your own practice, consider the following key questions:

- How could you adapt the homework grid to address out-of-school learning opportunities for your pupils?
- What opportunities can you build into the school day to promote extra-curricular learning?
- How can you motivate pupils to become engaged with extra-curricular learning?
- In what ways can you encourage parental/carer involvement?

Possible sources of evidence for Teachers' Standard 4c:

- Learning journals and homework diaries;
- Extra-curricular opportunities for pupils;
- Parental/carer consultation evening feedback;
- Pupil feedback;
- Pupil progress.

4d: Reflect systematically on the effectiveness of lessons and approaches to teaching

> Pedagogy involves two aspects of learning. The first is associated with what and how students are learning; the second is about the teacher as learner – learning about teaching and building expertise. (Loughran, 2010, p. 21)

Learning about teaching and the theories associated with pedagogy are essential attributes of the reflective teacher. As a teacher-learner, you can build the necessary skill-set in order to identify, more effectively, pedagogical issues relating to student learning and thus, support pupils as they progress.

Critically reflecting

Why reflect?

A quality of an effective teacher is the ability to engage in self-reflection, in the role of the 'reflective practitioner'. Reflection is an integral part of effective practice, due to the impact that this can have on teacher practice and ultimately, on pupil progress. By engaging in regular reflection activities, the teacher can adapt and improve practice in a timely manner, thus providing the best opportunities for the pupils with whom they work.

Reflection and learning

A plethora of research exists on reflective practice and it is important to develop an understanding of the benefits and impacts of reflection in order to advance professionally. Perhaps most notably, Ghaye (2011) considers four common reflection types: reflection-in-action; reflection-on-practice; reflection-for-action; reflection-with-action (p. 6). Building on the proposals of Schön (1983), Kolb (1984), Gibbs (1988), King and Kitchener (1994) and other researchers in the field, definitions of reflection are key to engaging in reflective activity and knowing how to evidence this effectively. Interestingly, Ghaye (2011) considered teacher perspectives on reflection-on-practice and concluded that different teachers thought many different things (p. 21). In addition, the research findings concluded that many do not know how to critically reflect or how to get the best from it (p. x). Ghaye and Ghaye (1998) muse:

> Teaching is value-laden practice. Values help teachers to make decisions on how to proceed. Evidence helps teachers make wise and principled decisions. Confident and competent teaching requires teachers to reflect systematically and rigorously on evidence derived from practice. Reflective teaching and learning then is evidence-based. (p. 9)

So, how is it that this evidence can be collected? Ghaye and Ghaye (1998) suggest that 'reflections-on-practice can be of different types. Five types are:

- descriptive reflection-on-practice which is personal and retrospective
- perceptive reflection-on-practice which links teaching to feelings
- receptive reflection-on-practice which relates your view of things to others' views
- interactive reflection-on-practice which links learning with future action
- critical reflection-on-practice which places individual teaching within a 'broader' system. (p. 9)

Examining this as a possible model for reflection-on-practice provides opportunities for teachers to develop, first, a purpose for reflection and subsequently, the evidence required to meet that purpose.

A deepened understanding of models of reflection is beneficial practice, but perhaps the simplistic model in Figure 4.3 may offer a practical and accessible view of ways in which evidence can be collected through questions, in order to inform purposeful reflection as the busy, reflective classroom practitioner.

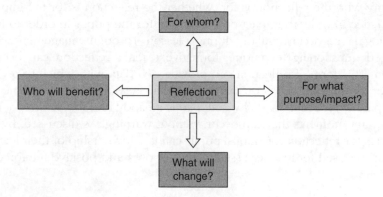

Figure 4.3 A question of reflection

Once answers to these questions have been considered, dedicated time for reflection could be planned for, both during lesson time and subsequently, in order to inform future practice. Where reflective practice, actively involving pupils, can have the greatest impact is during a well-planned lesson. By offering regular opportunities for pupils to engage in reflective activities, they can begin to take ownership of their own improvement *during* a lesson and the time can be used as an assessment tool for the adult with whom the pupils are working. Thus, pupils are actively involved in the reflective practice of the teacher.

Beere (2012) extends the idea of assessment *for* learning, suggesting that assessment should be embedded within lessons and the classroom ethos in such a way that it becomes assessment *as* learning. Reflection may also be considered as such. As discussed previously, reflection should occur frequently, throughout the lesson, with the encouragement of independent pupil reflection embedded within classroom practice. This act of 'active pupil reflection' could be found in the 'mini-plenaries' offered throughout a lesson. During the final stages of a lesson, the teacher is able to use this knowledge to adapt subsequent learning and teaching experiences in order to secure realistic outcomes. Of course, these 'next steps' should not be restricted to future lesson planning, but instead should be flexible enough to accommodate and support learning beyond the classroom.

How to reflect, ensuring future impact

Having considered some of the more common definitions and the purpose of reflection, there are several opportunities to engage with reflection in the primary classroom:

During the lesson

First, identify who the reflection is for. Whether the reflection is for the improvement of your practice in order to impact on learning or for the pupils in order to impact on their learning, it can occur regularly during a lesson. Through engagement with pupils and planned questioning technique, formative teacher reflection can occur within each lesson. This form of reflection can provide rich data with which to revise future planning or even adapt a lesson part-way. Being responsive to pupil needs is an important part of reflection. A sticky note pad is a handy tool in a lesson for capturing those important moments that can occur, without warning. As discussed, by planning opportunities for reflection for pupils, pupils can take ownership of their learning and the data can be used for teacher assessment purposes and positive reinforcement.

After the lesson

The annotation of lesson plans or lesson evaluation can impact on future planning. By reflecting in this way, it allows the class teacher to adapt future planning, make improvements and re-plan to suit the developing needs of the learners. Consider how you intend to reflect and for what purpose. It is with this deepened self-understanding that effective reflection can impact on practice.

Long-term examples of this may include:

- After formal observations of, or by, colleagues;
- During collegiate planning sessions;
- Through annual action plans and subject reviews;
- As part of performance management reviews or appraisals.

Whilst this is not an exhaustive list, it encapsulates the range of opportunities to assess in the learning and teaching environment. In effective practice, the class teacher should aim to engage with most of these areas, which, in turn, will impact on short-, medium- and long-term goals and more importantly, on pupil progress.

 Top Tip: Encourage pupils to record their own successes and developmental needs in their books (or, for younger learners, use images or another adult as a scribe). This communication can embellish your own assessments and responses can ensure that the pupil voice is being both listened to and acted on.

 Practice examples – Teachers' Standard 4d

DEACON
Deacon has created a reflective journal for each subject area. At the end of each session, Deacon makes reflective entries within the journal and uses these to adapt future planning.

NICOLE
At the end of each session, Nicole annotates her lesson plans. The plans have a dedicated space on which to notate reflections and these often refer to pupil progress and next steps. In addition, Nicole asks pupils to engage in reflective assessments at the end of sessions, whereby pupils are encouraged to share their own feedback with Nicole in a variety of ways.

In relation to Teachers' Standard 4d and your own practice, consider the following key questions:

- Consider the ways in which you engage in reflective practice. How do they impact on teaching and learning?
- What can you learn about types of reflection and how will you use these to enrich your practice?
- How will you build in further opportunities for reflection within your practice?

(Continued)

> *(Continued)*
>
> Possible sources of evidence for Teachers' Standard 4d:
>
> - Formatively, during lessons;
> - In annotated lesson plans;
> - Summatively, at the end of a lesson or unit of work;
> - After formal observations of/by colleagues;
> - During collegiate planning sessions;
> - In feedback to pupils;
> - As part of the planning process – adapt, improve, re-plan;
> - Through annual action plans and subject reviews;
> - As part of performance management reviews and appraisals.

4e: Contribute to the design and provision of an engaging curriculum within the relevant subject area(s)

Planning

What is a plan and what is its purpose?

A plan can be defined as 'the instructor's road map of what students need to learn and how it will be done effectively during the class time' (Milkova, 2014, n.p.).

First, we must consider the purpose of a plan – who and what is it for? The answer is to prepare for the progress of the learner and to orientate all adults working with the pupils. This may, of course, include senior leaders, managers or phase leaders.

What are examples of different types of planning?

Planning formats can vary considerably between settings, but the over-arching theme of all successful plans is the learning. As Bentley-Davies (2010, p. 57) suggests: 'The deepening of knowledge and understanding should be the key factors when planning lessons. Don't think about the *tasks* students will be doing, instead concentrate on the *learning*.'

Long term

Long-term planning provides an overview of a subject area or areas and usually considers key objectives or outcomes. Frequently, the long-term plan may include continuity and progression between age phases, or over a period of time within one age phase. Long-term plans act as a summary and inform medium-term plans.

Medium term

Medium-term planning varies depending on the school. The purpose of the medium-term plan is to provide a more detailed overview of a unit of work within a subject area, for example over one half term. Medium-term plans provide key objectives and intended outcomes; links to the National Curriculum (DfE, 2013b); detailed transitional steps in learning; opportunities for cross-curricular links; assessment opportunities; resources; and an overview of individual session content. Some schools place a great deal of emphasis on a detailed breakdown of lesson content, whilst others prefer a less prescriptive approach. Medium-term plans inform short-term plans.

Short term

Short-term plans are weekly or daily plans that detail the specifics of a lesson within a class or year group. Short-term plans may be developed as part of a team or may be individual. Short-term plans provide opportunities to 'think through' the lesson in significant detail.

Securing pupil progress through effective planning

Bentley-Davies (2010) suggests that:

> One of the most crucial aspects in planning a good lesson is in the effectiveness of lesson objectives. A good lesson needs to make it absolutely clear right at the start, midway through and certainly by the end of the lesson what it is that the students have been *learning*. (p. 75)

As identified previously, effective planning can be used as a tool to secure pupil progress. By designing engaging lessons, in which pupils are both supported and challenged, pupils have opportunities to thrive and therefore, make progress. Pupils should be encouraged to be autonomous learners and opportunities should be planned to facilitate this. Irrespective of the differences between short-term planning design in different settings, there exist key themes which should be considered by the erudite teacher. The model in Figure 4.4, courtesy of senior leaders at Robin

Hood Primary Academy, Birmingham, explores one such example of key considerations for short-term planning.

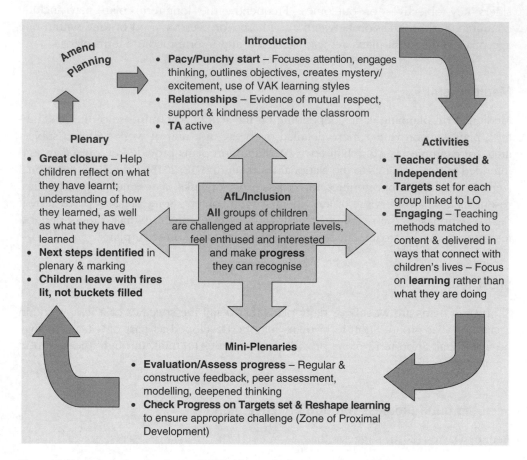

Figure 4.4   Amend planning (courtesy of Robin Hood Primary Academy, Birmingham)

The model in Figure 4.4 builds on the idea of a fluid and flexible lesson in which the teacher provides opportunities for learning, reflection, assessment and progress. Regardless of planning format, the key considerations here pave the way for effective learning and teaching. The example in Figure 4.5 demonstrates how this model can be applied; it focuses on a lesson in which pupil independence (VIPs = Very Independent Persons) is celebrated.

The example short-term plan in Figure 4.5 demonstrates an exemplar structure, clarity and essential 'ingredients' that could be considered when short-term planning. Whilst the planning format and style may not suit all tastes, it serves as a good example of the key stages of a lesson. Notable features include:

English focus: *Selecting vocabulary to convey characters effectively*		Term: Summer 2	
Objective: In narratives, describing settings, characters and atmosphere and integrating dialogue to convey character **We are learning:** To use descriptive techniques to convey characters effectively **Purpose and audience:** A skills-building lesson to develop descriptive writing to convey characters effectively to readers		**TA: Introduction:** Extend middle-ability (MA) pupils with questions, e.g. *How could you describe X more effectively?* etc. Prompt questions provided to TA **Main:** MA pupils to be supported in the improvement of their sentence structure through modelled examples and vocabulary **Plenary:** MA pupil extension and reflection on learning (tasks/questions provided to TA) **Other resources:** *Paper; whiteboards; film, success criteria, challenge vocabulary, tasks, questions*	

	Learning outcomes	Whole-class input	Activities to achieve outcomes (30 mins)	Plenary (5 mins)
W	**By the end of this lesson, children will be able to:** **HA:** I can include internal and external traits, description of actions and a range of figurative language when describing characters **MA:** I can include internal and external traits and description of actions when describing characters **LA:** I can include internal and external traits when describing characters **Building on prior learning:** Pupils need to improve on making character descriptions engaging, displaying a range of language and varied structure for effect	REVISE USE OF 'VIP' INDEPENDENCE POSTERS: *How will you demonstrate your independence?* **Introduce targets (2 mins)** **HA:** Include internal and external traits, a description of actions, a range of figurative language **MA:** Include internal and external traits and a description of actions **LA:** Include internal & external traits (paired support: writing buddies) **SEND:** Child with visual impairment to be seated close to the board with a specific set of tools to aid learning, accessed independently **Model:** Share model of character description. *Is this an effective description?* Relate to targets and reinforce (2–3 mins) **Launch:** Show clip from the film 'Up' to show character traits. Pupils record key words and phrases to describe internal and external character traits (5 mins) **Drama:** Think about 'Up' character traits. Move around the room as 'Up' character **Mix, pair, share:** *Why did you move in that way? (because he has arthritis etc.)* (5 mins) **Main task:** To describe a character effectively (2–3 mins) *In order to write an effective description, we need to …?* Ask pupils to generate criteria for success **Success criteria** **(Pre-lesson teacher ideas):** • Choose engaging, wide-ranging vocabulary (including figurative); • Vary sentence structure for effect; • Include internal and external traits. **Got it?** Move on to independent writing: *How will you improve on your previous description writing? How will you show you are a VIP when you think you have completed the task?* **Not?** Shared writing with teacher, before moving on independently	**Tasks:** **HA:** 'Up' character: Write a descriptive sentence, stop and improve independently. Use figurative language and vary sentence structure for effect and to engage the reader **MA: (TA)** 'Up' character: Write a descriptive sentence, stop and improve. Continue independently **LA:** 'Up' character: Guided support with vocabulary prompts from whole-class feedback **(Teacher):** Write a descriptive sentence, stop and improve through modelled examples. Continue independently **Challenge:** Pupils self-select differentiated challenge vocabulary from challenge boxes **Additional challenge:** *What additional language features could you include to engage a reader?* Write a character description that is the opposite of the character you have described **Support:** Key words available to prompt pupil thinking. Teacher/TA to support with modelling and questioning **Mini-plenaries throughout (adapt according to pupil needs):** (General) STOP! *Are you working towards your success criteria? How do you know you are being successful?* (Specific) *Underline three excellent vocabulary/phrase choices that convey character effectively and share with a partner (magpie)*	*How have you met the success criteria? Find evidence and pair-share, giving a 'wish and a kiss' (+&–)* Share effective examples of pupil descriptions. *Why is this description effective?* Relate to success criteria *What have we developed in this session – what are you better at?* *What still challenges you?* **Next steps:** *(notes added by teacher as lesson progresses)*

Figure 4.5 Example of a short-term plan

- *Key questions to support assessment:* pre-planned questions that support pupil progress and autonomous learning are crucial to the success of a lesson. Questions should seek to empower and challenge the learner and aid progression through carefully considered wording. They will also provide excellent opportunities for teacher assessment.

- *Clearly defined groupings:* it is important to identify with whom pupils will be working in all stages of a lesson. This will aid classroom management, in addition to careful consideration of the best arrangements to support learning. Pupils do not need to stay within these groupings for the entirety of the lesson and it is often useful to provide opportunities for movement, such as the 'Mix/Pair/Share' activity (Kagan et al., 1995), where pupils can learn standing up!

- *Detailed use of other adults (and support for them in* all *stages of a lesson):* a lesson plan not only needs to indicate with whom other adults will be working in all stages of a lesson, but, more importantly, what they will be doing to support learning. It is essential to pre-plan key questions and prompts for other adults in order to best support the learners.

- *Reference to key documentation and assessment criteria:* it is important for a lesson to be grounded in key documentation to support the subject area, such as the National Curriculum (DfE, 2013b). This will be considered more thoroughly in medium- and long-term planning, but it is still important to identify the focus in short-term planning in order to track continuity and progression. In addition, reference to specific assessment criteria can aid the teacher in identifying potential opportunities for pupil progress and shows that you know exactly where your pupils are.

- *Clearly outlined objectives and differentiated intended outcomes for all learners:* learning objectives are 'What we are learning…' Key objectives should link directly to national curricula and the intended outcomes for all pupils. It is essential to identify key objectives for the lesson, in order to provide a clear focus. All learning should link directly back to the key objectives/outcomes. Intended outcomes are simply the intentions for groups of pupils, in relation to the objectives, by the end of the lesson. Intended outcomes can be differentiated for learners and should include opportunities for pupil progress.

- *Criteria for success created* with *pupils* for *pupils:* if pupils are to understand how to be successful, they are more likely to achieve the intended objectives. By encouraging pupils to think about how they can achieve objectives, they are involved in success criteria creation and whilst this will have been considered beforehand by the teacher, it is often useful to compare pupil ideas with this in order to further aid understanding and thus, progression. Success criteria are, therefore, the steps a pupil needs to go through in order to achieve the objectives.

- *Challenge and support linked to progress and further learning (not just extra work):* challenge and support should be identified for *all* learners, not simply those with SEND. Whilst it is important to provide opportunities for pupils with SEND to make good progress, *all* groups of pupils should be provided with ways in which they can make *additional* progress, perhaps in the form of challenge. A challenge may simply be access to questions for consideration; extension activities that build on successes; independent creation of challenging activities and so on. Such challenges should be identified clearly on a lesson plan.

- *Consideration of prior learning and next steps*: this is not simply knowing where the learning fits into a unit of work, but also what learning pupils have been engaged in previously. Topics may have been introduced in previous year groups, or pupils may have accessed learning at home and it is important to know this about all learners, in order to provide the best opportunities for learning, pitched at the correct level. The next steps for learning can be considered during and at the end of every lesson through brief annotations, or by asking pupils to comment on their own areas for development.

- *Opportunities for autonomous and peer learning:* promoting pupil independence is paramount, whatever the age of the pupil. By setting up a learning environment that embraces the idea of pupils independently accessing resources, activities and learning materials, you are paving the way for success. Asking the teacher for support should be a last resort for the pupil, after all other possible considerations have been exhausted, including talking to peers (positive, productive talk is OK); using the resources around them (including the classroom displays, their books, journals or equipment); and thinking carefully before asking. Peer learning opportunities often provide pupils with opportunities to make improvements and mistakes within a safe, secure setting. Learning with a peer is often less daunting than worrying about whether or not you have got something right when you hand it in to the teacher.

- *Embedded reflection tasks and mini-plenaries:* these should be peppered throughout the lesson. As discussed previously, these tasks do not need to involve all pupils at the same time. Groups of pupils may be asked to reflect and improve at different stages in a lesson, specific to their learning needs.

- *Segments:* it is useful to consider the length of sections of a lesson beforehand in order to promote flow. However, lessons should remain fluid and flexible and constantly adaptive to the needs of the learners. The example demonstrates how a range of short, sharp, focused activities, balanced with more sustained pupil-led activities, can aid learner success and promote pupil progress.

- *Resources:* there is nothing worse than being part way through a lesson and realising that you have forgotten to sort out an important resource. By detailing resources on a lesson plan, it is a useful aide-memoire.

Whilst the above elements are intended as guidance, it would be useful to consider them in a range of learning contexts and age phases and to adapt the content to the type of learning experience and the pupils within your setting.

Top Tip: Try using the key elements of the above lesson plan in your own context and adapt it to suit your personal style and the learning needs of your pupils.

Practice examples – Teachers' Standard 4e

KENNY

Kenny works in a year group team in which joint responsibility is assumed for planning a weekly overview. Each team member takes a subject to plan for the year group for the week. In his planning, Kenny ensures that he adheres to the school's planning policies and provides detail for each key heading. In order that all adults working with the pupils are clear about the activities and outcomes, Kenny ensures that he states how pupils will be supported, in addition to describing the activities in which pupils will be engaged. Progress and outcomes are clearly differentiated and the structure of the lessons allows pupils to engage in a variety of learning experiences, including autonomous learning.

MARIE

Marie plans alone and has a challenging class. She has begun to involve pupils in the planning process and has elected class representatives to gather information on the needs and desires of the class, which they share with Marie. Pupils are more engaged as they feel that they are considered in the planning process.

 In relation to Teachers' Standard 4e and your own practice, consider the following key questions:

- Who is your planning for?
- What are the key ingredients of a successful lesson plan?
- Where can you find good examples of planning and engaging activities?
- When is a lesson plan unsuccessful?
- Why is pupil engagement important?
- How can you ensure the best learning opportunities for pupils?
- How will you adapt your current planning in order to facilitate the learning process and pupil progression?

(Continued)

(Continued)

Possible sources of evidence for Teachers' Standard 4e:

- Long-, medium- and short-term plans;
- Additional activities planned to engage pupils, such as a multicultural afternoon or an assembly;
- Notes from staff meetings and planning sessions with colleagues;
- Working walls within your classroom.

Chapter summary

Consider your understanding of learning. Develop your own philosophy of learning and teaching and you will better understand the kind of teacher you are and the values you hold dear. Write down your initial ideas and then refine them; it is a challenging process. Review your lesson planning strategies and consider how you can improve them in order to improve learning. Leave no stone un-turned. Trial new ways of planning and adapt your own good practice in order to incorporate those essential ingredients. Know your pupils really well and their developing needs. How will you accommodate these on a daily basis and how will you know that you are making the most of these opportunities? Plan for this. Make reflection an integral part of your daily practice. Develop your understanding of reflective practice through wider reading and research, but always bring it back to the children – they are at the heart of all you do. Plan opportunities for both teacher and pupil reflection and use the outcomes of this to impact on future learning. Develop further opportunities for pupils to learn beyond the classroom and listen to their interests. Encourage pupil sharing, thus fostering more significant home–school links, based on individual interests. In particular, know the interests of your reluctant learners and capitalise on them. Observe outstanding practice in your own setting and others and reflect on how it can impact on your own practice. Above all, be passionate about learning and encourage pupils to engage with the processes of learning and to love it – it's infectious! You have chosen a career as a teacher; it is your job to promote a love of learning.

CHAPTER 5

ADAPT TEACHING TO RESPOND TO THE STRENGTHS AND NEEDS OF ALL PUPILS

Teachers' Standard 5 – Adapt teaching to respond to the strengths and needs of all pupils:

5a Know when and how to differentiate appropriately, using approaches which enable pupils to be taught effectively

5b Have a secure understanding of how a range of factors can inhibit pupils' ability to learn, and how best to overcome these

5c Demonstrate an awareness of the physical, social and intellectual development of children, and know how to adapt teaching to support pupils' education at different stages of development

(Continued)

(Continued)

5d   Have a clear understanding of the needs of all pupils, including those with special educational needs; those of high ability; those with English as an additional language; those with disabilities; and be able to use and evaluate distinctive teaching approaches to engage and support them.

What is this all about?

Adapting to a potentially diverse range of pupil needs and building on pupil strengths are two of the greatest challenges faced by the primary teacher. Learning to view your class of pupils as a 'collective of individuals' is an essential mindset if you are to cater for their differing needs and allow all to make good progress. It is with a solid foundation of knowledge relating to what those needs might be and how and when to support them, that effective practice will result.

How can this be demonstrated?

Effective teachers pride themselves on knowing their pupils ... not just knowing them, but *really* understanding what makes them tick and perhaps, more importantly, what doesn't. Through interaction with the various support mechanisms in school settings and an effective integration of school policies, a teacher can build a repertoire of evidence relating to Teachers' Standard 5, by embedding good practice into their everyday planning, implementation and review cycle. Staff development opportunities allow teachers to build on their existing knowledge of a range of pupil needs and a deepened understanding and recognition of these can support learning in making exceptional progress through challenge and support. Being flexible in daily practice ensures that teachers are able to adapt when required in order to maximise learning potential and effective communication with all stakeholders allows teachers to collaborate, in order to provide the best opportunities for pupils in their care.

Chapter overview

Each child is unique and has a bespoke set of individual circumstances, specific needs and a range of abilities and it is the responsibility of teachers, in collaboration with parents/carers, senior leaders, teaching and support assistants, SENCos and external agencies, to provide a personalised education for all children.

This, of course, is no easy task, but it is an essential role of an effective teacher. Beere (2014, p. 78) states: 'Great teachers show that they know the individual needs within each class (not just as a list) and have short- and long-term plans to monitor and meet them as they change.'

It is this adaptability – teacher as the ever-adaptable 'chameleon' – that paves the way to success for pupils.

In this chapter, we will explore the following key themes:

- Differentiation in practice;
- Facilitators of and barriers to learning;
- Pitching lessons accurately;
- The physical, social and intellectual development of children;
- Inclusive practice.

Giving a background to theory in each of these areas, the chapter will explore ways in which teachers can provide evidence of excellent bespoke practice. This will be impact-focused and relate to practical examples and pedagogy. In the chapter, there will be opportunities to practise and apply the skills, knowledge and understanding you have acquired, through engagement with key questions and practical, relevant ideas. Finally, there will be sections on how and where to find sources of evidence and helpful resources.

Taking it apart and putting it back together

As in previous chapters, we will examine each of the sub-sets relative to Teachers' Standard 5 and encourage reflection on the key points to enable readers to consider how to put the principles into practice and how evidence can be sourced for each sub-set.

5a: Know when and how to differentiate appropriately, using approaches which enable pupils to be taught effectively

Adapting and being swiftly responsive to pupil needs is an essential attribute of an effective teacher if pupils are to remain engaged, focused and make progress. As discussed in Chapter 3, careful observation of pupil engagement and being both responsive and easily adaptable in order to cater for a wide range of pupil needs, are tools which must be considered thoroughly and refined. There are various potential barriers to the successful management of this, not least the fact that individual pupils and classes of pupils are different and an approach that may be effective for one pupil or group of pupils, may be ineffective for others. When considering Teachers' Standard 5a, the University of

Worcester (2015) suggest that teachers displaying outstanding characteristics 'consistently teach lessons which differentiate effectively to accurately match individual needs. Teaching takes account of the different progress made by each learner during the lesson. As a result of excellent differentiation all learners make excellent progress' (p. 8).

This drives home the importance of recognising pupils as individuals and being adaptable enough to stray from the 'script' and act on what is necessary, in order for pupils to make progress. This is called *differentiation* and it can be a very real challenge for teachers.

In order to add clarity to ways in which differentiation can be evidenced, let us first break down the term differentiation, before attaching meaning to how it may look in practice and how it may then be evidenced.

Isn't differentiation just about giving out three different types of worksheet?

Whilst adapting worksheets for learners has a place, when well-considered and targeted, this should not be an automatic 'go to' option. O'Brien and Guiney (2001) propose that differentiation should be integral to learning, not an add-on for those situations when things do not go as well as planned and problems occur. It is a concept that has to be seen in an inclusive way, applying to everyone (p. ix). They go on to suggest that: 'The process of differentiation presents the teacher with a variety of tools. Such tools lay foundations that allow learners to understand the potential for availability of choices and to make them' (p. 54).

If differentiation, then, is considered to be embedded in effective practice, how is this achieved for all learners? Returning once more to the idea of the three-way differentiated worksheet, as a solitary method, this may be insufficient to meet the needs of all learners, unless it is accompanied by rigorous monitoring and action processes in order to support and challenge throughout a lesson.

So, is it just about grouping then?

Frederickson and Cline (2009) identify that, historically, if children had particular difficulties in school, they were put together with other children whose needs were perceived to be similar (p. 69). Whilst pupil groupings can be an effective way of ensuring that learning is pitched at an appropriate level for groups of pupils, there is a danger of pupils being grouped together ineffectively and the potential of a perceived ceiling being put on the learning of individuals if this is not monitored closely. Pupil grouping, however, can have its merits. By placing pupils in ability groups, tasks can be more readily organised to suit a broader range of pupil needs, but support and challenge should also be part of the differentiated tasks: differentiating the differentiation!

Two things not to learn the hard way are:

1. Do not assume that by giving pupils interesting and original names you are 'disguising' the ability groups behind a shroud of mystery: the pupils know, *always*, how they are performing in relation to their peers.
2. Groups can be flexible. Just because you have made fabulously creative group signs and have excellent tracking records for groups of pupils, it doesn't mean that the pupils cannot move between groups. 'One size fits all' simply doesn't work in an adaptable, inclusive classroom. By all means, have a structure in place, but why not let them move fluidly between groups, identifying new challenges and next steps autonomously?

It is, of course, better for teachers to know individual strengths and areas for development and we will explore some ways in which this can be achieved.

Use what you know (or can find out)

As discussed in previous chapters, the importance of observation and accurate, timely assessment cannot be overstated. This is where you gather your evidence for how, what, where, when, why to differentiate and for whom. The '5W1H' approach (Who? What? Where? When? Why? How?) or 'The Kipling Method', named so due to Kipling's referral to each of the above questions in the opening to his poem 'The Elephant's Child' (1902), is a good starting point for teachers to begin examining the best course of action to enable all learners to make progress.

💡 *Top Tip*: Imagine your group of pupils and a recent lesson in which you reflected that some pupils may not have made as much progress as expected. Try writing down the six 5W1H questions on a large piece of paper. Use this assessment to map out the 5W1H approach and consider how you may answer these in relation to differentiation – for example, Who? Pupil X and Pupil Y (be specific about needs and how you will differentiate); What? Identify the task, questions, activities, etc. that will be used to support learning for specific learners. Continue to map out provision by answering the questions in as much detail as possible. This approach will allow you to: identify (but is not exclusive to) individual needs in relation to specific areas at various stages of a lesson (who and when); reflect on pupil seating arrangements and groupings and their effectiveness (where and how); review the tasks you had planned for (what); and consider the rationale for supporting pupils (why). The 5W1H approach may be effective in supporting your deepening understanding of how and why you differentiate. See if the system helps you to plan for subsequent interventions.

Use what you know about your pupils in order to differentiate more accurately. Talk to them about their developing needs and use assessment data in order to plan for each lesson, in each subject area, for each child. Once you have the data and really know your pupils, you can begin exploring exciting ways of differentiating alongside your pupils and then begin to evidence these.

Five commonly used methods of differentiating:

1. *Task*: plan a range of learning activities (throughout the lesson) in which pupils can experience both success and challenge. Encourage an element of choice and build in opportunities for pupils to move on to the next stage, autonomously. Your planned tasks, interventions, observations and pupil self or peer assessments are your evidence.

2. *Outcome*: there are some occasions when you may wish for your pupils to start on a level playing field and see where it leads them. In these cases, the evidence is provided in individual pupil outcomes and these outcomes can, in turn, impact on subsequent teaching and learning. Communicate with pupils and observe the outcomes, recording these as evidence.

3. *Teaching and support*: how you deliver a lesson, supporting and challenging individuals within it, is part of the puzzle. It is the easiest way to differentiate, as you can readily adapt to pupil needs as you go along. The danger arises when the teaching becomes the imparting of information, without ensuring that you are taking the children with you. Regular checks and communication with pupils are essential when teaching and the targeting of individuals can be seen through the expert use of questioning and seamless interaction with pupils.

4. *Questions (and answers)*: a powerful tool. Plan these – carefully. It is sometimes challenging to plan for questions when you want lessons to be responsive to pupil needs, but you can use your prior/current knowledge of pupils to plan questions that you think may challenge and extend them, suited to their needs. Perhaps employ the 5W1H approach to planning for questions and plan to target individuals. Rephrase to suit different learners and their abilities or understanding and always praise them, genuinely, for their efforts. Plan subsequent questions and perhaps most importantly, listen and respond to the answers. Never, ever just accept the answer and move on – delve a little deeper to find out why they think something or what more they know. This, of course, is 'live assessment'.

5. *Consultation*: just because you are the teacher does not mean that you have to do all of the work. Talk to pupils and ask them about their progress. Engage them in reflective activities and develop an ethos whereby pupils feel that they can talk about things they find hard or when they are 'stuck'. Ask them to identify their own developmental needs in order to be more successful and listen to what they tell you – the pupil voice is perhaps one of the most powerful tools in your teacher toolkit.

Allow time for them to identify clear next steps and scaffold this by providing them with options. Be ready to support them when they don't know and be there to challenge those who are ready for even greater success.

Your own steps to success

Herbert (2011) considers the various stages a teacher may go through in order to support pupil learning and notes that the curriculum will take account of the existing learning that they have in any subject or area and will plan to move the learner through the learning steps necessary towards meeting suitable learning objectives (p. 7). Beere (2014) focuses less on the process of planning to differentiate and more on the process of overseeing the progress of learners, stating that it's not the strategy you use – it's your ability to monitor and evaluate its impact and to adapt accordingly (p. 76). When considering the best way to meet the needs of learners in your care, it is not simply about selecting the right tool for the job, but also about monitoring the effectiveness of that tool in terms of the impact it has on pupil progress and finally reflecting on this in order to make necessary adjustments next time. It is about being adaptable in your teaching and showing this in your planning, implementation and assessment. Become familiar with school policy relating to meeting the needs of individual learners and use this as another tool to support your own differentiation within your class. Ekins (2012) considers twenty-first century approaches: one where difference/diversity is not seen as a problem to be dealt with, but rather where an understanding of the individuality and individual strengths of pupils is emphasised and encouraged (p. 163). Through effective identification of individual pupil needs and regular communication with them about this, differentiation is embedded in practice and as a result, allows you to develop approaches for pupils to be taught effectively.

 Practice examples – Teachers' Standard 5a

ISABELLE
Isabelle works in an early years setting. As part of each day, she sets aside time to communicate with as many of her pupils as possible, targeting them with key questions and learning about them. Isabelle records simple notes on a sticky notes pad and adds these to individual pupil profiles. The profiles are a developmental picture of the pupils, over time and allow Isabelle to make links between learning, progress, social and emotional development and to plan for specific tailor-made interventions in order to facilitate extra progress and development.

(Continued)

(Continued)

RON

Ron teaches mathematics to a large Year 4 class. When planning starter activities for lessons, Ron ensures that he provides a variety of options with which pupils can engage, depending on their stage of development. After a brief, engaging introduction, he displays five differentiated activities relating to the same learning objective and allows pupils to choose, then self-challenge. Ron uses adult support in the classroom to target a small group of pupils whom he has identified as requiring further challenge. Good use is made of peer talk and positive competitive spirit. Ron chooses to work with a group of pupils whom he has identified as requiring support to move on further, but maintains a watchful eye over the rest of the class, who work independently and with peer support.

 In relation to Teachers' Standard 5a and your own practice, consider the following key questions:

- How well do you know your pupils and their interests?
- What strategies do you employ to plan to cater for individual needs in your class?
- When you plan questions, how do you differentiate them for learners?
- How and when do you use pupil consultation as a tool for meeting individual needs?
- How adaptable are you when teaching?
- In what ways do you differentiate?
- What evidence do you have that your existing practice is effective?

Possible sources of evidence for Teachers' Standard 5a:

- *Pupils*: listen to their voice; plan for independent and peer assessment; consult;
- *Responses*: from pupils in written work and your accompanying comments (marking);
- *Display*: ensure that the classroom environment and displays are set up to facilitate support and to challenge and orientate pupils;
- *Other adults*: plan for other adults and ensure that they are well versed in the expected learning outcomes and the needs of individuals; invest significant time in this;

(Continued)

(Continued)

- *Planning*: this should offer clear information regarding differentiation, prior knowledge, pupil needs and challenge for all;
- *Teaching*: ensure that this is accurately pitched and learner-focused; adapt your teaching as the lesson progresses; consider how you respond to pupils and adapt questions for individual learners; use teaching to support and challenge individuals; and remember – they do not all have to be engaged in a whole-class introduction for a long period of time, if they can be moving on and making progress;
- *Groupings and environment*: be flexible and allow freedom of choice for learners; ensure that your classroom signposts learners to relevant support and challenge and that this is embedded in your practice.

5b: Have a secure understanding of how a range of factors can inhibit pupils' ability to learn, and how best to overcome these

As discussed in the previous section, knowing your pupils and their individual needs is a prerequisite to effective teaching. Having high expectations of pupils with various needs requires an accurate assessment of the barriers to their learning, then making effective interventions to help them make good progress (Beere, 2014, p. 92). What people construct from a learning encounter depends on their motives and intentions, on what they know already and on how they use their prior knowledge. Meaning is therefore personal. What else can it be? The alternative is that meaning is 'transmitted' from teacher to student, like dubbing and audio-tape, which is a common but untenable view (Biggs, 2003, p. 12).

A way in which this can be achieved is through pupil scrutiny and appraisal and this can be addressed through formalised assessments, or simply conducted through observation and formative assessment in lessons. What is essential here is that any potential barriers to learning are pre-considered, in order to support pupils in making progress.

Potential barriers to learning: how to recognise and help overcome them

Barriers to learning can come in a range of guises. They can be, but are not exclusive to, any one or a combination of those identified below:

1. *Needs*: pupils are, of course, unique and have a wide range of differing needs. These needs can manifest in a variety of ways and it is important to recognise when they may impact on learning and progress. These needs may sometimes be expressed in, what may be considered to be inappropriate ways, so recognising them and putting support mechanisms in place in order to pre-empt them, or be prepared when they arise, is essential. In recognising specific needs, you first need to engage with any information relating to individual pupils submitted to you by previous teachers and/or parents/carers. Be aware of any pupil support plans, in order to best cater for individuals. Make excellent use of parent/carer consultation times and listen to the voice of the child.

> 💡 *Top Tip*: Create simple pupil profiles. These do not have to be extensive and may be bulleted notes on the individual. Start off with any information you may have on them and then this can be added to throughout the academic year. It will come in very handy when planning for learning and later on, when report writing.

2. *Environment*: as discussed in Chapter 1, environmental factors can play a major role in pupil support. Being aware of stimuli, furniture, aromas, colours, display and proximity to the board, for example, are key considerations when preparing your learning environment. Similarly, knowing whether or not individual pupils have specific triggers for behaviours relating to environmental factors is crucial. As you become more familiar with your pupils, this information will inevitably self-present, but, in the early stages, use the information you have at your disposal in order to make sound judgements relating to this.

3. *Social*: for pupils, school is not simply about learning. As teachers, we are very learning-focused and it is important to remember that, for pupils, school is also a social experience. It can be very rewarding or totally disheartening. It can be enjoyable or very disconcerting. Social factors, therefore, have the potential to inhibit learning and the importance of equipping pupils with resilience and positivity relating to social difficulties cannot be overstated. Be aware of any social difficulties your pupils may encounter and develop a positive classroom ethos in which pupils feel that issues can be discussed and resolved. Beere (2014) considers rapport and empathy with pupils to be a key factor in securing behaviour for learning and pupil progress. Rapport is that deep communication with a class of

individuals that elicits wonderful states of cooperation and motivation (p. 174). Building a rapport with pupils and showing a genuine understanding of their interests, needs and challenges can help to secure a positive teacher–pupil relationship in which the pupil feels valued. In these cases, teachers consider the social elements of pupil development and are invested in ensuring that these are channelled effectively in order to support pupils as they learn.

4. *'I'm stuck!'* This is the classic barrier to learning. Pitching activities so that they are achievable for pupils, but also offer challenge, is essential when promoting progress. Equipping pupils with the independence to access support when it is required in order to help them move on autonomously is crucial if you are to minimise demands on teacher time and ensure fast progress, as discussed in previous chapters. Developing a classroom ethos in which pupils feel that they can engage with challenge is essential.

💡 *Top Tip*: At Robin Hood Primary Academy in Birmingham, members of the senior leadership team developed a series of printed whole-school posters aimed at promoting pupil independence. The posters simply stated: *'Stuck? Brilliant!'* and then proceeded to bullet-point some simple steps to support pupils in using the tools they had at their disposal, in order to self-help, before asking the teacher. By re-framing the concept of being stuck, the message was clear: it is OK to be stuck. It means that you are about to learn.

How do you balance individual pupil needs with whole-class demands?

Catering for individual needs can be a challenge, particularly when large class sizes act as a potential barrier to this. To what extent can children's learning be personalised when you have a class of 30? Ideally, this can be achieved through assessment by developing autonomous learning strategies whereby children actively participate in their learning (Harris and Lowe, 2014, p. 94). Refinement of assessment strategies is crucial when considering individual needs. As Robinson et al. (2013) accurately state, formative assessment is undertaken minute by minute as you ask the class questions and listen to pupil responses. The information you glean from pupils' answers should inform your teaching. You should adapt planned lessons based on the acquisition of the knowledge you witness in the pupils' responses (p. 80). When teaching, therefore, you are using all of the fine-tuned assessment techniques at your disposal in order to address individual needs and your teaching needs to have this in-built flexibility, if you are to ensure pupil progress.

Practice examples – Teachers' Standard 5b

LISA

Lisa is a teaching assistant and works with reluctant learners. The pupils in her care have a range of needs and with the support and guidance of the class teacher, she aims to offer bespoke learning opportunities for these pupils. Lisa does this by using her extensive knowledge of them. She has invested time in getting to know their interests and their triggers and uses these to engage and empower them, particularly when they face challenges. Lisa has exceptionally high expectations for behaviour and learning, as does the class teacher and she remains consistent in these, despite disruptive behaviours. Lisa cares for her pupils' well-being and tells them this. As a result of this supportive, learning-focused approach, the pupils are motivated and show respect for Lisa, each other and themselves.

DOMINIC

Dominic is a dinner supervisor working in Key Stage 2. During dinner breaks, Dominic has noticed that pupil conflicts often remain unresolved prior to returning to afternoon lessons, despite the best efforts of the dinner supervisors. Dominic approached the class teachers and has since set up a lunchtime club that pupils can attend in order to seek support in resolving problems. The club, which he calls 'Moving On', has attracted many pupils and the school has begun to train some of the children in mediation. Class teachers have commented that this has had an impact on afternoon sessions, with pupils returning to class much more focused.

In relation to Teachers' Standard 5b and your own practice, consider the following key questions:

- What barriers to learning have you witnessed in your own setting?
- What strategies have you seen employed by colleagues in order to overcome barriers to learning?
- In your own reflective practice, have you identified next steps and development based on your own assessments of pupil progress and those factors that have inhibited it?

(Continued)

(Continued)

Possible sources of evidence for Teachers' Standard 5b:

- *The pupil voice*: listen to what pupils have to say and act accordingly;
- *Observation*: pay close attention to what is going on both in the classroom and the external environment, such as the playground; these observations can help you capture those things that may be overlooked or those crucial pieces of information that pupils choose not to share;
- *The classroom environment*: how does this support learning and reduce barriers? A close examination of this, in collaboration with pupils, could yield results;
- *Planning*: how does your planning demonstrate an understanding of barriers to learning and how does it attempt to address these?
- *Your questions and responses to pupil questions*: plan questions carefully to maximise learning; tailor questions for individual pupils; take the time to respond in a way that promotes learning. Try to avoid 'brushing over' a pupil question in order to move on with the lesson – if time is short, ensure that you communicate that the question is valued and you will return to it later (and make sure you do).

5c: Demonstrate an awareness of the physical, social and intellectual development of children, and know how to adapt teaching to support pupils' education at different stages of development

An essential part of Initial Teacher Training (ITT) courses is the opportunity to engage in school experience in different key stages. In primary ITT, you may experience active setting engagement in Foundation Stage, Key Stage 1 or Key Stage 2 and it is during this essential stage of training that a developing understanding of pupil pedagogy, related to stage and development, is gleaned.

By developing an understanding of child development in relation to specific learning outcomes, your teaching can be pitched accurately in order to cater for the specific needs of your pupils, appropriate to their stage of physical, social and intellectual development. In an engaging talk delivered by Sir Ken Robinson, entitled 'Changing Education Paradigms' (RSA Animate, 2010), the concept of a standardised schooling system in the UK, whereby pupils are grouped according to their age, is explored. Robinson (in RSA Animate, 2010) considers that children are educated 'by batches', put through the education system by age group and questions why there is an assumption that the most important thing children have in common is how old they are. This, of course, is an important consideration when exploring pupil pedagogy and development and when planning interventions to support learning and progress at different developmental stages.

In order to examine adapting teaching to pupil needs, relating to child developmental processes, we will initially consider what is meant by stages of child development and then examine how a teacher can use this information in order to cater for individual needs.

It is well documented that children develop at different rates. Bulman (2006) categorises and defines the three key areas of child growth and development, as outlined in Teachers' Standard 5c, into the areas that follow (paraphrased):

Physical: the body increasing in skill and performance;

Social and emotional: the child's identity, self-image, relationships, feelings and learning the skills to live in society with other people;

Intellectual: learning skills, understanding, memory, concentration. (p. 2)

Let us now examine each of these areas in turn and explore the ways in which teachers can evidence this standard.

Physical development

The physical development of a child is a crucial component of the EYFS (DfE, 2014c) and can be observed by teachers as part of daily interaction with them. A child's physique will develop, over time, as will their ability to engage with objects, environments and people around them.

The EYFS (DfE, 2014c) defines physical development in early childhood as follows:

Physical development involves providing opportunities for young children to be active and interactive; and to develop their co-ordination, control, and movement. Children must also be helped to understand the importance of physical activity, and to make healthy choices in relation to food. (p. 8)

Whilst a child's physical development includes a range of developmental stages, two important considerations for teachers are gross and fine motor skills. Evangelou et al. (2009) examine these areas in depth, drawing on the work of a range of early child development theorists. The key gross motor skills are presented as walking, running, jumping, throwing, hopping and balancing (p. 67) and fine motor skill as 'manual control', which is described as the ability to use the hand and the arm to control objects (p. 69).

Social and emotional development

Social and emotional development of the child encompasses ways in which children develop relationships with others, know themselves and their feelings and learn to become 'social'. The EYFS (DfE, 2014c) state that:

> Personal, social and emotional development involves helping children to develop a positive sense of themselves, and others; to form positive relationships and develop respect for others; to develop social skills and learn how to manage their feelings; to understand appropriate behaviour in groups; and to have confidence in their own abilities. (p. 8)

Bulman (2006) suggests that this aspect is closely linked to the quality of parenting in the early years. A child's social and emotional development can manifest itself in a variety of ways in a school setting and it is how these developmental stages can be captured and used as a tool to support the learner that is a key consideration for the teacher.

Intellectual development

Intellectual development concerns cognition and is linked with other aspects of their development. Much of this book has examined ways in which a teacher can support a child's intellectual development and a closer examination of the works of established learning theorists, such as Dewey, Vygotsky, Piaget, Steiner, Montessori, Bandura (to name but a few), would provide an excellent overview of the intricacies of child cognition and the different perspectives from which to develop your own educational philosophy. Teachers need to be able to use this information to make informed choices when differentiating learning to suit pupil needs. When considering differentiation in teaching and learning, O'Brien and Guiney (2001) discuss four interactive factors – pedagogical, social, emotional and cognitive – which affect the learner's ability to learn. They suggest that, in seeking to account for these factors, within a differentiated teaching and learning system, key importance is placed on the need to synthesise these factors in order to enable the learner to develop autonomy and self-awareness (p. 55). Here, then, pupils have the potential to develop an active role as autonomous co-creators of bespoke learning opportunities and a self-awareness of their own personal learning needs.

Pitch perfect

Depending on the age phase in which you are teaching, evidence to support this should be self-presenting in the inclusive classroom. Evangelou et al. (2009) discuss the concept of creating 'enabling environments' for pupils in which all learners can learn, develop and succeed. This encompasses numerous strands:

a thoroughly differentiated curriculum; an inclusive ethos that can be readily identified; and effective dialogues with pupils, parents/carers and other professionals. As part of this environment, pitching and adapting learning opportunities for pupils within your care should be child's play. As discussed previously, excellent teachers *use what they know* (about the needs of their pupils) and *show that they know*, in what they plan, implement, say and evaluate. A deep knowledge and understanding of child pedagogy and developmental processes underpins effective practice and it is your use of this knowledge that enables pupils to succeed and allows your practice to be 'pitch perfect'.

Practice examples – Teachers' Standard 5c

MICAH

Micah teaches Year 4 and prides himself on engaging in regular professional peer observations in other age phases in order to develop his own practice. Micah has liaised with colleagues who teach in Foundation Stage through to Year 6 and has observed practice with a specific focus on how teachers adapt to the needs of their learners relative to their stage of development. Through engagement with professional dialogue and critical reflection with his colleagues, Micah has developed a repertoire of ideas and support mechanisms which impact on his daily practice.

AIMEE

Aimee uses the STEPS (CfSA, 2008) approach (see *Top Tip* box below) when planning learning opportunities for her Year 2 class. The STEPS approach is thoroughly embedded in the planning processes within her setting and Aimee ensures that all adults working with the pupils in her class are an integral part of the planning process. By using this approach, Aimee can readily identify those pupils for whom extra provision may be required in order to facilitate their learning and progress.

Top Tip: When considering a successful outcome and planning for this, you may wish to consider a STEPS approach. This popular, inclusive approach for the delivery of physical education in primary schools requires teachers to consider and identify five crucial elements in their planning and implementation:

(Continued)

(Continued)

Space, Task, Equipment, People and Success. In a publication entitled *Physical Education: Supporting gifted and talented children* (CfSA, 2008), the STEPS approach is broken down into the following key considerations:

Space: Where? *Task*: What actions? How? *Equipment*: With what? *People*: With whom? *Success:* Observed success (p. 2). By building these considerations into your planning for pupil provision, you can provide evidence of pupil support in *any* lesson, not just physical education.

We would encourage you, at this point, to reflect on the content of this chapter up to this point, with specific regard to adapting to meet pupil needs.

In relation to Teachers' Standard 5c and your own practice, consider the following key questions:

- How well developed is your understanding of the developmental process of the pupils you teach?
- In what ways could you further enhance your understanding and thus, provision for pupils?
- In which activities could you employ the STEPS (CfSA, 2008) approach?

Possible sources of evidence for Teachers' Standard 5c:

- *The pupil voice*: what do the pupils say about how they are supported and is an inclusive classroom ethos present and visible, at all times?
- *Observations*: what do your observations (and the observations of others) say about your ability to pitch activities which cater for the needs of *all* pupils? How do you use observations to impact on future practice?
- *The learning environment*: is this an 'enabling' environment in which pupils can flourish and succeed?
- *Planning*: how does your planning demonstrate that your learning opportunities are well-pitched and suitable for the pupils in your care?
- *Evidence*: how do you use evidence of pupil development, including learning inhibitors, in daily practice? Can you show that you are responding to this?

5d: Have a clear understanding of the needs of all pupils, including those with special educational needs; those of high ability; those with English as an additional language; those with disabilities; and be able to use and evaluate distinctive teaching approaches to engage and support them

'Miss! I'm brilliant at this!'

Have you ever experienced that amazing moment when pupils share their sense of pride and achievement? This 'outcome' should consist of a range of contributing factors, including your relationships with pupils, pupil engagement, well-pitched learning opportunities and pupils being a valued and essential part of the assessment process. Such a moment is great and hopefully there will be some clear next steps in order to challenge and extend, but pupils don't always tell you, so how do you go about identifying strengths and needs and motivating pupils to persevere and succeed?

Identification is the first stage of the process of differentiation and the intended outcome is pupil success. Identification is, in essence, assessment. By utilising fine-tuned assessment tools in your teacher toolkit, you will be able to observe, listen, adapt, stretch, support and respond to pupil needs during a lesson. Referring back to the pupil exclamation: *'Miss! I'm brilliant at this!'* let us examine how we can use this to cater for the needs of the pupil. In order to do so, you will need to be a responsive, reactive and proactive teacher. First, ask yourself, what does this tell you? The child considers that they have 'mastered' this particular element and it is your role, or the role of a supporting adult, to ascertain whether or not this is the case. Simple, effective questioning can aid this, preceded by praise. Once you have 'assessed' the situation, you will be able to decide on next steps *with* the pupil, whether challenge, support or additional practice, in order to develop further.

In the sections that follow, we will examine inclusive practice incorporating provision for pupils with SEND. In addition, we will focus on effective provision for pupils with English as an additional language and on how best to meet their specific needs.

On inclusion, integration and segregation

It is an understatement to say that education has experienced significant change throughout history and this is never truer than with the subject of pupil needs. Frederickson and Cline (2009) remind us that: 'Historically, if children had particular difficulties in school they were put together with other children whose needs were perceived to be similar … This solution was also applied to children learning EAL' (p. 69).

In serving the needs of pupils, particularly those children with special educational needs and disability (SEND), there is much debate regarding effective provision. In more recent years, inclusive practice has featured high on the agenda in mainstream settings, alongside effective integration and the limiting of segregation. Frederickson and Cline (2009) go on to suggest that: 'Where inclusion is embraced, educational provision carefully structured to meet a diversity of needs, and flexible, personalized programmes delivered, research into social and academic outcomes for pupils with SEN has identified net benefits' (pp. 100–1).

Many educational researchers consider that embracing inclusion should be a whole-school ethos, rather than an over-reliance on targeted intervention being a cure-all (Frederickson and Cline, 2009; Herbert, 2011; Ekins, 2012). Ekins (2012) further considers that the key stages of identifying needs, planning interventions, pupil progress and review and action planning enable impact (pp. 138–42) and that our perceptions need to be re-framed, so that 'difference and diversity is not seen as a problem to be dealt with' (p. 163).

So, how can teachers in busy classrooms, with large class sizes, ensure that they are providing for all pupils and ensuring that provision is tailor-made for pupils with special educational needs and disability?

The importance of supporting and challenging pupils with SEND

The UNESCO 'Salamanca Statement' (1994) describes the fundamental rights of children to education and goes on to acknowledge that all children are unique and should be provided with opportunities to achieve. This inclusive perspective, amongst others, has revolutionised the way in which pupil needs are met within the primary classroom. Pupil needs can be wide-ranging. Needs may be short-term and related to minor disruptions in a child's 'normal' routines, such as the loss of a relative, or more long-term, such as a physical disability or specific learning needs, such as dyscalculia. Ensuring that you are aware of individual pupil needs is a prerequisite to meeting Teachers' Standard 5d and it would be useful to engage in wider reading regarding specific needs, particularly if you have not encountered them previously. Listed below are some of the more common needs you may encounter in your setting:

- Learning difficulties: some pupils may encounter difficulties in a range of subject areas, the acquisition of basic skills or perhaps have a diagnosis of dyslexia or dyscalculia.
- Physical needs: this may be an impairment or physical disability that impacts upon a pupil's ability to engage in learning or social activities.
- Communication: some pupils may experience difficulties in communicating with others, or perhaps in understanding or interpreting.

- Emotional needs: these needs may impact upon a pupil's behaviour, affect how a pupil interacts with others or how they engage with learning. These needs may also impact on a pupil's ability or willingness to work within the rules of the class/school.

The above examples of course, may overlap and some pupils may exhibit a combination of a variety of needs.

Adapting practice to meet these needs of pupils may range from minor classroom furniture and resource adaptations to significant adaptations to the curriculum and support mechanisms being put in place. Once pupils with SEND have been identified, it is your role, alongside the SENCo and other adults with whom the children may be working, to adapt provision in order to cater for their needs and as highlighted in the Salamanca Statement (UNESCO, 1994), to provide opportunities for all pupils to achieve. In all cases, adaptations to provision are necessary in order to maximise the learning experiences for pupils in your care. For many, individual education plans (IEPs) or individual behaviour plans (IBPs) will need to be developed and will provide clear guidance on individual needs. Often, parents/carers, medical professionals, teaching assistants and teachers work alongside one another in order to create bespoke support plans for pupils with needs. These documents are useful when used alongside teacher assessment processes and provide evidence that interventions are embedded in practice. Teachers use these strategies in order to plan for a differentiated curriculum and this is usually evident in planning. It would be useful to invest time in learning about the range of some of the more common pupil needs and the ways in which experienced teachers adapt their practice in order to help support these pupils. There is, however, a wider debate concerning how a 'need' can be defined and of course, the notion that *all* pupils have needs in a variety of ways. As Glazzard (2011, p. 62) reminds us: 'You might think about inclusion only in relation to the education of children with special educational needs and disabilities in mainstream environments. However, inclusion is a broad concept which embraces all learners.'

In your daily practice, the expectation is that you will show how you adapt and cater for the needs of all pupils, not simply those pupils with *additional* needs. Whilst it is vital to identify and provide support, an ingredient that is frequently missing from lesson plans is how all pupils will be challenged, *including* those with SEND. It is evidence of this that will ensure you are catering for the needs of all and demonstrating that you are an inclusive practitioner.

As Ekins (2012, p. 132) reminds us: 'Any approach to coordinating provision has to be based on setting high expectations of progress for all pupils: including those pupils with SEN and/or disabilities.'

Herbert (2011) suggests that, rather than focusing on the differences between learners, there are common strategies with which teachers (and pupils) can work in order to enhance learning for all. These areas are memory, motivation and communication and Herbert (2011) suggests that, through engaging with these areas more thoroughly, teachers can maximise opportunities in their daily practice to develop these areas, in order to support learning for all in an inclusive way.

EAL learners

Supporting pupils with English as an additional language is often a challenge for teachers and a thorough understanding of EAL provision is essential for the inclusive teacher. Historically, when pupils have had little or no English, they have been grouped together with pupils for whom learning is a challenge, despite the fact that, of course, learning may not be the challenge for EAL learners (Frederickson and Cline, 2009). In their 'mother tongue', pupils may be successful in their academic studies and it is therefore a para-doxical situation when teachers of EAL pupils try to cater for their poor English abilities by grouping them with pupils for whom higher order academic studies may be challenging. Haslam et al. (2005) state that there is a big difference between the acquisition of social English and a mastery of the language of academic success (p. 19). EAL learners may acquire much of their English through social means and it is therefore essential that these social opportunities are maximised both within and outside of the classroom. Cummins (1980) identified a distinct correlation between age and the development of cognitive academic language proficiency (CALP) in additional language learners. The findings concluded that, where CALP was better developed, older learners manifested additional language CALP more rapidly than younger learners, as it already existed in their first language and therefore, was available to use in a new context (p. 184). Cummins (1984) also explored the relationships between basic interpersonal communication skills (BICS) and cognitive academic language proficiency (CALP), developing the popular 'iceberg' model to illustrate this. BICS refers to social, 'surface' language proficiency (considered to be cognitively undemanding), such as language used in face-to-face conversations, whereas CALP refers to academic language (which is considered to be cognitively demanding), such as language used in reading or writing. It would be useful at this point to consider where you think the pupils with whom you have had contact have acquired their additional language: perhaps the playground, at home or in the classroom? You may wish to consider wherever this occurs, what kind of language is being acquired e.g. colloquial. It is useful to reflect on the impact of these considerations on the EAL learner's ability to both acquire language and make progress.

Douglas Brown (1980) considered 'critical period hypothesis' (the ideal window of opportunity to acquire an additional language) and the notion that an optimal stage exists during which a person successfully acquires fluent control of a language (p. 157). Douglas Brown (1980) also examined the effects of the 'culture shock' in additional language acquisition. He described this as the learning of a 'second culture' in addition to an additional language and suggested that teachers can help the experience of learning a 'second culture' to become one of increased cultural and self-awareness, as well as being a successful language learning experience (pp. 163–4).

For teachers of EAL learners, it is essential to consider the overall impact of immersion in what is potentially a new and very different culture, in addition to the constraints of learning and mastering a new language. Catering for the diverse needs of EAL learners requires a holistic approach to teaching, involving attention to social factors, in addition to academic integration. On scaffolding as a support mechanism for EAL learners, Baker (2006) suggests that: 'rather than instruction being teacher-directed or student-centred, teacher-student cooperation appears important for these students. In such a social collaboration, the key issue is how that teacher supports the student by a careful pitching of comprehensible language' (p. 301).

This is easy to demonstrate in effective classroom practice, as it can be identified in planning and should be visible in learning situations.

Haslam et al. (2005) identify the key elements of teaching EAL learners:

'Anti-racism;

Language exists within context; we need to be aware of this when assessing and planning. Therefore:

i.   Skills are practiced and language is taught in a meaningful context, rather than in isolation, drawing on and reinforcing the National Curriculum, and

ii. We use context-embedded teaching to support meaning, and when we build on responses to support further production.

There is a distinction between social and academic English.

The pupil's prior knowledge and experience should be accessed, used and built on.

Oracy and collaboration.' (p. 8)

In summary, there are several aspects to contemplate when planning to meet the needs of EAL learners and it is a thorough consideration and understanding of these areas that will provide evidence that you are meeting Teachers' Standard 5d. We would advise that you engage in wider reading concerning the successful support of EAL learners and work alongside those professionals in school settings for whom this is their specialist role.

Practice examples – Teachers' Standard 5d

LOLA

Lola has a new child in her class who has been diagnosed with dyspraxia. In particular, the pupil, Alex, has difficulties with fine-motor skills. Lola has liaised with Alex's previous school and examined previous provision made for Alex. In addition, Lola has contacted the Dyspraxia Foundation (www.dyspraxiafoundation.org.uk)

(Continued)

(Continued)

in order to seek out training opportunities to allow her to better cater for Alex's specific needs. Lola has invited Alex's parents into school to discuss building confidence in her own abilities and how best to support Alex, in partnership. As a result of this meeting, Lola learned that Alex has an aversion to writing, in part due to difficulties in holding a pencil and that this has impacted on Alex's confidence in making progress in writing. Lola, on the advice of the SENCo, has provided Alex with a pencil grip and a support assistant to work alongside him during extended writing activities. By investing time in learning about Alex's specific needs and through close parental partnership and good communication, Lola has been successful in working with Alex to provide the best possible support. Alex is now settled and happy at school and is making good progress.

HARRISON

Harrison has teamed up with the National Association for Language Development in the Curriculum (NALDIC) in order to develop effective assessment procedures within his setting for EAL pupils. Using formative-level descriptors (NALDIC, 2009), Harrison has begun a staff development programme in order to help teachers within his setting support next steps learning for EAL pupils. As Harrison works in a large three-form-entry primary school, Harrison has also developed an EAL pupil project called 'SEALL: Supporting English as an Additional Language Learner', in which more accomplished EAL learners work alongside less developed EAL pupils and adults in school as a supportive mechanism. This inclusive, whole-school ethos has also manifested itself in an annual 'International Day', planned with all pupils in school, in order to celebrate the rich and diverse cultures within the setting.

 In relation to Teachers' Standard 5d and your own practice, consider the following key questions:

- How do you cater for the needs of pupils with Special Educational Needs and Disability?
- If you do not have EAL learners in your current setting, how could you develop your professional understanding in this area?
- How do you provide challenge and extension for *all* pupils, including those with SEND?

(Continued)

(Continued)

- How do you meet the needs of higher ability pupils?
- In what ways does your setting recognise and support pupils displaying additional talents in non-curriculum areas?
- Reflecting on your own SEND provision, how can you improve on your practice?
- Access www.naldic.org.uk/eal-teaching-and-learning/eal-resources [accessed 4 February 2015]. How can you use this resource to support you in developing effective EAL provision?

Possible sources of evidence for Teachers' Standard 5a:

- Individual education plans (IEPs) or individual behaviour plans (IBPs);
- Working collaboratively with the SENCo and external agencies;
- Identification of individual pupil needs in planning that goes beyond task and activity differentiation.

Chapter summary

In this chapter, we have explored various theories concerning adapting practice in order to cater for a diverse range of pupil needs within an inclusive classroom. We have examined the importance of an inclusive whole-school ethos and investigated ways in which pupils can be supported effectively through a range of strategies and practical examples. But how is this achieved in a Key Stage 2 class of 30 or a busy Foundation Stage? Effective use of other adults is a crucial consideration when planning to meet pupil needs, but, often, adults, arguably the most expensive classroom resource, are not available. It is up to you, therefore, to establish rigorous routines and support mechanisms with which pupils can engage autonomously in order to maximise the potential to meet pupil needs. Establish an excellent rapport with your pupils and encourage respectful peer relationships in which learners are motivated to learn and support one another. As stated previously, just because you are the teacher, you do not have to do all of the work! Lay the foundations for a successful classroom environment and plan for exciting learning opportunities that motivate pupils to make extra progress and overcome potential barriers to learning.

CHAPTER 6

MAKE ACCURATE AND PRODUCTIVE USE OF ASSESSMENT

Teachers' Standard 6 – Make accurate and productive use of assessment:

6a Know and understand how to assess the relevant subject and curriculum areas, including statutory requirements

6b Make use of formative and summative assessment to secure pupils' progress

6c Use relevant data to monitor progress, set targets and plan subsequent lessons

6d Give pupils regular feedback, both orally and through accurate marking and encourage pupils to respond to the feedback.

What is this all about?

The key point made throughout this standard relates to how teachers monitor and assess the needs of all pupils. As the chapter unfolds, it will become clear how assessment is integral to teaching and learning. The standard enables you to consider how constructive, formative feedback is used to support learners to make progress, as well as how summative assessment is used. Teachers are expected to demonstrate an understanding of the assessment requirements for National Curriculum and EYFS testing, as well as those for optional tasks or tests. You are required to know about national and local performance data and how this can be used to compare and inform teachers on the attainment of pupils.

How can this be demonstrated?

There will be short-term, daily activities which may be classroom-based as well as longer-term whole-school activities, which will all provide opportunities for you to consider how assessment is used to support pupil progress. The range of strategies you use when monitoring progress, the interventions you use when working with pupils and the impact of your feedback will all provide valuable examples and should be included to demonstrate how you are meeting Teachers' Standard 6. You may draw on the professional discussions you have had with colleagues about assessment arrangements, including any involvement in moderation of work. This Standard requires teachers to demonstrate how they have accessed and interpreted the range of local and national data to raise achievement. Through your practice, you will be able to show how you have used data to generate realistic, achievable targets for pupils.

Chapter overview

The chapter reflects on the purpose of assessment for learning and assessment of learning and considers the place of formative and summative assessment in raising achievement. 'Assessment refers to all those activities undertaken by teachers, and by their students in assessing themselves, which provides information to be used as feedback to modify the teaching and learning activities in which they are engaged' (Black and Wiliam, 1998: 2). Effective teachers know their pupils well and 'ongoing, teacher-led assessment is a crucial part of effective teaching' (DfE, 2014a). They have made use of assessment to find out about their pupils. This assessment has enabled them to plan work that is appropriate to the age, interests and ability of the pupils, which impacts on pupil engagement and behaviour, resulting in a positive learning environment in which pupils can achieve and succeed.

Effective assessment involves the cyclical process of 'assess, plan and teach', which is a never-ending cycle. An analogy can be made with health. Imagine a patient who visits their doctor with a sore throat. In order for the doctor to plan to use the best medicine to treat the condition, an assessment has to be made. We would not expect a doctor to pre-scribe medication without first making an assessment of our needs. In the same way, as a teacher you would not be able to ensure a pupil makes progress without first finding out, i.e. assessing, where they are in their learning.

In this chapter, there will be an exploration of the statutory requirements and we will consider what these are as well as how they are used in schools. The assessment requirements for the Early Years Foundation Stage (EYFS) are outlined, as are sign-posts for assessments in the National Curriculum subject areas. Essential to effective assessment is the process of monitoring and tracking progress and the organisation of this is highlighted. Following these activities, we look at some ideas for record keep-ing. Thorough systems of assessment not only support the teacher to demonstrate the impact of their teaching, but also support identification of the learner's next steps. The chapter continues with an emphasis on the value of both oral and written feedback to pupils, which is regarded as a critical skill for all teachers.

Taking it apart and putting it back together

When we start to disentangle the elements of Teachers' Standard 6, it is imperative that we do not think of assessment as sitting in isolation. A teacher has to have a solid work-ing knowledge of what a child can do, what they understand and what they know, so that they can plan appropriate teaching and learning opportunities. Assessment, plan-ning and teaching are all parts of one cyclical process. Teachers know their learners well and identify the achievement, progress and attainment made by each individual child. Glazzard and Stokoe (2011, p. 76) provide the following, helpful definitions:

- Achievement refers to a measure of what children know and can do at a given point in time.
- Progress is a measure of achievement, taking into account children's starting and exit achievements within a given timescale.
- Attainment compares an individual's achievement with national standards.

6a: Know and understand how to assess the relevant subject and curriculum areas, including statutory requirements

Teachers assess learners against national benchmarks at all phases of a pupil's education and this starts in the Foundation Stage. The requirement when addressing this sub-set is to consider how national benchmarks can help to secure a judgement about a learner's progress. Teachers should demonstrate that they can use assessment strategies to assess a pupil's learning and can set realistic targets based on the analysis of assessment data. We will consider each of these key areas in detail. To do this, we will discuss what assessment looks like on a short-term weekly basis and how to use assessment over a termly and annual basis. Whatever the timescale, teachers will be using systems that are relevant for the school they are in and in line with national requirements.

Statutory requirements

There are national assessments at key points in a child's primary education. These aim to provide information to parents about their child's progress and to present information about the performance of the school. There are different approaches to assessment at each key stage, which includes tests and ongoing teacher assessment. The Standards and Testing Agency (2015) provide useful updates and guidance on teacher assessment frameworks for both Key Stage 1 and Key Stage 2.

To support schools with assessing pupils the government introduced a scaled score system. A description of pupil performance at a national standard is included in a framework which is used to set a raw score that links to a scaled score. In the scaled score, 100 will always represent the national standard. A pupil's scaled score will be based on their raw score. The raw score is the total number of marks a pupil receives in a test, based on the number of questions they answered correctly. The pupil's raw score will be translated into a scaled score using a conversion table. A pupil who achieves the national standard will have demonstrated sufficient knowledge in the areas assessed by the tests. This will mean that they are well placed to succeed in the next phase of their education (Gov.UK, 2015).

In the EYFS, a baseline will be used within the assessment framework to support teachers in the Reception class to make a judgement about progress and attainment. The baseline is used as the starting point from which to measure progress and is usually administered by the Reception teaching staff. It sits within teachers' broader assessments of children's development. The Reception baseline is the only measure used in this key phase to assess progress for children who start Reception in September 2016 and beyond.

In Key Stage 1, there are statutory assessments. This includes a phonics check near the end of Year 1. At the end of Key Stage 1, there are teacher assessments in mathematics and reading which are informed by externally set tests. There are also externally set tests in grammar, punctuation and spelling which will help to inform the teacher assessment of writing. The tests reflect the new National Curriculum and are expressed as a scaled score. For mathematics, reading, writing and speaking and listening, teachers assess pupils as meeting one of several performance descriptors. For science, there is a single performance descriptor.

Performance descriptors are used in both key stages to describe the range of skills and knowledge that is required by a pupil, to demonstrate the expected standard in each test, in each subject (Morgan, 2015).

In Key Stage 2, there are national tests at the end of Key Stage 2 in: mathematics; reading; grammar, punctuation and spelling; and a teacher assessment of mathematics, reading, writing and science.

Minimum requirements are set nationally for schools and if a school falls below this minimum they will come under additional scrutiny through inspection. This minimum standard is called a *Floor Standard*. Teachers are aware of the national expectations for the learners in their class and make use of national data to identify the needs of individuals, ensuring they are supported to make progress.

Subject and curriculum areas

There are different expectations for the assessment of subjects/curriculum areas within each key phase of education. In the Foundation Stage (FS), children are assessed in the prime and specific areas of learning. Importantly, teachers observe and make a judgement about each child based on the characteristics of learning. In Key Stages 1 and 2, English and maths have statutory tests. Teacher assessments are made in Key Stage 1 for science and in Key Stage 2 there are science tests. There is no requirement to conduct an end-of-key-stage assessment in non-core subjects for Key Stages 1 and 2. Teachers are required to teach the full programmes of study for each subject and to report progress in the subject each year using their professional judgement to determine the most effective method of gathering evidence and reporting children's progress.

Weekly assessments

Teachers use a range of assessment tools to capture development and to track daily and weekly pupil progress. The data provide information which supports teachers to plan appropriately for the pupils in their class. Teachers use the data from assessment tools to plan appropriately for the pupils in their class. Tracking pupil progress takes many different forms and teachers develop their own way to record daily observations in the classroom, alongside using the school system. A simple and yet effective system is to use a table which includes the names of children being assessed with the learning objective(s) at the top. Teachers use a range of symbols to record achievement, such as a triangle if a child has achieved the learning objective, two sides of a triangle if they have partly achieved it and one side of a triangle if they have not achieved it. Other symbols can be used such as colour coding, letters (A, B, C) or numbers (1, 2, 3), stars or ticks. Whatever system is used must be convenient for the class teacher, appropriate and fit for purpose. Each teacher will have a class assessment folder where all assessment documents are kept. There will be an assessment folder for each child where assessments from their current year and their previous year will be kept as evidence.

Planning should show how you will support learners to make progress. This cannot be left to chance and at the planning stage teachers are able to identify next steps in learning. Lesson plans can be annotated to demonstrate how formative assessment has been used and how individuals and groups of learners have made progress. Glazzard and Stokoe (2011, p. 72) make a valid observation about using systems that are manageable to 'record children's achievements against intended learning outcomes at the end of every lesson'.

Termly assessments

Progress, as well as attainment and achievement, will be discussed with colleagues, parents and children as part of ongoing good practice. Moderation exercises take place within and sometimes between schools to allow teachers to discuss their judgements of pupil progress. This ensures judgements are secure and consistent. Pupil progress meetings may be held termly to identify progress as well as gaps in learning. Formal school assessment may take place half-termly using a specific record of tracking. One such system is Assessing Pupil Progress (APP). APP is a nationally developed and standardised approach which provides a framework of assessment to support teachers to make judgements about the standard of pupils' work. It supports teachers to develop an understanding of the needs of each child through tracking pupil progress and then adapting their planning and teaching. Teachers use national benchmarks and draw on a range of evidence to make their judgements.

At the end of each term, some schools may use a formal test such as QCA, or devise their own tests, to assess and support teacher assessments for each child in different subjects.

Annual assessments

Earlier, we discussed the range of statutory tests and tasks which are carried out annually. Key Stage 1 (Year 2) and Key Stage 2 (Year 6) statutory tasks and tests (SATs) are carried out during the first half of the summer term. The results are used by schools as a way of tracking progress and attainment for individuals and for the projection of results for cohorts of children. This supports target setting and the data are used to highlight school trends and inform the School Improvement Development Plan (SIDP). The school results and levels are analysed and then tracked to show both statutory and internal assessment results. Assessment data are reported to parents/carers at parents' evenings, SEN reviews and in the child's annual report.

Reports

Schools have a statutory responsibility to send a written report to parents/carers by the end of the summer term. All schools send an annual written report but some schools may send reports more frequently (Ewans, 2014).

As a minimum, the report must cover the pupil's achievements and general progress as well as their attendance record. It is likely to also include areas for development and results of statutory assessments. Parents/carers will have an opportunity to give their response to the report which may be a written comment through to a meeting with the school staff.

> *Top Tip*: Familiarise yourself with the relevant guidance and legislation for the age range you are teaching. This will help you to locate information about how the frameworks relate to the age and ability ranges of the learners in your class.

Practice examples – Teachers' Standard 6a

JAMES

James was able to demonstrate how he confidently assessed pupils' attainment against the national benchmarks with his Year 2 class. He used the performance descriptors for Key Stage 1 to inform his teacher assessments for mathematics. James had attended moderation meetings with teachers from several primary schools and worked closely with them to make a judgement and agree the levels for the moderated work. In his evidence, he included several pieces of annotated work which had been moderated with other teachers.

ROSE

Rose used assessment records as evidence to demonstrate how she had met this standard. She had a confident grasp of the expectations within science for the age group she was teaching, which was evidenced through her records. These illustrated the progress the children in her class had made throughout the term in science. Rose was aware that children can make good progress but that their attainment may not meet national expectations. However, through her records she was able to show each child's level based on prior knowledge, then track their progress through current achievements and finally, compare attainment against the national standards.

In relation to Teachers' Standard 6a and your own practice, consider the following key questions:

- How does planning take into account the curriculum expectations for the pupils you are teaching?
- How do you find out how attainment is measured in the EYFS and at the end of Key Stage 1 and Key Stage 2?
- What evidence do you keep to support teacher assessment?
- What moderation meetings do you attend to ensure your judgements are accurate?

Possible sources of evidence for Teachers' Standard 6a:

- Results from statutory assessments such as SATS, key stage tests;
- Formative and summative tracking data;
- School-based training/staff meetings/external courses on statutory assessment;
- Annotated children's work and written feedback;
- Lesson plans and lesson evaluation.

6b: Make use of formative and summative assessment to secure pupils' progress

There is plenty of research and literature related to formative and summative functions of assessment (Harlen and James, 1997; Black and Wiliam, 1998; Black et al., 2003; Brandom et al., 2005; Cremin and Arthur, 2014). Petty (2009) suggests that the breadth and depth of learning are measured through assessment and highlights that each method of assessment has a different aim, with each carried out in quite different ways within the classroom. Petty (2009) argues that formative assessment requires a specific conceptualisation if it is to contribute directly to helping children learn. Learning is at the heart of assessment and each is a vital component of the other. A good understanding of learning is critical in helping teachers to improve pupil progress. What do you understand by learning? A good place to start is to explore some of the frameworks that have been presented, such as Kolb's theory of learning (Kolb, 1984) or Herrmann's whole-brain model and there are further sources to examine which detail these theories (Petty, 2009; Cooper, 2014).

Teachers' Standard 6b refers to formative and summative assessment and these are recognised as the main categories relevant to assessment in the primary classroom.

Formative assessment

Formative assessment is also termed as assessment for learning. It is ongoing and is continuous throughout effective teaching and learning. Cooper (2014) refers to it as a process in which the learner and teacher interact as learning is reviewed. The Assessment Reform Group (2002) devised 10 principles which summarise assessment for learning. Figure 6.1 sets out these key points.

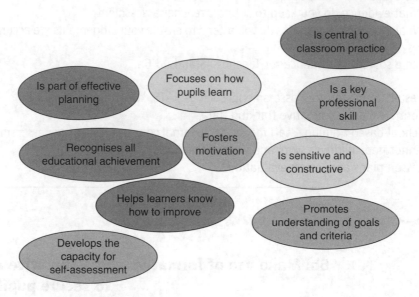

Figure 6.1 Assessment for learning principles (Cooper, 2014)

The key points highlight the need to include teachers and learners in assessment and for active engagement in the process. Assessment should not be something that is done to the learners. In the classroom, a culture needs to be developed in which learners understand how they can improve their work and what they need to do next. Put simply, learners need to know what their starting point is and how to attain their goals.

Using formative assessment

Teachers who are effective at using assessment understand that both teacher and learner need to be engaged in the process of assessment. In this way, learners can take responsibility and ownership of their learning to understand how they can make progress. The opportunities teachers create to support assessment for learning include sharing the learning objective with learners. A word of caution is needed here as children can just learn to recite the learning objective with no real understanding – ensure the language used is understood by the children and that child-friendly words are used. The learning objective is used by teachers and learners to make a judgement about whether pupils have achieved what they set out to learn. A key role of the teacher is to implement strategies to support children to assess their own work and that of others. This includes planning for self and peer assessment opportunities in lessons. It takes time to implement assessment strategies and build a culture of trust in the classroom to support honest judgements to be made. In self and peer assessment, learners are encouraged to contribute to discussions, ask and answer questions and comment on their progress. Feedback becomes a two-way process in which discussions about the learning will help the learner to identify what they have done well, what they want to improve on and how they might achieve the next steps in learning.

Questioning forms an integral part of assessment for learning and is a valuable pedagogical tool that teachers use. The following ideas clarify the key points when using questioning:

- Allow time for pupils to respond to questions.
- Consider when to use closed questions (requiring a yes or no response) and when to use open questions (where explanation and detail are given).

Although we have discussed feedback through talking with learners, effective feedback can also be given in marking work.

Marking

Children can be actively involved with feedback and marking. This can be through marking their own work based on a set of criteria and through marking each other's work. In this way, they can focus on understanding the work that has been covered rather than on the pressure to be correct. Deeper learning is enhanced as it promotes learners learning from each other as well as recognising their own mistakes. When a child assesses their own work and that of their peers, they need to have a good understanding of the assessment criteria, which promotes deep-seated learning rather than a superficial understanding. With deep-seated learning, they are likely to remember the concepts as they are more meaningful and set within a context for learning where the learner has made links between what they already know and new learning. Pupils need to be clear about what can be done better and offer guidance on how work can be improved. For the marking process to be effective, pupils should be trained in giving feedback on the work so that they understand the objective of their learning, know what to do to achieve and can identify how work can be improved.

Summative assessment

The purpose of summative assessment is to find out how much a child has learned from a unit of work. It is concerned with accountability and looks back to find out what has been attained so that information can be given about what a child has achieved. The assessment may take the form of a test or exam and some schools may require teachers to carry out summative teacher assessments to assess children's attainment at a given time during the school year (Ewans, 2014). This evaluation of learning provides information which helps teachers to review the process of teaching and learning.

Using summative assessment

At the end of each key stage, children will be set national statutory tests and tasks. At other times, schools may administer their own or published tests to identify pupil attainment and progress at interim points between the key stages. The goal of summative assessment is to measure the level of success by comparing it against a specific standard – for example, teachers may use it to find out how well a child has learned their spellings or maths facts. The outcome of such a structured, summative assessment can be used formatively when the teacher uses the information in their planning of subsequent lessons. The assessment provides information about the level of attainment achieved, allowing the teacher to plan for the next steps in that child's learning to enable them to make progress. The information from summative assessments is used not only by teachers, but may also be useful for other members of the school staff and for parents.

Diagnostic assessment

All children will have specific, individual needs, with some children more confident in certain subjects than others. How do you find out what a child knows before starting a new topic or area of learning? This is where diagnostic assessment can be used. It is a means of exploring what children know and understand, as well as finding out about misconceptions, before starting something new. There are different ways that teachers capture this information, such as orally through questioning, asking questions about things children want to know, peer discussion and visual representation such as jotting down ideas and mapping or drawing pictures. This information helps the teacher to start the work at an appropriate level but can be seen as a continuous process (Petty, 2009).

A word about 'praise'

It is important to spend some time discussing the significance of praise. This should not be underestimated.

Praise can be ineffective or effective, depending on how it is used to support learning. Brophy (1981) suggested that there are specific aspects that contribute to praise being valuable and helpful to a learner. The main features of effective praise are listed in the box below.

- Praise is effective when it is used in response to a specific behaviour.
- Praise is effective when the behaviour is described in specific terms.
- Praise is effective when it is sincere, reliable and spontaneous.
- Praise should reward the attainment of clearly defined and understood performance criteria.
- Praise should provide information about the student's competencies.
- Praise should be given in recognition of noteworthy effort or success at a difficult task for that particular student.
- Praise should attribute success to effort and ability, implying that similar success in the future is achievable though such effort and ability.

An effective example of using positive praise would be: 'Jade, that is good work. You have used alliteration in your work. This makes the writing interesting.'

Consequently, it follows that ineffective praise would be the opposite of all of these features. It is likely not to relate to what the learner has achieved and Brophy (1981) points out that it attaches credit to ability alone or to how easy the task was.

Top Tip: Assessment is a continuous process and should not be viewed as an 'add-on'. As you plan, you will consider how you use assessment in lessons, starting with the introduction, then in the main activities and at the end. This will help you to focus on how assessment has enhanced learning.

 Practice examples – Teachers' Standard 6b

BECKY
Throughout her science lesson with a Year 3 class, Becky used questioning as a way of encouraging the children to think deeply and to demonstrate their understanding. She used open questions and realised that a closed question would give a limited response. If she had asked, 'Is air resistance a type of friction?', the answer given would be 'yes' or 'no'. In contrast, she asked the question, 'Why would an object

(Continued)

(Continued)

moving through air slow down?' This requires an understanding of friction and a deeper response. By engaging the children in talk, Becky was able to listen to responses and ask further questions. This type of formative questioning provided her with information about what the children understood as well as their misconceptions.

RICHARD

When planning a unit of work for a Year 3 class in science, Richard used summative assessment to make a judgement about what the children had previously learned and the level of attainment reached. This gave Richard information to help him plan how to recap on previous learning to check for understanding and misconceptions, to plan for progression and to differentiate appropriately, as children were working at different levels of ability. The summative assessments gave Richard a starting point for planning his science lessons – for example, he had noticed that there was a small group of very able children working above the expected level. He would now be able to plan lessons that provided challenge for this group by looking at the National Curriculum expectations for the attainment of these pupils.

 In relation to Teachers' Standard 6b and your own practice, consider the following key questions:

- How do you keep detailed and up-to-date records of assessment?
- How do you use this information to inform planning?
- How do you use this information to contribute to subsequent assessment?
- Are books regularly marked?
- How does the marking support progress?
- What opportunities do you include to ensure pupils have opportunities to engage with and respond to marking?
- Do you use a range of formative assessment strategies?
- How do you justify the specific strategies being used?
- How do you use assessment to form a view of pupils' learning?

Possible sources of evidence for Teachers' Standard 6b:

- Formative and summative tracking data;
- Planning to show individual/group targets;

(Continued)

(Continued)

- Records of CPD with assessment coordinator;
- Lesson observation records from induction tutor and other staff;
- Examples of pupils' marked work, with pupils' comments;
- End-of-year pupil reports;
- Work trawl focusing on the quality of marking and feedback; and identifying next steps;
- Interventions including more able and other, vulnerable groups.

6c: Use relevant data to monitor progress, set targets and plan subsequent lessons

It would be helpful here to examine what is understood by relevant data. Data will come from a range of sources, such as marking, observations, target setting, recording evidence and tracking records. The standard requires the teacher to use records and targets to identify specific needs that children may have, such as those who are gifted and talented as well as those with special educational needs. The teacher needs to have an awareness of the level and ability of each child, or else how can the teacher plan for pupil progress?

Relevant data

The use of data is an important tool for schools in supporting the school improvement process. Schools track the progress of every child. Tracking pupil progress supports teachers to know where each child is in their learning and to set targets which are realistic and challenging. It supports head teachers and governors to identify how the attainment and progress of pupils in their school compares to the national average and to identify pupils who may not be performing as expected. The information is useful in ascertaining how the school is doing in comparison to other, similar schools, alongside considering the school's strengths and areas for development. Pupil progress is tracked through using different tools and some of these are discussed next.

Data Dashboard

Ofsted provides the Data Dashboard. It is used by school governors and the public to find out how the school is doing in terms of performance. A summary of results data for Key Stages 1, 2 and 4 over a three-year period can be viewed. There are no National Curriculum tests at KS3, so the Data Dashboard does not provide information for this key stage (dashboard.ofsted.gov.uk).

Fischer Family Trust

The Fischer Family Trust (FFT) is a registered charity. It provides information to support schools to improve and to support pupils to achieve their potential. Data are presented through interactive dashboards, which support schools to examine past performance, to identify strengths and weaknesses and to set challenging future targets (www.fft.org.uk).

The dashboards can be used within school by teachers, subject leaders, department heads and senior school leaders, as well as by local authority advisors. They are used to set targets and these can be for individual children, for a phase, in specific subjects or for the whole school.

RAISEonline

RAISEonline supports teaching and learning with the aim of helping schools to analyse their data about performance as part of the school's self-evaluation process (www.raiseonline.org). The tool provides data about pupil attainment and progress in Key Stages 1 and 2 and there is an interactive feature allowing schools to explore hypotheses of pupil performance.

The increase in tools for management of data has been helpful in supporting schools to evaluate their performance as well as in tracking pupil performance. Schools are held accountable and they are judged by the available data. This makes it critical that any information is analysed and up to date and is considered as a shared responsibility by all school staff because all staff are accountable for pupil progress (www.sec-ed.co.uk). Performance and progress do not sit in isolation from behaviour and attendance. The data from academic and social aspects are used to link these areas and to consider the wider, holistic aspects of a child's progress. Alongside the central sources of data, such as those from FFT, RAISEonline and Data Dashboard, schools use teacher assessments to make judgements about the level pupils were performing at previously, where they are now and to examine the trajectory of each pupil's progress. The analysis and interpretation of data should lead to robust discussions about how schools will act on this data, in order to identify areas where there are issues, understand why this is and then put strategies in place which are effective.

Target setting

Targets are indicators of progress which lead to a potential improvement in performance. Targets can relate to academic progress as well as to social aspects, for example behaviour or attendance. Whatever the aim of the target, they have common features and these are often referred to as SMART (specific, measurable, attainable, realistic and time bound) targets (Ewans, 2014). Where a target is specific and well defined, it is easy to know what has to be done to achieve it. The learner needs to know what they have to do to be successful. If this is measurable, then it is motivational because small steps can be identified on how to make progress. Targets need to be attainable and agreed so that ownership can be taken and rather than something being done to the learner they can become empowered. Realistic targets take account of the resources and time that may be available to ensure a positive result and if they are time bound there is likely to be a sense of urgency in order to achieve the target, rather than it being loosely bound. Drawing the learner's attention to the target at the start of the lesson and discussing the target at the end of the lesson are important in supporting the learner to recognise the progress made (Briggs et al., 2009).

Recording progress

Ongoing assessment during a lesson is an element of effective practice and is integral to a teacher's practice. Teachers will assess some children's learning through marking their work and sometimes it will happen when the teacher is working with individuals or groups. A system of recording this information will identify children who have met, exceeded or not met the learning objectives (LO). A table with a list of children's names down one side against the LO stated across the top works well to record how each child has performed. Further notes can be added. Each school will have its own system of recording and each teacher may have a preferred way of recording their assessments. It is important to have an understanding of the whole-school policy on record keeping and tracking, whilst developing a simple, easy-to-use recording system which is useful to the class teacher.

> *Top Tip*: The head teacher and senior leaders in school will ultimately be responsible for responding to data. Look at the data available for your school (FFT, RAISEonline or Data Dashboard) and consider what is happening in your school and what the school staff are doing to address data issues.

Practice examples – Teachers' Standard 6c

LIAM

In a mixed ability class of 30 Year 3 children, Liam had identified three pupils who were working well below the expected level in Phonics. He had used data from the previous year, including teacher assessments and data from the school senior management team from RAISE online. This led to discussions with other teachers about how these children could be supported. It was decided to introduce an intervention programme for this group and to monitor progress over the half term. Liam spoke to the school's English coordinator to agree on the level of support and to set targets for each of the children within the group.

OLIVIA

In her daily practice, Olivia keeps records of how well the children are meeting the learning objectives in lessons. Using this information, she records academic progress and attitude to learning. She was aware of the average level of groups and of the spread of levels within groups. Olivia noticed, over time, that one child was performing exceptionally well and exceeding expectations and shared this information with the head teacher. After looking at the trajectory of progress since starting school, the child was deemed to be gifted and talented in maths. Consequently, Olivia was able to set challenging targets to ensure the child continued to make good progress.

 In relation to Teachers' Standard 6c and your own practice, consider the following key questions:

- How does your school use data to raise standards?
- How is data shared with parents?
- What interventions can be used to support pupils who are working below the expected level?
- Are you clear what is expected of you as a teacher and what your role is in the process of monitoring pupil progress?
- How do you use assessment to make a judgement of pupils' learning?
- How do you review learning throughout the lesson?

(Continued)

(Continued)

Possible sources of evidence for Teachers' Standard 6c:

- Planning;
- Assessments and tracking data, including teacher assessments;
- Assessment for learning feedback.

6d: Give pupils regular feedback, both orally and through accurate marking and encourage pupils to respond to the feedback

This sub-set of the standard considers how to give feedback to pupils and how to support them to be part of the assessment process so that each child can take ownership of their learning. This formative method of assessment is mostly considered to be informal (Jacques and Hyland, 2010). You will give feedback based on three different ways of knowing: (1) through observation, (2) verbally through discussion or questions and (3) through marking. There are essentially two types of feedback – verbal and written. Ofsted (2015) recognises that marking and feedback to pupils, both written and oral, are important aspects of assessment.

Verbal

Discussion and questioning allows the teacher to quickly assess a child's understanding and can be evaluative or diagnostic (Jacques and Hyland, 2010). Throughout daily practice, teachers identify opportunities to discuss and question children on their understanding. This is shown on the planning or appears in practice as a spontaneous opportunity. Support is given to children when it is both appropriate and timely which makes it meaningful. As a lesson progresses, it may be fitting to give immediate feedback to move learning on, or to guide children who have not grasped a concept securely. Misconceptions can also be identified through supporting a child to discuss their work. This form of feedback can be highly motivating in helping pupils to remain on task and to build confidence. Through discussion, feedback becomes a conversation between teacher and learner, in which the learner should be able to identify what they have done well and what steps they need to take to make further progress. It is very often the immediate feedback to children that is the most meaningful and effective. Questioning, whether open or closed, needs to be planned and the more a teacher can consider questions the more prepared they will feel in supporting learning. Often, teachers include a mixture of questions, although open questions will encourage a deeper level of thinking (Ewans, 2014). Effective teachers are able to use good questioning and through collaboration with children, teachers scaffold learning. Children then have the opportunity to engage more deeply with learning as they develop strategies to ask their own questions and find answers, as opposed to the teacher telling them the answer. In this way, children move from a surface to a deeper level of learning and are more likely to retain information, as it is more meaningful to them. When did you last ask a question that you did not want to know the answer to? Verbal feedback can happen at any point in the lesson and an effective strategy is to include mini-plenaries or pit stops at significant points during a lesson. This has the advantage of sharing good examples, of addressing misconceptions or of broadening and deepening understanding.

Written

What is meant by 'accurate marking' will depend on the individual school. It is up to the school's management team to make it clear what is expected in terms of marking through the marking policy. Ofsted (2015) makes the comment that: 'Marking and feedback should be consistent with that policy, which may cater for different subjects and different age groups of pupils in different ways, in order to be effective and efficient in promoting learning.'

Tracking progress over time, through marking and providing feedback, has been found to be more important than a single one-off when seeking evidence that a child has made progress. This tracking can provide solid evidence to demonstrate the level of progress made by children. Yet, feedback is of no value unless it is acted on by the learner and the teacher plans an opportunity for children to respond to comments made on work. Marking should show children that their work is valued and teachers will be able to refer to examples of their own marking, highlighting feedback that is positive and constructive. This helps to raise a child's self-esteem. Marking is used to highlight areas for development or next steps and to evaluate how well the child has understood the learning objective. Effective marking is used to create a discussion and dialogue between the teacher and the learner, so that comments made can be debated. This encourages the child to be actively involved in the feedback process. Essentially, marking needs to be understood by children and by having a consistent whole-school approach children are more likely to know what is expected.

Self- and peer assessment

Quite simply, self-assessment is about children knowing where they are in their learning. Peer assessment is concerned with others knowing where a child is in their learning. Through engaging in discussion about the assessment criteria and sharing the success criteria with children, they can be more involved which can help promote active engagement and deeper learning (NFER, 2007). This is because they can understand what they have to do and so make a judgement about how well they have achieved it. An example is where children have been working on improving their writing through using personification. A child can go through their work and check whether they have included this. This has the benefit of encouraging a child to reflect on their work and understand what they have done well. The teacher's role is to ensure that a child has been given enough time to go through their work and to provide an opportunity for the child's learning to be acknowledged. Teachers use different systems for this, such as encouraging the child to mark their work in a specific colour, to signify what they have achieved or what they need to understand better. Another method to consider is putting a feedback box at the end of the work so that a dialogue can emerge between teacher and child. An important aspect of self-assessment is that it should take account of children's motivation (ARG, 2002). Research shows that improving skills in self and peer assessment is essential to helping children become effective learners and these include the skills of taking greater responsibility for their own learning, reflection on learning and enhanced self-esteem and motivation (Briggs et al., 2009). However, it must be recognised that self and peer assessment do not just happen. The teacher is pivotal in ensuring a culture of trust and respect is evident in the classroom where it is OK to fail and to learn from mistakes. This form of assessment requires children to be trained in using it, which includes understanding its purpose, how to identify features of the work and to suggest ways to improve using an appropriate vocabulary. Ewans (2014) suggests that some self-help strategies that could be used by children are re-reading work, using post-it notes as reminders and asking questions that encourage further thinking. Through such activities, children are given the chance to go and reflect on work and improve it before sharing it with the teacher. Giving children such opportunities to discuss and reflect on work encourages the development of problem-solving and reasoning strategies. The teacher can use this approach to encourage children to learn to evaluate and identify their next steps. It supports a classroom climate where the ethos recognises the need for continuous improvement resulting from reflection and investigation.

Top Tip: Generic praise is not helpful. It serves to distract from what is really important and fails to identify the skills that are needed. Keep the focus on comments that are specific and challenging for the learner. Encourage dialogue and discussion.

Practice examples – Teachers' Standard 6d

EMILY

In a Year 1 maths lesson on halving, Emily realised that one particular child was confusing numbers and making uneven groupings. Emily encouraged the child to count out 12 counters and share 'one for you, one for me' until all the counters had been shared evenly. Questions focused the child to say how many were in each half and that each half had about the same amount. Emily praised the child for recognising these concepts and encouraged the child to apply this through sharing out counters for her and a friend so that each had equal amounts. As well as consolidating the skill of halving, the child was reminded to use her knowledge of halving 2, 4, 6, 8 and 10 and was challenged to use this when working with larger numbers.

LYN

James struggled to form letters correctly. When his teacher, Lyn, observed him practising his handwriting, he formed the letter h perfectly. In her feedback, Lyn told the child that he had started the letter at the top which was very good and he had sat the letter neatly on the line. The teacher asked James what he felt he could do to further improve the letter and asked about the size of the ascender. James suggested that he could make the ascender nice and tall next time. James felt pleased, gained confidence in recognising what he had done well and was able to articulate how he could make progress.

 In relation to Teachers' Standard 6d and your own practice, consider the following key questions:

- What strategies do you use to ensure a range of methods are used to give feedback?
- How do you monitor and record progress?
- How does your planning demonstrate that you work with all groups of learners over the week?
- How do you record which group is working independently, which with a TA and which is supported by the teacher?
- How do you plan opportunities for self and peer assessment?
- What processes are in place to support children to make a decision about their learning?
- How can pupils feed back on your marking? When do you build time in to a lesson to support this?

(Continued)

(Continued)

Possible sources of evidence for Teachers' Standard 6d:

- Marking with feedback and pupil responses;
- Lesson observations;
- Self and peer assessment work;
- Target setting;
- Examples from success criteria.

Feedback is effective when it focuses on what the child has done well and how to further improve, rather than being linked to a grade or level. This is because children need to be able to think about how to make progress which is about the process of learning (Cooper, 2014) and a grade has a focus on the product of learning which does not support the learning process.

Chapter summary

The sub-headings relate to the main Teachers' Standard. Teachers will be able to demonstrate compliance with sub-sets by engaging in a discussion to show that their knowledge is up to date. In terms of monitoring progress, setting targets and provision of feedback through marking, this will all be apparent through documentation. Referring to the use of whole-class and individual feedback as well as to the use of self and peer assessment activities would be relevant:

> As you gain confidence and deepen your understanding you will begin to realise that professional attributes, knowledge and understanding, planning, teaching and learning and assessment are interlinked. Consequently an understanding of assessment is pivotal to fully achieving many standards for QTS. (Glazzard and Stokoe, 2011, p. 68)

Assessment for learning can be linked to most of the Teachers' Standards and does not sit alone. Consider the links between assessment and pupil progress (TS2), between assessment and planning (TS4) or meeting the needs of all learners (TS5) and you will appreciate the overlap and transition between the Teachers' Standards.

CHAPTER 7

MANAGE BEHAVIOUR EFFECTIVELY TO ENSURE A GOOD AND SAFE LEARNING ENVIRONMENT

Teachers' Standard 7 – Manage behaviour effectively to ensure a good and safe learning environment:

7a Have clear rules and routines for behaviour in classrooms and take responsibility for promoting good and courteous behaviour both in classrooms and around the school, in accordance with the school's behaviour policy

7b Have high expectations of behaviour and establish a framework for discipline with a range of strategies, using praise, sanctions and rewards consistently and fairly

7c Manage classes effectively, using approaches which are appropriate to pupils' needs in order to involve and motivate them

7d Maintain good relationships with pupils, exercise appropriate authority and act decisively when necessary.

What is this all about?

Classroom behaviour is going to be an ongoing consideration for teachers at any stage of their career. Every school will have a behaviour policy that sets out the rules for discipline within that school. This chapter clarifies what teachers need to do to meet this standard set within the school's policy. This includes exploring how to promote consistent expectations, how to apply them and how to adapt to different circumstances. The use of behaviour management strategies is underpinned by having positive working relationships so that the management of learning and behaviour is the foundation for an effective and successful learning environment.

How can this be demonstrated?

Clarity, consistency, commitment and confidence form the building blocks for effective behaviour management in an orderly classroom. We will return to these principles later on when we look at the sub-sets. But let's make it very clear that you will never be able to tick a box that says you have sorted out behaviour. This is because each year the children will be different, with different needs and teachers will form different relationships with them. What works for one group may not work for another group of children. A constant in all of this is the school's behaviour policy. This 'Teachers' Standard can be evidenced through reference to how you uphold the school policy, how you use a range of strategies to manage learning and behaviour, including sanctions and rewards, how you address issues of bullying, how you support pupils to take responsibility for their learning and behaviour and of course, through the way that you respond to and tackle any issues that may arise.

Chapter overview

Behaviour management is a hot topic, it is in the public eye, on government agendas and will always be a key focus within all schools. The behaviour and safety of pupils is a key priority and more recently, it has been acknowledged how disturbing low-level disruption can be (DfE and Morgan, 2015). Developments from the government have taken place to address poor behaviour through support for teachers, making it clear that teachers can use reasonable force to maintain behaviour (DfE and Morgan, 2015). As we explore the issues around managing behaviour, there will be some thought given to how school policies and government legislation translate into daily practice. Every teacher's toolkit will have a range of behaviour management strategies. This includes strategies used in a whole-school and classroom context. Whilst recognising the holistic nature of behaviour management to ensure consistency across the school, there is discussion about the value of class teachers implementing rewards and sanctions that are personal to their class. These will be implemented because each teacher knows the children well and recognises their interests and what motivates them. The value of including children in decision making about the rules for learning and behaviour are highlighted and this is set within an understanding that children have a right to feel safe and should not have to put up with disruptive behaviour from others. Learning and behaviour cannot be separated and this is a complex field, so an overview of some of the theories on behaviour will be included. There are many theories of managing behaviour and teachers will use approaches they find effective and are comfortable with. Teachers are not clones of each other, so it is vital that an approach is used that feels natural, that suits the children and with which each teacher can identify. The chapter takes a look at some of the causes of poor behaviour with respect to the social and emotional aspects of learning. Schools are concerned with both the academic and social aspects of a child's development, which are the fundamental elements of teaching and learning. At the same time as promoting independence, teachers will sometimes need to support children to learn how to manage their behaviour so that they, as well as their classmates, can learn. The teacher is responsible for ensuring trusting relationships develop which promote a positive classroom ethos. The final purpose of this chapter is to support you to explore how a teacher develops confidence and authority when managing difficult situations. At some point, a teacher may need to plan specific intervention to support a child with their behaviour and learning, although an unexpected situation may also arise and we explore how to modify teaching to deal with this. Teachers need to be aware of the school systems that are in place to support them if they find themselves in such a position.

Taking it apart and putting it back together

Learning and behaviour should be seen as entangled, in as much as behaviour is an aspect of learning (James, 2013). To feel secure in our own knowledge about behaviour, we must think about the importance of the learning environment. The focus is on managing behaviour and therefore learning, through setting out clear expectations and this includes being confident in managing different parts of a lesson. It is not enough to know just what has to be done; a theoretical understanding of behaviour will help to develop an understanding of why an approach is valued. So through the synthesis of theory and practice, we will look at strategies for managing behaviour. There are layers and like an onion they need to be peeled away to get at the core. Here, the core of understanding about behaviour is learning, so we set this chapter within the context of behaviour for learning. The layers are represented as relationships, rules and routines, sanctions and rewards, strategies, teacher authority and the empowering of pupils. It is through these lenses that we will establish an understanding of how to meet Teachers' Standard 7, whilst acknowledging that it takes patience and tenacity to become an effective teacher who can manage challenging situations.

7a: Have clear rules and routines for behaviour in classrooms and take responsibility for promoting good and courteous behaviour both in classrooms and around the school, in accordance with the school's behaviour policy

Clarity

The start of a lesson has a big influence on the creation of a climate for learning. Equally, how transitions between different parts of a lesson are managed needs to be considered, as these are the times when valuable learning and behaviour can be lost. How children behave outside of the classroom, in the playground and the hall are all equally worthy issues in relation to this Teachers' Standard. These aspects of practice are set within the framework of the school's policy on behaviour and discipline. The clarity of how this is transferred from policy to practice is explored next. Although school policies differ from school to school, it is law that all schools must produce a school behaviour policy (DfE, 2014b). This policy sets out how the school will promote good behaviour, including self-discipline and respect and how the school will prevent bullying. Along with the governors, the head teacher will determine the rules and principles which all children and staff, at that school, will adhere to. It is critical that there is clarity in the way the policy sets out the principles, so that the policy can be followed and applied with consistency. By law, the head teacher must publish the school's behaviour policy, at least annually, on the school website (DfE, 2014b).

Many school policies will include reference to the following areas:

- A consistent approach to behaviour management;
- Strong school leadership;
- Classroom management;
- Rewards and sanctions;
- Behaviour strategies and the teaching of good behaviour;
- Staff development and support;
- Pupil support systems;
- Liaison with parents and other agencies;
- Managing pupil transition.

As you consider suitable evidence for Teachers' Standard 7a, think about how your understanding of the school policy has informed you to make decisions about your daily practice. This may be in the way you have used reward systems to encourage good behaviour or how you have been decisive and confident in handing out sanctions because you are aware of the school rules on this. In having a consistent approach to behaviour management, you may draw on times when you have used a particular strategy, such as dealing with low-level disruption in the same way each time. By having this coherent approach, the teacher is sending a clear message to the children about the expectations for behaviour and learning. The policy sets out rules for inside and outside the classroom and as teachers maintain discipline within the school environment, there will be opportunities to consider how a teacher's actions are based on knowing the school rules. The school policy guides teachers to consider not just their actions but also their way of managing the learning environment. This includes how the classroom is organised to ensure pupils are engaged, motivated and responsible for their learning. Teachers consider how children are grouped and seated to ensure learning is effective and children behave in an appropriate way. Amongst the evidence needed to meet this standard, think about how intervention strategies may be used to encourage acceptable behaviour. This includes how nurture groups or parenting groups may be implemented and importantly, the impact of such groups. Some schools have 'time out' spaces and within classrooms teachers use strategies such as setting up a quiet place where children can go and calm down, reflect on their behaviour and remove themselves from any conflict. This helps a child to recognise their behaviour and manage it, taking control of a situation and being proactive. Mosley (1996) provides many useful strategies which can be applied practically in the classroom. Teachers can include such strategies as evidence of the rules and routines within their classroom. It is also relevant to refer to specific interventions, such as social and emotional aspects of learning (SEAL), to show how they are incorporated into classroom practice to demonstrate how the teacher plans for and manages learning and behaviour.

More recently, government policies have recognised how damaging low-level disruption can be and how this can interrupt learning. Set in context, Ofsted commented that up to an hour of learning a day is potentially being lost, due to low-level disruption. In response, new teachers will be given training to learn how to deal with low-level disruption and to gain confidence in this area of practice (DfE and Morgan, 2015).

A whole-school approach and understanding of how behaviour and discipline are managed, is supportive for teachers. It provides teachers with a protection and confidence to know that certain practices are in place to deal with disruptive behaviour (Rogers, 2011a). Evidencing your understanding of whole-school practices will be obvious in the way that you deal with issues of discipline in line with the school behaviour policy.

> *Top Tip*: Teachers act as role models and how you speak to the children as well as other adults will all form part of the child's understanding of respect for others and expected behaviour.

Practice examples – Teachers' Standard 7a

SAROJ

The start of a lesson sets the tone for learning and Saroj has a few strategies that she feels comfortable using to ensure the children know what is expected of them. She always makes sure she is not late to a lesson which sends out a signal about punctuality. She stands by the door when the Year 5 pupils enter the classroom and thanks them for coming in quietly and she speaks calmly to settle them after lunchtime. When pupils start the afternoon session, they follow the same routine where they choose from a list of activities and carry this out for 5 minutes working on their own. Following this activity, the children prepare for the lesson. Saroj reminds them that they need to be facing her and showing they are ready for learning through actively listening and contributing, as well as not talking when someone else is speaking. The children are clear about their teacher's expectations as they follow the same routine every day.

JODIE

A climate of trust does not just happen and Jodie has spent several weeks on providing a consistent framework of expectations to ensure the children feel safe and secure. She ensures all pupils are listening to her or to each other and instantly addresses any children who are talking when someone else is speaking. At the start of term, this was a constant feature of lessons but now there are very few times when this occurs. Jodie makes sure that the children have a go and it has taken time to build up their confidence to do this. Initially, the children laughed if someone made a mistake but she dealt with this every time it occurred in a calm manner so that the children understood that this behaviour was not acceptable. This has resulted in more children willing to speak out and ask or answer questions and a supportive climate has developed so that rather than laugh at others the children now work together more closely.

 In relation to Teachers' Standard 7a and your own practice, consider the following key questions:

- How do children know what your expectations are for behaviour?
- Are the classroom rules negotiated with the children?
- Are these rules displayed in the classroom?

(Continued)

(Continued)

- How do you use the school's behaviour policy to promote positive behaviour?
- How do other adults who work with the children know about your expectations?
- What opportunities do you provide for children to show respect for each other?

Possible sources of evidence for Teachers' Standard 7a:

- School behaviour policy;
- Classroom rules;
- Observations carried out of your teaching;
- Observations of pupils;
- Notes of critical incidents that have happened in school;
- Lesson plan showing routines that are consistently used.

7b: Have high expectations of behaviour and establish a framework for discipline with a range of strategies, using praise, sanctions and rewards consistently and fairly

Consistency

There are times in our lives when a measure of consistency is needed to ensure everything runs as expected. We expect to get the same train to work each morning and if the train is delayed or cancelled it causes frustration and perhaps even chaos. We may be working hard in the gym to prepare for a half-marathon but if we run once a week this will not reap the same benefits as exercising consistently through running several times a week. The same principle can be applied to classroom practice in that we need to have consistency in what we do, to send out the same messages about the rules and principles that guide behaviour and learning. If we stray and apply different criteria, then a child may become confused and not know what the truth is: 'Being consistent in dealing with the behaviour of your students means they know what will happen if they choose to break the rules and equally they know what will happen if they choose to follow the rules' (Dix, 2010, p. 21). As you evidence this standard, you will be able to consider how you have ensured a consistent approach is achieved through your expectations of behaviour. This will not vary from day to day and is based on the school values as well as your own values. High expectations relate to the way that children speak and listen to each other and towards adults within the classroom and outside of it. A typical example can be seen daily in the way that children speak to teaching assistants or the lunchtime supervisor, which should be the same way that they speak to the teacher. It is the teacher's role to ensure that there is consistency in the way this is managed and addressed if the children do not meet the teacher's expectations. High expectations relate to behaviour and attitude towards work and you can monitor this throughout a lesson, to assess who is motivated, involved and interested as they work. A teacher's record of how this is tracked can provide evidence of your high expectations along with how you address any issues. Issues of a child not meeting a teacher's expectations may of course be as a result of the work being inappropriate, too easy, too challenging or not well explained or modelled. Equally, a child may be off target and any unacceptable behaviour needs to be addressed. Consequently, how a teacher deals with this will be based on the school and class rules for sanctions.

Praise, rewards and sanctions

Praise

A very easy and yet effective way to acknowledge that expectations have been met is to use praise. A generic 'Well done' is of no use as it does not tell the child what they have achieved. When a teacher acknowledges that a child, or children, have behaved in the way that is expected of them, such as not calling out but putting a hand up when they want to speak, it sends a clear message to them that they have behaved correctly and the teacher recognises this. It is motivating and encourages others to do the same: 'When you sincerely communicate to students how pleased you are with them it builds trust in the relationship and motivates them to sustain their efforts' (Dix, 2010, p. 31). As you include evidence to meet Teachers' Standard 7b, you may think about how you manage the use of praise in the classroom. Schools have a range of different ways of praising pupils, including a call home to parents, a word to the parent in the playground or a certificate to take home and share. Find out what the systems of praise are at your school. Whatever practice is used, praise and encouragement will benefit children as they seek 'acknowledgement and affirmation' (Rogers, 2011b, p. 135).

Rewards

When handing out rewards and sanctions, children need to see that there is a fair system in place and understand how they are applied consistently. Cowley (2014, p. 81) offers a suggestion: 'When using rewards and sanctions aim for a ratio of about five to one in favour of rewards.' There will be times when you give out rewards which will be linked to behaviour, attitude and academic progress.

Ultimately, teachers are aiming for children to behave in the correct way because they are intrinsically motivated and want to do the best they can. Cowley (2014) suggests that rewards have a valid place as children learn to move from extrinsic and externally driven motives to that of a motivation from within. Rewards help children to focus on what is important and a teacher must ensure that the type of reward given is appropriate for the children. What works for one particular age group or class will not automatically work for another. So teachers naturally adapt and change the rewards, using, for example, a mix of stickers, house points, zone boards, certificates and golden time, which is a dedicated amount of time to follow a particular interest, such as extra time on an ipad. A teacher who encourages the class to put their chairs under the table may reward one child who has made a particular effort to do this, by giving them the magic shoes for that day. This is a pair of shoes with a hole in the centre so they slide on to the legs of the chair. Teachers find many creative ways to offer rewards to encourage children when expectations are met.

Sanctions

No teacher likes having to sanction a child. Here, consistency plays a vital role in helping a child to understand boundaries and to learn what is expected of them on a regular basis. Teachers establish a framework for behaviour and learning through having a fair and calm disposition, which builds trust and demonstrates a predictable pattern of actions and responses. The behaviour policy will guide teachers to apply the most appropriate sanctions, so that all staff and pupils within the school follow the same principles and expected behaviours which are 'best for staff and fairest for students' (Cowley, 2014, p. 87). One of the golden rules all effective teachers adhere to is to follow through on sanctions, as not doing this will leave a child confused. Take the example of a teacher asking children not to talk at a certain point in a lesson, then a child starts chatting – if this is not addressed, then soon others start talking because the rule they thought applied does not seem to be relevant. This sends very mixed messages to the children and although it may be tiresome for the teacher to have to keep reminding them, the consistency of doing so will support the children to realise that this is the rule for everyone and then they will not talk. There is a wide range of different sanctions which may be applied by teachers. These are likely to be more successful if a whole-school approach is used because it demonstrates how all staff define the expectations for behaviour (Rogers, 2011a).

> *Top Tip*: The sanctions and rewards may be different for every class you teach. Be clear about the key messages outlined in the school policy and consider how you implement and uphold them in your daily practice.

Practice examples – Teachers' Standard 7b

DEB

In the class of 28 Year 4 children, only six were girls and there was a lot of conflict between the boys who did not work well together. Deb was aware that she needed to implement strategies to help the class work together rather than separately, as pupils were often quick to get each other into trouble or to compete with each other. She set up a class reward system where all of the children on a table had to work together as a group. For example, at the end of a lesson the table had to be tidy and all resources put away, with the children showing they were ready to move on. The group who completed this together first gained a star. The group who achieved the most stars over the week had an additional reward. If the whole class achieved a certain number of stars over the week, then the whole class got an extra 5 minutes of playtime. Over the following weeks, Deb noticed the behaviour changing as the children encouraged each other to behave in the expected way and they started to help each other to get tasks completed first.

GERRY

Gerry noticed how one particular child, Kyle, was often in trouble at playtime and how other children would be quick to blame him for things that had gone wrong, or not include him in their games. So Gerry set up a reward system where children were encouraged to tell the teacher good news based on something positive that had happened at playtime between themselves and Kyle. Each time a child shared an example of how they had played well together, both the child and Kyle received a house point. Gerry gradually observed how friendships grew and the poor image Kyle had received changed as the children became more friendly and inclusive in their play.

 In relation to Teachers' Standard 7b and your own practice, consider the following key questions:

- How will you share the sanctions and rewards system with children and other adults?
- Which whole-class and individual behaviour management systems will you develop?

(Continued)

(Continued)

- How will you allow children to contribute their own ideas for praise and reward systems?
- How will you know that the systems you use are effective?
- How will you ensure parents are aware of the behaviour management strategies?
- In the class, what do you think are the key barriers to learning and behaviour?
- Do you notice and acknowledge pupils who are well behaved?

Possible sources of evidence for Teachers' Standard 7b:

- Photographs of reward schemes in the classroom;
- Examples of individual reward systems;
- Individual behaviour plans;
- Tracking records which monitor behaviour and attitude;
- Pupils' work with comments about their attitude to work.

7c: Manage classes effectively, using approaches which are appropriate to pupils' needs in order to involve and motivate them

Commitment

Classroom management is at the root of Teachers' Standard 7c. This covers a range of strategies that teachers use to ensure there is a positive learning environment in the classroom. It includes the relationship the teacher has with the pupils, which shows mutual respect and which relates to Teachers' Standard 1. The physical classroom environment is the stage for this, with displays valuing children's work, reward systems such as zone boards that signal children are meeting expected behaviours and resources that are well organised. There may be a list showing which child has the responsibility for managing different aspects of the environment, such as keeping the reading corner tidy, putting pencil pots on tables or giving out the ipads. These are all examples of how children are involved. There is a need for structure as it sets the boundaries and guidelines for children. It provides security and is well recognised as an effective behaviour management strategy: 'For the most difficult students in our schools, this structure is probably missing from their worlds' (Cowley, 2014, p. 12).

As well as the physical environment, the classroom ethos is at the root of how teachers manage behaviour and learning. Think about the way the teacher uses body language to set expectations and contribute to showing interest in children as well as maintaining discipline. The way a teacher demonstrates presence and authority, through to the way that the class is organised, all show how an ethos rooted in a disciplined, positive working environment is established. Teachers show a commitment to their class, to the school rules and to maintaining, day after day, a secure environment in which all children can learn: 'Class rules should be based on educational, moral and safety criteria only' (Petty, 2009, p. 123). All children have a right to learn and the relationships between children as well as between the teacher and children set the tone for the classroom ethos. This means treating children and other staff in the way that you would like to be treated. Remember, teachers are role models and whether they like it or not, they are being judged by children, parents and the general public. As well as using positive body language, teachers use positive language, such as praise and show a genuine regard for a child's interests or progress through offering specific feedback. Rogers (2011b) suggests that the use of positive language may not come easily in a context where a child is being disciplined, due to the emotional attachment. It may take some practice to develop a calm, confident use of positive language, but it is worth persevering with because this can help to refocus on teaching and learning and a positive working relationship. As teachers provide evidence of how they use positive language, they will be demonstrating how they employ effective strategies and approaches to manage behaviour.

The links between the Teachers' Standards start to emerge as teachers understand how managing behaviour is integral to learning, to having high expectations, giving appropriate feedback and creating a climate in which pupils make progress.

Barriers to learning

If teachers are to understand how to manage behaviour effectively, then they must get to know the children well. An approach that is holistic, that takes into consideration the development of the whole child, is central to behaviour management. The knowledge of the child will help the teacher to identify groups of learners who may present challenges and disrupt learning in the classroom. No child should have their education disrupted, which has been acknowledged and recognised: 'Last year Ofsted found children could be losing up to an hour of learning a day because of low-level disruption, the equivalent of 38 days lost every year' (DfE and Morgan, 2015, p. 1). Any child can misbehave and this may sometimes be as a result of the child expressing feelings of anger or frustration. This behaviour must be addressed and once dealt with the disruption can be dispersed reasonably quickly. Disruption can be defined as low level, such as simple non-compliance, through to medium, such as repeated work avoidance, or high level, including violence and disrespect for others. On the high end of the spectrum are the persistent offenders who display undesired behaviour and any level of unacceptable behaviour may come from external or internal sources.

External sources may be relationship difficulties between a parent and child, between a teacher and child or between different children. It may be a problem that the child has with their own self-image which causes frustration and attention seeking. Getting to the root of the issue is important so that teachers can monitor and manage the situation through implementing specific strategies. The home environment is another external factor that can have an impact on a child's behaviour. This is to do with relationships too – for example, a child who has a new baby brother or sister may experience different feelings, perhaps of excitement or feeling left out, or a realisation that they are suddenly not the centre of attention. In situations where new members join a family, teachers may notice a change in a child's behaviour. This situation can be managed through including parents/carers in the discussion, so that consistent approaches can be used at home and at school to help the child adapt to change. Many of the internal sources include the needs recognised by Maslow, who stated that there is a hierarchy of needs concerned with survival (at the bottom), then safety and security, social and family fulfilment, status and self-actualisation or fulfilment (at the top) (Denby, 2012). This hierarchy 'implies that children must feel safe, secure and socially accepted before there is any real motivation to learn outside of this structure' (2012, p. 102). If this is the case, then children need to have their basic needs met if they are to feel motivated to learn and so engage and behave in the expected way. A child who has not had a good night's sleep or who comes to school hungry will not feel motivated and will not meet expectations for learning and behaviour. Just as diet may be a factor, we also need to be aware that language could be a barrier for some children in particular circumstances. Some hide barriers to learning through presenting challenging behaviour and the child then follows a pattern where he 'misbehaves because he doesn't understand; because he's misbehaving, he doesn't access the learning' (Cowley, 2014, p. 121). This situation is carefully handled by teachers through differentiating the work to make it more accessible and through dealing with it sensitively so that the child is not embarrassed or made to feel inadequate. Strategies such as involving the child in listening and talking activities and having an individual reward system can be productive. The curriculum can be the cause of a poor attitude as a child may find the work too easy or too challenging. In their planning, teachers need to get the pitch just right so a child is able to access the work and make progress.

Involving children in their learning

Next, we explore approaches that can support children to feel included in their learning and behaviour, so that they do not feel like something is being done to them but are empowered and can make decisions about their work. Children are more likely to invest in the class rules for behaviour if they have suggested what these may be and have jointly discussed and agreed them. This approach is known as social constructivism (Cooper, 2014). The language of choice involves children making a decision about their actions, which helps them to take ownership of their next steps, rather than the teacher telling them what they must do. Yet the teacher is very much in control because the choices given to the child are determined by the adult. In your classroom, you may have a child who decides to play with a toy rather than get on with their work. Here, the choice can be given to the child to put the toy in their tray or on the teacher's desk. The teacher would be able to refocus the child on their work whilst supporting the child to put the toy away, although where the toy goes is a decision made by the child.

When thinking about praise and rewards, these should outweigh the number of sanctions applied. Taylor in DfE (2011) recommends that teachers should praise children who are meeting expectations, more than reprimanding those who are not doing the right thing and refers to this as parallel praise. Praise that is specific to the expected behaviour will help children to understand what they have done well; they are then likely to repeat this behaviour and act as good role models for others. This strategy is concerned with overt behaviour often defined as behaviourism. The main principle of behaviourism is that all behaviour is learned and so can be unlearned and replaced with alternative behaviour, by offering the right reward. It is suggested that children are mostly a blank canvas when it comes to behaviour and their behaviour is dependent on what they have been exposed to, although it is recognised that some behaviour is not learned but instinctive (Chaplain, 2003). We tend to learn (repeat) things for which we receive a reward, which Chaplain (2003) explains in the following way, suggesting that the reward of praising children for their effort in class, which is the stimulus, may motivate children to work harder, in order to gain more praise. It is worth noting that children will have different views on what a reward is. Some children will be embarrassed to have their good behaviour highlighted in front of their peers and for some children stickers or house points work well. Chaplain (2003) recognises that some children's behaviour is self-reinforcing, meaning that their success is implicitly recognised and they do not need external incentives. Teachers who use the behaviourist theory draw on a 'rewards and sanctions approach to managing behaviour and punishing inappropriate behaviour' (Cooper, 2014, p. 195). Pupils who are involved in their learning, who are motivated learners, are more likely to be active than passive. They are likely to have a voice in shaping the classroom environment, thus building a culture of mutual respect for the children and adults within it.

> *Top Tip*: Get to know what interests and motivates the children in your class. Be consistent in the use of strategies as children need to know that they are being treated equally and fairly. Think about how you can encourage children to be independent and offer choices so they feel empowered.

Practice examples – Teachers' Standard 7c

DARYL

When children feel involved in their learning, they are more motivated and interested. A core value of Daryl's practice is to ensure all children feel their contribution is valued. In the Year 6 class, as part of Literacy, he planned an activity on persuasive writing. Through linking this to a product that the children were going to make and sell at the school summer fete, they showed passion for their own product, enthusiasm to prove that they had a great product and used powerful, persuasive writing to encourage people to want to buy their item. The children engaged because the activity was set in a real context and they could relate to it personally. They were immersed in their work and supported each other, showing collaboration and cooperation. Daryl found this a powerful way for the children to learn and consequently there was no disruption or poor attitude displayed.

MARILYN

In Marilyn's class, the pupils found it difficult to work together. Marilyn implemented a system of peer assessment to encourage greater cooperation between the children. Over time, they learned how to use positive language to feed back to each other and how to identify what was good about another child's piece of work. As well as the children being involved in their learning and enjoying their work, Marilyn noticed that relationships between pupils improved and there was less low-level disruption. It took time to train the children to work in this way but Marilyn saw huge long-term benefits for this method, which has now become an approach that is used across the whole school.

 In relation to Teachers' Standard 7c and your own practice, consider the following key questions:

- What opportunities do you give children to make decisions for themselves?
- How do you encourage independence in learning?
- Are children given responsibility for looking after the learning environment?
- Do you take time to reflect on the impact of an approach or strategy?
- Are children clear about how they should behave when they are moving around the school/classroom and between different activities or parts of a lesson?
- How is praise used to motivate children?

(Continued)

(Continued)

- Are the classroom and resources organised to enable independence and a responsible attitude towards learning?

Possible sources of evidence for Teachers' Standard 7c:

- Children's work with comments from peer assessment;
- Planning which is annotated to evaluate an approach that has been used;
- Observations carried out of children;
- Feedback from TAs;
- Evaluations of lessons;
- Feedback from observation of your teaching.

7d: Maintain good relationships with pupils, exercise appropriate authority and act decisively when necessary

Confidence

> When children know that teachers will stick to the behaviour policy and class routines, they feel safe and happy, and behaviour improves. (DfE, 2011)

Teachers' Standard 7d recognises that teaching involves responding to change. At times teachers will need the confidence and resilience to make decisions and manage particular situations. Additionally, managing behaviour is complex because poor behaviour can surface at any time and from any child. A positive relationship with each child is going to help the teacher to handle any unexpected situation in a calm manner. Maintaining a positive relationship includes developing trust with children and this is achieved through having clear boundaries for behaviour and being confident in implementing strategies. The pupil who trusts the teacher will learn that they can rely on the adult and will feel safe. How a child thinks (the cognitive) and feels (the affective) is very powerful as it can influence how receptive and engaged they are in their learning. This in turn leads to the promotion of positive behaviour. The confident teacher will think about their body language, how they use non-verbal cues and the tone of their voice as they assume responsibility and portray an authoritative stance (Cowley, 2014). These aspects of practice show authority and a relationship that is respectful to children. Sometimes the relationship may be tested, for example when teachers have to deal with minor disruption and in these situations reprimands can be sandwiched between positive comments. If a child is distracting others, the teacher may make a comment about something the child has done well, then firmly comment on how to behave, followed by a positive remark. When teachers have to discipline children, it can put a strain on the relationship, so it is important that they quickly regain a sense of calm to dissipate any tension. Strategies include praise for the child when they do something right, being calm and using humour: 'Humour can relax, engage, encourage – even defuse tension' (Rogers, 2011b, p. 68). As a role model, teachers are able to demonstrate the behaviour they expect to see, which includes managing emotions in difficult situations. Whilst maintaining discipline within the classroom, teachers have a sense of fun as they know children learn better when they are not under pressure.

Exercise authority, act decisively

This sub-set of the Teachers' Standards highlights the need to exercise appropriate authority and act decisively. When considering this, teachers need to think about unexpected situations and how they have been managed. A teacher who thinks that all children must be well behaved all of the time is going to become frustrated. They almost need to expect the unexpected and be prepared for how they might react and take control of a situation. To do this, the school policy will be drawn on. This sets out the rules and sanctions for how teachers should deal professionally with any unacceptable episodes. It may be necessary to use interventions and there are many different approaches teachers take here. This includes ignoring low-level behaviour, which Rogers (2011b, p. 139) calls 'tactical ignoring'. In this situation, the teacher chooses to ignore the child and is still very much taking control, then takes the opportunity to refocus the children or provide reminders to the whole class about the expected behaviours. Other strategies teachers employ include giving hand signals such as fingers to lips when a child talks over the teacher or another child, waiting time, acknowledging children who are behaving in the correct way or reminding children of the class rules. Repositioning within the class, either the teacher or the child may provide a helpful solution in changing a child's behaviour. A method that recognises the power of emotions, such as anger or anxiety and low self-esteem and their impact on thinking and behaviour, uses a cognitive behavioural approach (Chaplain, 2003). This involves the teacher in a directive role, supporting the child to identify and restructure their behaviour, which results from internal thinking linked to the way the child is feeling (their emotions) and thinking.

More serious issues involving the safety of children, issues of bullying and high-level disruption must be acted on swiftly. Teachers must have authority and be assertive when dealing with these situations. Being decisive is vital, even if underneath the teacher is feeling less strong, as an authoritative stance conveys clarity in terms of the boundaries. Sometimes a child may have an individual behaviour plan as their behaviour is so disruptive and is ongoing. Rogers (2011b) reinforces the significance of using a whole-school approach and involving appropriate colleagues in this.

In all cases of managing behaviour, the teacher must focus on the behaviour rather than on the child, making it clear to a child that it is their behaviour the teacher does not like, rather than the child thinking the teacher does not like them. Having a clear vision of actions and confidence in an action plan for how to deal with unacceptable and unexpected behaviour will support the teacher to be proactive in, rather than reactive to, situations.

Top Tip: Get to know the children in your class – not just their academic ability, but find out about their interests so that you can show pupils you have an interest in them. Build trust quickly to secure a positive working relationship with every child in the class. Remember that parents are a valuable resource and can be drawn on to find out more about the child.

Practice examples – Teachers' Standard 7d

CHRIS
As soon as anyone entered the classroom, the good rapport between the children and Chris was evident. It could be seen in the high quality dialogue as Chris worked with individuals, groups or the whole class. She used questioning which encouraged the children to use higher-order thinking skills and guided learning. Chris showed a genuine interest in children's achievements, which encouraged them further and when a child was struggling to understand, she explained again calmly so that the child did not become frustrated. Later on, she checked the child's understanding through using open questions. The children enjoyed learning and there was mutual respect and trust between Chris and the children.

GWYN
During a design and technology lesson, a child had a toy car out which had been brought from home. Following the school's policy and guidelines, Gwyn was aware that children should not bring toys from home into the classroom. He dealt with the

(Continued)

(Continued)

situation by using the language of choice, calmly asking the child to choose one of two actions. The child could either put the car in their tray or give it to the teacher where it would be kept safely on the teacher's desk. By being offered these choices, the child was able to take responsibility for their actions, comply with the school rules and feel empowered. The impact was that the other children saw the equity as the child was following the rules in the same way they were all expected to. The teacher was showing confident authority and clearly setting out the expected rules whilst following the school policy.

 In relation to Teachers' Standard 7d and your own practice, consider the following key questions:

- How have you worked with other colleagues or drawn on specialist advice to help develop strategies to deal with disruptive pupils?
- What do you do to build a respectful relationship with children?
- How do children know that you care for them?
- When have you needed to deal with an unexpected situation and what strategies have you used to deal with it?
- How have you used the school policy to support you in managing a challenging situation?

Possible sources of evidence for Teachers' Standard 7d:

- Feedback from lesson observations;
- Accounts of critical incidents;
- Letters from parents;
- Individual plans for children;
- Intervention strategies;
- Relating to a theoretical approach, such as cognitive behavioural, to say how you have used this with a specific child;
- Planning – annotated to show how you modified teaching within a lesson;
- Highlighting the school policy to show when you have used it.

Chapter summary

The discussion and examples given throughout this chapter will support teachers to identify times in their own practice when they have used strategies to address issues of managing learning and behaviour. It is not intended that these are taken as the only ways to address Teachers' Standard 7, for in practice there are likely to be many different situations that occur. However, through recognising how teachers develop clarity, consistency, commitment and confidence in their practice, teachers will be able to transfer these skills to highlight how, in their own practice, they employ competence in managing a positive learning environment. Throughout the chapter, the association between learning and behaviour has been stressed: 'Consistent experience of good teaching promotes good behaviour. But schools also need to have positive strategies for managing behaviour that help children understand their school's expectations' (DfES, 2006). Alongside a focus on teaching and learning, teachers use the school policy to implement effective strategies for managing a positive, working environment. Colleagues are drawn on for guidance in setting up interventions for specific children and the value of talking to parents has been raised. The most effective classrooms, in which behaviour is managed, are the ones where teachers motivate and involve children in their learning, where learning is fun and meaningful and where everyone is engaged. The importance of the school behaviour and discipline policy has been acknowledged, in helping teachers to maintain an effective classroom environment, in which all children feel safe and secure and in which all children are able to learn. Every child has the right to learn and every teacher is entitled to teach in a safe and secure environment.

CHAPTER 8

FULFIL WIDER PROFESSIONAL RESPONSIBILITIES

Teachers' Standard 8 – Fulfil wider professional responsibilities:

8a Make a positive contribution to the wider life and ethos of the school

8b Develop professional relationships with colleagues, knowing how and when to draw on advice and specialist support

8c Deploy support staff effectively

8d Take responsibility for improving teaching through appropriate professional development, responding to advice and feedback from colleagues

8e Communicate effectively with parents with regard to pupils' achievements and well-being.

What is this all about?

This standard has a focus on the roles and responsibilities of the school workforce. It includes exploring who is involved in the school team, what their individual roles are and how these roles complement each other. The education and development of pupils is the responsibility of everyone in school and the role of a teacher requires them to work effectively as part of that school team. There is an opportunity to reflect on how teachers do not work in isolation but how they work both independently and within a professional group. The standard focuses on how effective teachers contribute to teaching and learning through developing ways to work with other colleagues, how they liaise with others and when it is important to seek help from others. The subject of communication between teaching staff, support staff and parents is raised as we consider ways of developing effective communication channels between all groups. The important responsibility that teachers have in upholding the school mission statement is discussed and how this is achieved through working with parents, teaching staff and support staff. There is a consideration of the different ways that teachers become involved in the life of the school. Teachers contribute to school life through supporting and leading teaching and learning within and beyond the classroom and examples of how this is achieved are included.

As well as advice, suggestions are given for how teachers can take responsibility for their own professional development and seek opportunities to meet their own development needs. It directs you to additional ideas on how to reflect on practice and take action to further improve understanding. Through addressing this standard, you will be able to consider why effective teachers are also life-long learners who value feedback from colleagues and the importance of acting on advice in a professional manner.

How can this be demonstrated?

Teachers' Standard 8 requires teachers to demonstrate how they contribute to all aspects of school life to support the learning and development of pupils and how they uphold the school values. When finding evidence for this, teachers will be able to reflect on how they demonstrate that they have the knowledge, skills and understanding to communicate effectively with both their colleagues and with parents. The standard requires teachers to consider how they deploy support staff and to show awareness of collaboration and cooperation with others in relation to their daily practice. Teachers are required to make judgements about their professional development needs and to maintain a professional dialogue with other teaching staff and managers about their experiences and progress. In summary, the key aspects of this Teachers' Standard can be outlined as communication with colleagues and working as part of a professional team, reflection on classroom practice and awareness of continuing professional development needs and working with and effectively deploying support staff.

Chapter overview

This chapter draws on the good practice that exists in schools locally and nationally. Reference is made to the major UK educational policies which have had an impact on the way that schools are working and in turn how this has changed the way that teachers and support staff currently work in schools (DfE, 2011; Ofsted, 2012). After setting out the background for change and presenting the context, the chapter goes on to look at each standard and its sub-set, leading to a deeper exploration of the hidden aspects of the school curriculum as we consider the teacher's role in this world. In particular, looking at the aspects of school outside of the four walls of the classroom will help you to consider how, in your setting, you can identify the many different ways to become involved in the broader aspects of school life. The importance of school ethos is discussed in the context of developing a positive learning environment. Within this, we look at how as a member of the community you are able to demonstrate the mutual values and principles which are shared with the rest of the school community. Following this, the challenges and opportunities of working as part of a team will be explored. We consider who does what in school and when it is appropriate to draw on specialist advice. Then we consider the different roles of other adults who may be working in school and how to go about effectively deploying them to support teaching and learning. Models of working are drawn on, as well as thinking about how to work alongside support staff on preparation, planning, teaching and assessment.

Continuing your professional development is of sufficient importance for us to address it here and then return to it in Chapter 10. The chapter concludes with a focus on communication with parents, guiding you to reflect on the critical role they play and the different ways teachers interact with parents to both inform them and work with them on the development and education of their child.

Taking it apart and putting it back together

So, let's start the task of straightening out what you need to do to evidence the standard. To do this, we will separate each sub-set to explore the detail, then we will consider some of the opportunities you will have from your daily practice that will support you in finding evidence from your practice, in order to meet the standards.

8a: Make a positive contribution to the wider life and ethos of the school

Every school has an individual identity and this is set out in the school mission statement. This is what gives the school its own character and no two schools are the same. The school ethos is developed through the principles and beliefs of the adults and children who are connected with the school (Taylor and Woolley, 2013). This is evidenced through the way that these people interact and behave within the school community. This may be through their actions and their words and through the things they do on behalf of the children and adults in the setting. Every individual within the school will make a contribution to the character of the school. Your own values will impact on the teaching and learning environment in your classroom (Taylor and Woolley, 2013). Sometimes, as teachers, we get lost in the little things and may lose sight of what the school is aiming to achieve. So the organisation of the school serves as a reminder of what the people in the school are trying to achieve. Schools use their mission statement as a form of communication, through discussing the values and beliefs of the school with the children.

In finding evidence from your practice, consider what actions you take to contribute to the school culture and uphold the school values. This may be through activities with classes other than the ones you normally teach and may be outside the times of the school day. There may be a particular interest or skill that you have which you can use to further support the school. Class teachers may be expected to accept responsibility for an area of the curriculum as part of their normal professional duties. This provides an opportunity to develop your interests and skills as well as demonstrate how you are supporting the school more widely, which may be evidenced through the way you support colleagues or how you have developed the curriculum within the school. Even if you are unable to take on a subject responsibility, there are often opportunities to become involved in projects within the wider community outside the school. Some examples may be the opportunity to organise Christmas carol concerts, sports events or school trips, or even to organise a themed day based around a topic you have been studying where, for example, you arrange for visiting speakers to come along to school to talk to the children. Additionally, school assemblies may provide a chance to share your values with children, parents and staff. Alongside organising and supporting events, it is the teacher's day-to-day behaviour, attitude and actions that are influential in contributing to the school ethos. This includes how you speak to colleagues and the opportunities you seek to interact with them.

Top Tip: Although you may be working within a specific key stage, you can contribute to the whole school and work with other age groups. This could be through offering an extra-curricular activity or joining an existing after-school club. It will give an opportunity to work with other age groups and to develop your interests and skills.

Practice examples – Teachers' Standard 8a

RUTH

After talking to other teachers and the head teacher about the school's philosophy and ethos, Ruth read through the school mission statement. She discovered that collaboration on upholding school values includes how teachers work with pupils, how pupils work with each other and how school staff work together as well as with parents. Ruth realised that 'working together' was an important value within the school. Included in the mission statement was the value of building on and developing individual talents and personal strengths. This was aimed at supporting both children and adults to recognise what they do well and to use these skills. Ruth had trained in pilates and held qualifications for this. She decided to use her skills and knowledge of pilates to run an after-school activity for her colleagues. She discussed her ideas with the head teacher who supported Ruth and encouraged her to organise and deliver a weekly pilates class for teachers in the school. The school staff were very keen to attend and really appreciated the class because it gave them an opportunity to relax and have fun as a staff team. Ruth was able to demonstrate how she could contribute to the school values and support her colleagues through a skill she had. She used this example as evidence to show that she was able to contribute to the wider life of school. As well as developing her skills, she reflected on how it upheld the school values in supporting her to demonstrate and use her own individual strengths.

MATTHEW

Matthew worked in a very small village school, consisting of one class in the Foundation Stage, one class in Key Stage 1 and one class in Key Stage 2. There were just 60 children in total. The head teacher encouraged staff to develop opportunities to deliver a more creative approach to teaching. Matthew had specialist subject knowledge in geography and enjoyed teaching this. He belonged to the local geography teachers' group. When the head teacher explained that the whole school was going to be involved in a themed week, he expressed an interest in developing the ideas further through having a geographical focus. Matthew was able to contribute new ideas and share his expertise as he was confident in teaching geography. He worked alongside other teachers to plan and organise a week of events, for the whole school, based around the theme of water. He liaised with the local nature group and arranged for an outside speaker from this group to visit the school and talk to the children in an assembly. Through organising the themed

(Continued)

(Continued)

week, Matthew was able to evidence how he had made a positive contribution to the school through using his passion for geography alongside his geographical knowledge. As evidence for this, he drew on how he had encouraged all teachers to be involved in planning activities and how he had worked alongside them. Additionally, Matthew was able to demonstrate that he had supported the values of the school because of the way he had developed a creative approach to teaching and learning, which demonstrated his commitment to using creative approaches in teaching and learning.

 In relation to Teachers' Standard 8a and your own practice, consider the following key questions:

- What have you done to show that you support the values of the school? Think about your behaviour and your actions.
- How have you used your initiative to support the ethos of the school? What was the impact of this?
- What contribution have you made to the school or local community? This may be through working with other adults or with the children.
- How have you supported extra-curricular activities (for example, sports, the arts, subject-specific clubs or activities linked to environmental issues)?
- How have you used your individual talents and skills (perhaps to set up a special area within the school grounds or a new initiative for the school)?
- How will you use your specialist knowledge? (Consider taking on a role of responsibility or supporting colleagues with planning or resources.)
- What have you done at breaks or lunchtimes that demonstrates you are an active member of the school staff?
- How do you know you are making a valid contribution? Consider responses from children, parents and school staff.

Possible sources of evidence for Teachers' Standard 8a:

- Planning from extra-curricular activities;
- Letters from parents and colleagues;
- Lesson observations from senior colleagues.

8b: Develop professional relationships with colleagues, knowing how and when to draw on advice and specialist support

The daily practice of all teachers involves working alongside colleagues within school. There are many people who work as part of the school staff, to support learning and development. How you fit into your school will really depend on the staffing structure. This will vary from school to school, depending on the size of the school and what type of school it is. For the majority of schools, the structure will include the head teacher, deputy head teacher, assistant head teacher, early years coordinator, key stage coordinators special educational needs coordinator (SENCo), subject leaders and curriculum coordinators and class teachers. Each of these roles has additional responsibilities and staff in these roles are experienced, have an expertise and have specialist knowledge in the area. For example, subject coordinators are responsible for the leadership and management of a particular curriculum subject and the SENCo is responsible for day-to-day provision for pupils with special educational needs. There will also be staff with responsibilities for other aspects of practice such as safeguarding or health and safety. Sometimes teachers will work with external agencies on children's learning and development. These include integrated specialist support and learning support teams, such as speech and language or behaviour support teams, who work with pupils with special educational needs, physical needs and learning needs. Other external agencies may include educational psychologists, social workers and occupational therapists. Within the wider community, there will be specialist groups who support specific learners such as the local early childhood organisation (EChO) or subject teachers' groups. You will be able to find out more about your local groups from colleagues at school.

The ongoing dialogue that you have with colleagues is an integral part of your practice and this is equally as important as the more formal meetings you will have. To meet the requirements of this standard, you will be expected to draw on the experiences you have had of working with school staff such as the SENCo to discuss progress of children in your class who have a learning difficulty. Other staff may include the designated senior person for child protection (DSP), the English as an additional language (EAL) coordinator or subject coordinators. You can include occasions when you have discussed your planning or ideas for resources or learning activities with subject coordinators, as well as sharing your ideas for the development of this area of the curriculum within the school. You may have been on a course or training where you have gained further ideas which you can share with colleagues in school. There may be times when working with advisors or specialists and therapists has been essential to support the individual needs of learners, such as a child's speech and language, physical or sensory development, or to manage behaviour.

Finally, remember what a valuable colleague the teaching assistant (TA) is. It is likely that they will know the school, the children and the community well. Consider how you have worked with the TA and drawn on their knowledge and area of specialism to support learning.

> *Top Tip*: Think about the special skills and knowledge you have and how you can support your colleagues. Your area of specialism may be concerned with the research you carried out as part of your initial teacher training course.

 Practice examples – Teachers' Standard 8b

ANDREW

Andrew was working in a Key Stage 1 class which included a higher level teaching assistant (HLTA) as part of the teaching staff. The HLTA had been working in the school for ten years, had a qualification in supporting children with autism and worked closely with the SENCo. Andrew realised that the HLTA had a wealth of information about the children and the school. Although initially he felt that she knew more than he did and he was a little worried about this, he realised that he should make use of her deeper understanding. He quickly developed a good working relationship with the teaching assistant through asking her about her area of specialism and deploying her to ensure her strengths were used. This led to Andrew and the HLTA working together to support a child in the class with autism. This included jointly planning appropriate learning activities, developing strategies to support the child in class with turn taking and sharing and ensuring he was fully included in all aspects of the curriculum. Andrew was able to show how he had drawn on the specialist knowledge of the HLTA, to work more knowledgeably with a child in his class with autism.

ELEANOR

Eleanor was keen to develop her knowledge of the design and technology curriculum but lacked some confidence in this. After speaking to her class teacher, she discovered that the school had very close links with the high school next door and that the D&T teacher in that school was a specialist in this curriculum area. Eleanor worked with her class teacher to set up a meeting with the secondary teacher to discuss the possibility of working together on a topic for that term. At the meeting, she discussed her planning and ideas for making pulleys based on the children's book *The Lighthouse Keeper's Lunch*. The high school provided specialist equipment to enable the children to make pulley systems – equipment that they did not have in the primary school. Eleanor and the secondary D&T teacher then did some team teaching which

(Continued)

(Continued)

supported Eleanor to gain confidence in teaching this new area of the curriculum. She also gained valuable knowledge of the design and technology curriculum and became much more comfortable in using some of the technical vocabulary. Eleanor evidenced how she had worked with the teacher from the high school to draw on the specialist support she needed to improve her subject knowledge and build her confidence to enable her to deliver the curriculum in a creative way.

 In relation to Teachers' Standard 8b and your own practice, consider the following key questions:

- How have you worked effectively as part of the school team?
- How do you show that you work with other colleagues to support the development of children?
- How do you know who to contact for advice?
- How have you disseminated information to colleagues?
- Who have you spoken to, to gain further advice about a pupil, strategies, the curriculum or a child's development?
- How have you disseminated any knowledge or information you have about a pupil's progress or development?
- How have you collaborated or worked with colleagues in school or with external agencies to gain specialist advice?

Possible sources of evidence for Teachers' Standard 8b:

- Planning;
- Information shared with colleagues;
- Notes from meetings with colleagues, parents and specialists.

8c: Deploy support staff effectively

The idea of a team of professionals working together is not a new one. Throughout practice, you will have worked with other adults in the classroom and this is an essential part of working as a teacher. Yet, this has not always been the case and the change from a single teacher in a classroom to a team of professionals working together has occurred over time. In particular, over the last three decades, the increase in government control over teaching has been seen mostly as a drive to raise standards (Hammersley-Fletcher, 2008). Simultaneously, schools and school staff have become more accountable as the emphasis has shifted away from society to individual schools. The Workforce Remodelling Agenda, in 2003, was part of a government plan for improving the effectiveness of public sector services. It also provided an opportunity for schools to consider their staffing structure and make radical cultural shifts (Ofsted, 2010). The agenda centred around raising standards and tackling workload with a focus on how the change in adult roles will bring benefits for pupils. The vision was to have a children's workforce that is supported by shared systems and processes. The phasing of change over three years (Figure 8.1) marked the beginning of an evolving process for schools, in the way that staff were to be deployed.

Phase one – 2003	Routine delegation of 24 non-teaching tasks
Phase two – 2004	Introduce new limits on covering for absent teachers
Phase three – 2005	Introduce guaranteed professional time for planning, preparation and assessment

Figure 8.1   Phasing of change (Ofsted, 2013)

The idea of thinking of oneself as an integral part of a system, rather than as an individual, is necessary for collaborative working to be effective in schools. Inter-professional work relies on interactive learning and attention needs to be given to the changes that occur as support staff work alongside teachers in the classroom, to support teaching and learning. A key feature of an outstanding teacher is that they are able to manage and deploy other adults in the classroom effectively (Ofsted, 2008). This is through having a shared vision so that all adults know what their individual role is and what the shared expectation is for teaching and learning. It is usually in the role of a teaching assistant that a member of the support staff works alongside the teacher in the classroom. It is important to remember that the roles of teacher and teaching assistant are different. These roles must be defined in terms of how they work in cooperation and collaboration to meet shared goals. Support staff represent a significant group of the school staff and work in many important roles in a school. There are five main categories of support staff: pupil support roles include those responsible for pupil welfare, such as lunchtime supervisors; technical roles include those who help with a subject, such as IT or design and technology, music specialists or librarians; administrative roles include those who provide day-to-day office or financial support, including business managers; site staff roles include those who look after the school environment, such as site managers and cleaners; and learning support staff roles include those who work closely with teachers to support teaching and learning and this includes teaching assistants.

The presence of another adult in the classroom does not automatically improve the achievement of children. Blatchford et al. (2012) note that one of the main concerns in the deployment of teaching assistants has been their pedagogical role and the ambiguity with regard to this role. The authors suggest that teaching assistants are not always being deployed effectively and there needs to be greater clarity over roles and responsibilities. Consideration needs to be given to how to maximise the potential contribution that this extra adult can offer. The relationship between teacher and teaching assistant is important in supporting teaching and learning and raising achievement. To develop a good working relationship, the teacher needs to find out about the teaching assistant's role, interests, skills and strengths. Teaching assistants will have a job description and will be carrying out responsibilities relevant to the grade they are paid at. As a teacher, you need to be aware of the teaching assistant's role. Some teaching assistants will be working as a higher level teaching assistant (HLTA) and will be able to plan, teach and assess whole classes as well as work with individuals and groups. It is the teacher's responsibility to plan the work of the teaching assistant and to be clear what they will be doing throughout the lesson (Jacques and Hyland, 2007). The teacher will consider who they will be working with, how they will record observations and how they will feed back to the teacher on pupil progress. Ideally, the teaching assistant and teacher will have an opportunity to discuss the planning beforehand and the teacher needs to be confident that the teaching assistant is clear about their role within the lesson. TAs should always be given a copy of the planning well in advance of the lesson. A responsibility of having another adult in the classroom is to consider how you will support them to work independently so that they can consolidate the expectations of behaviour and learning and ensure consistency in the messages children receive. This will help you both to work together as a team. The teaching assistant should be involved in all aspects of the cyclical process (see Figure 8.2).

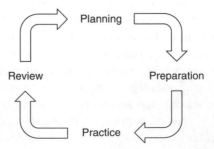

Figure 8.2   The virtuous circle of support for the curriculum, teachers and pupils (TDA, 2007)

The need for clear training and progression in all parts of the workforce and the need to have a highly skilled workforce is further highlighted in the 2020 Children and Young People's Workforce Strategy (DCSF, 2008). Brighouse (2008) recognised the importance of continuing professional development (CPD) and suggests that standards can be raised when staff work as an integrated school workforce and engage together in CPD. This was given greater credibility when Christine Gilbert, Her Majesty's Chief Inspector of Schools, commented on the correlation between professional development for the diverse school workforce and raising standards (Ofsted, 2010). Research in schools is becoming an accepted part of professional development. School staff are central to raising the standards of teaching and learning and work with parents/carers to ensure standards are high. Teachers must commit fully to developing themselves professionally, taking responsibility for their own learning as well as managing the effective deployment of the staff who work alongside them.

💡 *Top Tip*: Get to know who is who on the support staff team. Find out about the people you work with, including their hobbies and interests. Relationships are like bridges: the stronger you build a bridge, the more they can carry; the stronger you build your relationships with people, the more they will invest in you.

 Practice examples – Teachers' Standard 8c

NICOLA

The teaching assistant who worked with Nicola in YR was very experienced and knew the children well. Nicola was able to draw on the teaching assistant's knowledge of the children to plan appropriate activities that would interest them. Initially, it was difficult to find time to plan with the teaching assistant but, after raising this with the head teacher, it was decided that, once a week, during planning, preparation and assessment (PPA) time, the teaching assistant and Nicola would meet to share ideas for planning. This meant that Nicola could incorporate the teaching assistant's ideas into the learning activities. The weekly planning was emailed to the teaching assistant so that she had a copy at the start of each week. Nicola noticed how this helped the teaching assistant to feel more prepared for the lessons. It enabled the teaching assistant to think ahead about the resources she might use and about the kinds of questions she would ask the children to encourage them

(Continued)

(Continued)

to use higher order thinking skills. Nicola was able to show, through her planning, how she managed the work of the teaching assistant. This included stating on the plan who would be working with each group of children. She also showed how she had planned for the teaching assistant and teacher to work with different groups so that they were both involved with supporting all learners in the class.

VERITY

Verity was able to evidence how she deployed and respected the teaching assistant as a very valuable resource in the classroom. Verity demonstrated how she had effectively deployed the teaching assistant to carry out formative assessment. In her preparation for the lesson, Verity had planned for the teaching assistant to use a record sheet with a group she was supporting in a mathematics lesson. The teaching assistant was asked to record each child's academic progress, linked to the learning objective, as well as recording children's attitude and behaviour. She noted the responses from the children based on their written work and the discussions between her and the child. These data were valuable to Verity as they gave her further information about the children's progress. Additionally, it helped her to provide evidence not only of the effective deployment of the teaching assistant but also of the impact of their work.

 In relation to Teachers' Standard 8c and your own practice, consider the following key questions:

- How do you manage the work of other adults in the classroom?
- How do you communicate with the teaching assistant? (What are the opportunities for listening and speaking?)
- Are you clear about the role of the teaching assistant in this setting?
- How are the roles and responsibilities of the teacher and teaching assistant shown on lesson planning?
- What have you done to find out about the teaching assistant's skills and strengths?
- How do you share the planning with the teaching assistant?
- When do you discuss the assessments and observations the teaching assistant has made?

(Continued)

(Continued)

- Have you discussed how you will work together and agreed on ground rules?
- How will you work together to make sure the teaching assistant does not always work with the same group of children?

Possible sources of evidence for Teachers' Standard 8c:

- Lesson plans to show teaching assistant deployment with groups and individuals;
- Assessments and observation notes from teaching assistants;
- Medium-term plans to show the contributions of the teaching assistant.

8d: Take responsibility for improving teaching through appropriate professional development, responding to advice and feedback from colleagues

Learning is a life-long process and through this standard you will be able to evidence how you have met your continuing professional development needs. Teachers are expected to be independent and show a genuine commitment to improving their practice. The responsibility is on each individual to identify their needs and seek opportunities that will support these emerging needs. However, this is not always easy and Ewans (2014) identifies two approaches that may be supportive in helping you to decide what your professional development needs are. These are set out as: (1) aspects that are identified from your day-to-day classroom practice; and (2) aspects that arise from outside your practice (such as government policy, school priorities). This is a helpful way to organise your thinking about how you can identify professional needs.

Taking responsibility for your own professional development and being proactive are key considerations for any teacher. This relies on you being reflective and able to identify, from your practice, what those needs are. Moon (2004) defines reflection as thinking about something that is known and then adding new knowledge to make sense of what is being reflected on. If we consider this for a moment, think about a recent experience from your practice and consider what could have improved the lesson. Perhaps it was knowing more about strategies to support more able learners or better understanding of assessment in science. Thinking in this way will help you to identify which aspects of your practice you want to improve. Through reflecting on teaching and classroom practice, teachers make judgements about how effective they are and what they can do to further their skills and knowledge. There are different ways to consider impact, including keeping a personal learning journal, feedback from children and colleagues and observations from colleagues.

Like other aspects of your practice, recognising your professional needs does not sit in isolation from your role and responsibilities. Gaining further knowledge will impact on your wider role in the school and of course, on pupil outcomes. As a teacher, you will be expected to demonstrate the value of feedback from experienced colleagues, through acting on advice and engaging in further professional development activities. Ongoing dialogue with classroom teachers, as well as discussions with mentors and colleagues, will provide opportunities for you to discuss strengths and areas for further development.

Sources of professional development

Much of a teacher's development will centre on carrying out further reading, personal research and communicating with colleagues to improve their knowledge and understanding. There may be opportunities to attend staff meetings and professional development days within the school, as well as to engage in external activities such as courses or conferences. Observations of other practitioners will form an important part of making judgements about elements of teaching styles, approaches and strategies that can be added to your own range of teaching skills, in order to further develop your teaching and learning.

Responding to feedback

The chance to receive feedback on your teaching will provide a valuable professional development opportunity. This will help you to identify what is going well, your strengths and areas for development. During feedback and discussion, you will be able to engage and respond, taking responsibility for what you have to do next to improve your practice. Hansen (2012, p. 64) suggests that: 'the "assessment" of your teaching is something that should be done *with* you, not *to* you, and therefore you have a responsibility to be involved in the discussion'.

Future aspirations

Effective professional development involves recognising your own needs and being committed to developing yourself. This means being able to recognise what you need to fulfil your aims and ambitions. It may include shadowing a colleague in your own school or in a different setting, attending specific courses in order to carry out a role, developing new skills such as mentoring or coaching, carrying out research, attendance at or participation in conferences and training events, or acquiring professional qualifications. Perhaps your aspiration is to move on to a leadership and management role in school or to lead a subject or key stage. Your head teacher will support you with meeting your professional development needs through ensuring an effective appraisal system is in place. The appraisal provides a supportive and developmental framework so that all teachers receive the provision they need to carry out their role effectively. It helps teachers to be able to recognise how to improve their professional practice and to develop as teachers. Ultimately, this will have an impact on pupil outcomes.

> *Top Tip*: What aspirations do you have and where do you see yourself in five or ten years' time? If you would like to take up a leadership role, look at training that will support you to develop the skills needed to be a leader. Observe how the leaders in school demonstrate their ability. Start to think about the qualifications and experiences you may need to take a leadership role.

Practice examples – Teachers' Standard 8d

SAM

Sam's mentor observed him teaching a mathematics lesson to his Year 4 class. Following feedback from the lesson, Sam reflected on his subject knowledge. He realised that he needed to improve his understanding of teaching methods and mathematical vocabulary when teaching methods of multiplication. He actively responded by speaking to the school mathematics coordinator to discuss the teaching methods used in the school. He followed this up by arranging to jointly teach a mathematics lesson with the subject coordinator. Following further advice, Sam looked at teaching resources online to access ideas for activities to use in the lesson; he also read a chapter in a book to further consolidate his understanding of teaching methods as well as the use of appropriate mathematical vocabulary. He was able to provide this as evidence of acting on and responding to feedback from experienced colleagues which impacted on improved confidence and on pupil progress.

(Continued)

(Continued)

SUE

Sue was based in a Year 1 class for her first teaching post within a small primary school. She had identified that, through setting personal targets, she would like to further improve her understanding of children's writing at this age. Her main experience was of working with older children. She spoke to the mentor in school about the opportunity to observe some 'emergent writing' sessions. She followed this up with a discussion with the literacy coordinator who arranged for Sue to visit the foundation stage in school, where the teacher was recognised within the local authority for her experience in supporting and promoting early writing skills. A focused observation helped Sue develop her understanding of ways to help beginning writers become more confident and independent. This helped Sue to gain a greater awareness of the stages of development and gave her some interesting ideas for activities to help stimulate pupils' early writing skills. Later on, Sue used these ideas in activities within her lessons and she was able to draw on this as evidence of how she had reflected on and changed her practice. The impact was improved confidence which led to more interesting and varied ways to engage learners.

 In relation to Teachers' Standard 8d and your own practice, consider the following key questions:

- How will you identify any development needs?
- What opportunities will you seek to engage in professional dialogue with colleagues?
- What are your personal targets and goals?
- When and how will you reflect on practice?
- Who can help you to identify your CPD needs?
- How do you show that you can respond positively to feedback?
- What are you doing to develop your knowledge and skills and how are you incorporating new ideas into your practice?

Possible sources of evidence for Teachers' Standard 8d:

- Professional development meetings;
- Feedback from observations;
- Continuing professional development opportunities.

8e: Communicate effectively with parents with regard to pupils' achievements and well-being

Parents play a vital and critical role in the development and well-being of children. They are the child's first educators and hold valuable information about their child. The links between home and school are a vital bridge for the pupils' well-being. This standard requires teachers to demonstrate an understanding of the importance of communicating and liaising with parents/carers to promote and support learning. Teachers are encouraged to consider how they will maximise opportunities for parental, or carer, involvement. An important aspect is to provide evidence of how the role of parents/carers has been taken into account in relation to the needs of individual children. This could include how the teacher has developed or supported different initiatives to involve parents/carers in a child's learning. An example may be asking parents/carers to contribute specific resources or to think about how they have been included in sharing their knowledge and skills on a topic. Trainees should include examples of how they inform parents/carers of initiatives relevant to their child, such as information about school visits, assemblies or special events. Teachers should take into account the ways in which they engage parents/carers in understanding a child's needs in relation to attainment and personal development. You could consider asking parents/carers of the children in your class to attend a special event where you explain the process of the Key Stage Statutory Assessment Tests (SATs). There will be specific points in the school year which teachers have a duty and responsibility to contribute to, such as attending parents' evenings and providing observations and records for written reports. These formal occasions are important stages where you can discuss the child's academic progress, as well as their attitude and behaviour in class, special interests or medical conditions.

Parent consultation events

In preparation for parent/carer consultation events and to make sure everything runs smoothly, it will help if you have all marking completed and up to date and any attendance records and attainment levels easily accessible. Sometimes you may feel less confident about seeing a parent who is known to be difficult and it is sensible to talk to the head teacher or a senior member of staff so that they are aware and can try to be near the classroom at the time of the consultation.

Written reports

Government guidance states that teachers in England, Wales and Northern Ireland are required to produce at least one report to parents per student per academic year

(ATL, 2013). When you are writing the child's report, remember to follow the school's guidance. A good report will include comments relating to the achievements and progress of the child as well as what they could do to further improve. Remember that the less formal events are equally as important as the more formal, planned sessions. Some parents/carers may find it very difficult to approach a teacher and may be reluctant to go into the classroom. Having an open-door policy may be helpful in providing them with a space to talk about individual children in a more relaxed manner, as well as inviting them to address small issues so that they do not escalate into larger problems. Good communication is essential and parents/carers are more likely to share important information with you, about home or family circumstances which may impact on the child, if you have a trusting, supportive professional relationship with them. As well as the face-to-face contact, think about the ways that you contribute to the school newsletters, pamphlets on specific subjects or online information, guidance or advice.

Top Tip: Keeping parents/carers fully involved in and informed about their child's education will be important. This includes making sure you have effective systems in place to support good communication. Parents need to know that you are interested in their child and building up trust needs to happen quickly. Talking through problems and difficulties a child may be experiencing can help both you and the parents to find solutions so that issues do not escalate.

Practice examples – Teachers' Standard 8e

KELLY

Kelly was teaching in a Year 6 class in which parents/carers were keen to support their children's learning as much as possible. Kelly communicated with them in several ways. She initiated and developed the idea of sending emails to update them on the topics the class was going to cover. In particular, Kelly was able to provide evidence of the time she had asked for personal memories or artefacts of India, which pupils were studying as part of a geography theme on distant localities. There was a very encouraging response and Kelly had several offers from parents to either provide resources or come into school to take part in a planned day of activities. One parent offered to do some Indian cooking and came into school to work with the class. The result was that parents/carers were keen to support pupils' learning. Kelly was also aware of the school policy regarding contacting parents by

(Continued)

(Continued)

phone, or using the daily communication book if appropriate, which she continued to follow. She used these examples as evidence of how she effectively communicated with parents and was able to demonstrate the impact of these strategies.

OLIVER

When working in a Reception class, Oliver regularly spoke to parents/carers in the playground, before and after school. He used this time to develop a good working relationship with parents and to share his knowledge of the children with them. He was able to provide evidence of an occasion when he had worked with a parent of a child who was unhappy about coming into school each morning. One morning, when Oliver spoke to the parent it emerged that the child was worried about entering the classroom on his own because he was worried about leaving his mum. Oliver suggested that the child be greeted in the playground each day by the teaching assistant, who would, alongside the child's mother, take the child into the cloakroom to help settle him before going into the classroom. This worked well and after a few days the child began to build up a relationship with the teaching assistant. He was then able to go into the classroom with the teaching assistant without worrying about leaving his mum. This example from practice demonstrates how Oliver dealt with a sensitive issue and worked with parents to ensure that the issue was resolved and the child was happy.

In relation to Teachers' Standard 8e and your own practice, consider the following key questions:

- What methods of communication are used to keep parents/carers informed about pupils' needs?
- How do you know that certain methods have been effective?
- Have you had an opportunity to attend a parents' evening or contribute to a child's report through sharing your observations on a child's learning and development?
- What home–school links have you either established or continued to support?
- Are you aware of the school policy relating to the role of parents?
- Are there any events arranged through the PTA or friends of the school that you have been involved in?

(Continued)

(Continued)

- Have you sent any information home about the topic for the term?
- How do you encourage parents/carers to support their child with their homework?

Possible sources of evidence for Teachers' Standard 8e:

- Home–school liaison opportunities;
- Parent consultation events;
- Newsletters and information sheets.

Chapter summary

As a teacher, you have responsibilities on an individual level, as part of a team and as a member of the whole school. A principal duty is to gain a clear understanding of your school's role as part of the local community. Consider who is involved and how you could be involved more fully. In doing this, you will begin to understand the different ways in which teachers contribute to the life of the school and how this supports the development of relationships between school staff, children, parents, governors and members of the community. Through the interactions between school staff, pupils and parents, you will be able to observe how the school values and mission statement are evidenced. Having a clear focus on what your contribution is as a member of the school staff and where you see yourself in both the short and long term will be helpful. Be aware of how you work individually and as part of a team. How do you show that you value the contributions of your colleagues? As you consider your professional development needs, think about achieving a balance between addressing what you need to do to develop day-to-day classroom practice, the needs of the school and your long-term goals and aims. Finally, try to make every effort to build positive working relationships with parents in the life of the school. Developing strategies for including parents will enable them to feel valued as partners in their child's learning.

CHAPTER 9

PERSONAL AND PROFESSIONAL CONDUCT

Teachers' Standard Part Two

A teacher is expected to demonstrate consistently high standards of personal and professional conduct. The following statements define the behaviour and attitudes which set the required standard for conduct throughout a teacher's career:

- Teachers uphold public trust in the profession and maintain high standards of ethics and behaviour, within and outside school, by:
  - treating pupils with dignity, building relationships rooted in mutual respect, and at all times observing proper boundaries appropriate to a teacher's professional position

(Continued)

> *(Continued)*
>
> - o having regard for the need to safeguard pupils' well-being, in accordance with statutory provisions
> - o showing tolerance of and respect for the rights of others
> - o not undermining fundamental British values, including democracy, the rule of law, individual liberty and mutual respect, and tolerance of those with different faiths and beliefs
> - o ensuring that personal beliefs are not expressed in ways which exploit pupils' vulnerability or might lead them to break the law.
>
> - Teachers must have proper and professional regard for the ethos, policies and practices of the school in which they teach, and maintain high standards in their own attendance and punctuality.
> - Teachers must have an understanding of, and always act within, the statutory frameworks which set out their professional duties and responsibilities.

Since April 2012, the National College for Teaching and Leadership has been able to use Part Two of the Teachers' Standards when hearing cases of serious misconduct, regardless of the setting in which a teacher works (DfE, 2014b).

What is this all about?

Part Two encompasses one whole standard with a focus on how a teacher conducts themselves in both their personal and professional life. This is integral to all other Teachers' Standards and should not been seen as separate or unconnected. The foundation of Part Two is centred around relationships and being a role model, which takes account of an individual's values and beliefs about how to be an effective teacher. This includes considering issues of keeping children safe, safeguarding, in line with statutory policies and ensuring that teachers behave according to expectations so that they abide by the law. By developing respectful relationships with colleagues, parents and children, teachers can demonstrate how they behave in a professional manner and uphold policies. A key theme is British values and how these translate from personal beliefs to understanding and practice within the school context.

How can this be demonstrated?

Through everyday practice, teachers are able to show how they consistently uphold school policies to meet Part Two of the Teachers' Standards. This may be through observation of practice, where the observer can see how the teacher's values are evident in the way the teacher interacts, talks to others and creates a positive classroom ethos. There is a clear synthesis between practice and policy through the way the teacher manages relationships within the classroom, across the whole school and within the wider community. Evidence gained from attendance, punctuality at meetings, contribution to school events and preparation for teaching can all contribute to show how this standard is being met. In line with school policies, teachers can show how they are professional through their day-to-day behaviours, the support they provide for colleagues, advice given to parents and of course, the way that they work with the children in their care. How school policies are applied through the teacher's practice can also provide valuable evidence, for example in how the teacher manages the following in the classroom:

- health and safety issues
- behaviour management whole-school policies
- risk assessments
- staying safe online
- safeguarding
- inclusion
- equal opportunities.

Chapter overview

In this chapter, we consider what it means to be a professional and how the idea of professionalism is understood. Next, we explore what it means to be a professional in education and we go beyond defining the term to encourage you to reflect on the kind of teacher you want to be through recognising your own beliefs. The world of education is constantly changing and so the public view of how a teacher should behave and present themselves continues to be an area of importance. Yet teachers do not sit in isolation from other professionals. Cunningham (2008) notes how interdisciplinary working may result in issues of professionalism arising which go far beyond the remit of education. The impact of this places a greater onus on teachers to be aware of some of the challenges that could arise as they consider how being a teacher sits alongside being a professional in another field, such as psychology or health. In the remit of considering teaching as a profession, the chapter continues with guidance on teachers' pay and conditions, drawing on current legislation (University of Bristol, 2014) to give an overview of the statutory frameworks. There is a focus on the duties and responsibilities of education professionals, which include safeguarding, equality and inclusion, pupil safety and well-being.

Every school has its own identity. You sense this as you walk around the school and you see it in the school's mission statement and in the way staff and children interact with each other and all of this contributes to a school's unique and individual ethos.

This character of a school comes from each teacher's own values and beliefs and this will vary from one teacher to the next but all staff will be working to a shared vision. The importance of individual and shared values and beliefs within the school setting will be discussed next. The development of beliefs is considered in the context of a wider look at values in education, including what is understood by British beliefs and values.

Taking it apart and putting it back together

Part Two can be set in the context of three levels: national, school and personal (Figure 9.1). On a national level, a teacher is in the public eye and has a duty to uphold the trust of the public and have confidence in the profession. This includes an awareness of how a teacher's image is perceived and an acceptance of the

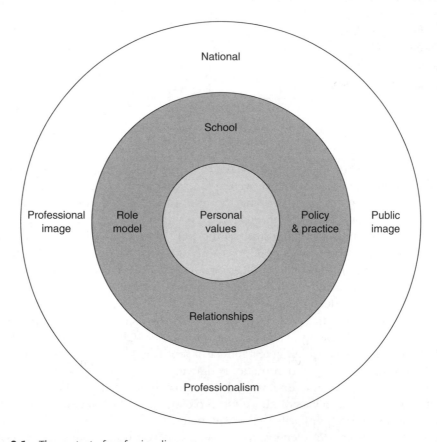

Figure 9.1 The context of professionalism

professional duties of teachers. The school context requires a teacher to follow the relevant policies and statutory professional requirements, to assume responsibility for the implementation of workplace policies and frameworks. It involves how policy is communicated in a teacher's practice. On a personal level, a teacher must examine how their own values and beliefs about education support the ethos of the school to ensure that as a teacher they do not exploit pupils.

To evidence Part Two, we will need to look at links to the other Teachers' Standards. We will take separate themes from Part Two and explore how these fit into classroom practice, for example how ideas about mutual respect can be found in behaviour management or having high expectations and how tolerance of other beliefs can be found in planning and teaching. There will be a deeper look at how teachers can evidence this standard through their daily practice in the classroom and across the school. To start this journey, we explore the notion of being a professional to encourage a deeper look at how you relate to this on a personal and professional level.

The wider context: professionalism

There is a lack of agreement about how professionalism is understood (Eraut, 1994; Sachs, 2003; Evans, 2011) and it continues to be a source of debate: 'Indeed, lack of consensus over the meaning of professionalism is widely acknowledged' (Evans, 2011: 854). The definition of teacher professionalism is informed by historical and ideological assumptions. However, Crook (2008, p. 23) suggests 'that the application of historical perspectives confirms professionalism to be an artificial construct, with ever-changing and always contested definitions'. This perspective defines professionalism as a complex process and as time-specific. Integral to this debate is a recognition of socio-cultural dimensions which provide a context for re-negotiation of professional identity over time. As Davey (2013, p. 163) explains, 'such an identity is not created in isolation from the distinctive groups of others with whom we interact in our work lives'.

Evans (2011) uses the term 'enacted professionalism' to describe a meaningful understanding of professionalism: 'enacted professionalism is constantly re-shaping itself through the dynamic agency of its practitioners' (p. 863).

A further proposition offered by Sachs (2003) defines professionalism in relation to responses to change and suggests that as professionals we have a choice in making decisions about this. Wilkins (2013) suggests that it may have been easier to shape professionalism in the past, when there were fewer directives from government: 'The old professions grew their structures and identities in this way, in the days when governments were less bothered about regulation' (p. 11).

In contrast to this belief is the notion that teaching, as a professional organisation, has a history which has been constrained by being under successive government control. As Eraut (1994, p. 3) reminds us, 'They have had some difficulty in articulating a distinctive knowledge base, and have also suffered from being under much greater government control'. Eraut (1994) recognises that teachers have less power than in other 'ideal' professions, such as law and notes that teaching has been described as a 'semi-profession'. The term 'semi-professions' grew out of public sector and educational growth and recognised that such occupations did not exhibit the traits of formal professions, such as those where practitioners work under strict ethical codes and training is controlled through a professional body, as with medicine. Millerson (1964) defined the specific characteristics of a profession and recognised that some traits appear realistic whilst others may seem restrictive. Amongst the essential traits, Millerson (1964) concludes, the following are important: 'theoretical knowledge, training and education, passing a test, code of conduct, service is for the public good and the profession is organised' (p. 4).

Whilst qualifying these characteristics may provide some understanding of what it means to be a professional, it also suggests ambiguity. Eraut (1997) examines this and puts forward the idea that a definition of professional traits has not made it any easier to characterise professionalism; rather, it has highlighted the characteristics of 'powerful professions which others seek to emulate' (p. 1). Contributing to the discussion, Watt (2014) proposes that Tristram Hunt, Labour Shadow Education Secretary, has further ideas to 'raise the standard of the teaching profession'. The agenda is to suggest that teachers are licensed which will place the professionalism of teachers in a stronger position:

> This is about growing the profession. This is about believing that teachers have this enormous importance. Just like lawyers and doctors, they should have the same professional standing which means relicensing themselves, which means continual professional development, which means being the best possible they can be. (Watt, 2014)

The introduction of the Teachers' Standards in September 2012 (DfE, 2013a) set a baseline for the conduct and practice of teachers, formally acknowledging a code which suggests a form of unity for education professionals. Evans (2011) further confirms that the Teachers' Standards 'collectively represent the professionalism that the government introducing them wants its teachers to manifest' (p. 854).

The government has currently placed importance on teaching competence with Initial Teacher Training (ITT) becoming more school-based. Blandford (2013) suggests that this is a result of recognition from political leaders that ITT is fundamental to meet the needs of societal demands and for the development of the economy. Saunders (2013) concurs: 'The rationale for this so-called new professionalism was to make England more economically competitive with its global rivals' (p. 13).

A further current government drive is encouraging all new teachers to study for a Masters' degree (DfE, 2011). Jackson (2013) offers the view that Masters' qualifications are integral to the professionalism of teaching: it supports teachers to be reflective, suggesting a move away from teachers as technicians who simply reproduce curriculum knowledge.

A further conceptualisation of professionalism is offered which defines theory and practice as co-existing, where the label of being a professional is associated with having a body of knowledge (Etzioni, 1969) and expertise (Schön, 1983). Schön (ibid.) describes the features of expertise as having expert knowledge and being able to apply that knowledge to solve problems and this includes the way in which this becomes integral to discursive practice. Integral to the discussion on understanding professionalism is a recognition that historical and social contexts have influenced educational policies and this has impacted on how the professionalism of teacher educators is understood.

Teaching as a profession

There are many challenges facing teachers, including the implementation of government policies, school structures and public ideas about what professionalism means in the context of teaching (Eraut, 1997; Evans, 2011; Jackson, 2013). You will have developed your own identity partly in response to external pressures, but hugely influential will be your own goals, pedagogy and philosophy about teaching and learning. Petty (2009) uses a teacher self-analysis questionnaire to help teachers evaluate their approach. The analysis from the questionnaire provides the reader with an overview of their preferred style as a teacher, which is loosely based on being either a facilitator, where pupils are in control, or an instructor, where the teacher is in control. Do you believe it is the child or the teacher that has the power over learning? For many teachers, control is very likely to be on a continuum between instructing and facilitating as teaching and learning are negotiated within the classroom. Buckler and Castle (2014) relate the instructor model to teacher-centred, where learning is seen as passive. Conversely, they suggest that the learner-centred approach supports active learning using a constructivist approach. Where you fit on the continuum will not only be based on your outlook but the context within which you work will also be significant.

Something all effective teachers have in common is the ability to reflect, take responsibility for their professional development and act as a role model for life-long learning. Where do you think you best sit? Are you engaged or sitting on the sidelines? McMahon et al. (2011) have located teacher development within school improvement where there is a connection between the wider context and the teachers' skills and knowledge. However, a teacher must take responsibility for their own development through recognising areas in need of improvement and taking action to address any gaps in knowledge and skills. This action could take the form of professional discussions with colleagues, attending an external course, reading, in-school training sessions or meetings, taking qualifications or carrying out research in the classroom. This is not an exhaustive list but the point is that teachers need to take ownership of and drive their own professional development, rather than have it imposed on them. Ewans (2014) outlines the value of professional development and links this to being a reflective practitioner: 'since the aim of reflective practice is the improvement of performance, and a self-critical disposition can assist in this' (p. 144). Effective professional development opportunities include recognising the synthesis between theory and practice, which need to work hand in hand (McMahon et al., 2011). In this way, teachers can take an element of their practice and through enquiry, using literature and research, 'critically reflect on their personal and professional values, past experiences and educational practice' (ibid. p. 81). In the Teachers' Standards, TS 8 makes clear the importance of professional development where teachers 'keep their knowledge and skills as teachers up to date and are self-critical'. Effective teachers understand that professional development is ongoing throughout their career; there is no quick fix answer or one-off solution. There is ebb and flow within practice where teachers gain knowledge, apply it and other needs emerge. There is a spiral effect within the teaching profession where teachers never stop learning and there is a recognition of and commitment to life-long learning.

The school context: the responsible job of teaching

So far, we have attempted to define what it means to be a professional and how it is understood. As a professional, teachers make a difference to the lives of the pupils they teach. As you consider your qualities as a teacher, you will be able to reflect on the teachers that have inspired and motivated you throughout your education, both as a child and as an adult. There is a plethora of literature about how to become an effective teacher or be successful in your chosen career (Castle and Buckler, 2009; Loughran, 2010; Barton, 2015; Rubie-Davies, 2015). Menter (2010) identifies the following four models of perceptions of teachers:

- The effective teacher: standards and competences. This concept has a political stance and is embedded in the testing and accountability regimes. The introduction of Teachers' Standards in September 2012 (DfE, 2013a) set a baseline for the conduct and practice of teachers, formally acknowledging a code which suggests a form of unity for education professionals. Evans (2011) further confirms that the Teachers' Standards 'collectively represent the professionalism that the government introducing them wants its teachers to manifest' (p. 854).
- The reflective teacher: Menter (2010) acknowledged that the roots of the reflective teacher were embedded in views from John Dewey who proposed that this approach 'was based on teachers becoming active decision-makers in their professional work' (p. 22). The work of Donald Schön (1983) is equally as influential in recognising the dedication of practitioners to their professional development, based on an individual's values.
- The enquiring teacher: the approaches evident in this practice suggest that the teacher is involved in enquiry and research. This may be through action research, for example.

- The transformative teacher: reflection and enquiry are evident in this approach. It recognises that teachers contribute to changes in society through the way that they prepare pupils to also contribute to societal changes. Given this stance, it acknowledges that there may be tensions between the education system and the values of the teacher and it is part of 'bringing about a more just education system, where inequalities in society begin to be addressed and where progressive social change can be stimulated' (Menter, 2010, p. 25).

You may identify aspects of different models which fit your own paradigm of the way you view education. The models represent extremes but 'not necessarily polar opposites' (Menter, 2010, p. 24) and you may find that there is a continuum where you place yourself on the spectrum between models. An example may be the way you reflect on practice in order to develop professionally, whilst recognising a need to be transformative in the way that children are supported to be able to cope with and contribute to changes in society.

A responsibility of teachers is to be true to their own vision of education whilst upholding the values of the school and being sincere as they demonstrate their understanding through their daily practice.

Policy and practice

The professional duties of a teacher are shaped by statutory legislation and guidance. A teacher needs to be aware of legal frameworks and acts which relate to professional conduct and conditions of service (Jacques and Hyland, 2010). Legislation includes the latest School Teachers' Pay and Conditions statutory and non-statutory guidance (DfE, 2014e), which changes annually, The Education Act 2011 and Schools: Statutory guidance for schools and local authorities (DfE, 2014e). Teachers will identify with the policies and endorse them in their professional practice. Teachers have rights and should be aware of these, drawing on the support of colleagues and teaching unions as well as government and teaching websites as useful sources of information. *The Bristol Guide* (University of Bristol, 2014) is an invaluable book which provides a friendly overview of a teacher's statutory responsibilities. The key areas to be aware of are equality and inclusion, child protection and child safety and well-being. These are all important and it is critical that you become familiar with and confident in managing issues relating to these aspects of practice.

Equality and inclusion

These aspects include having an understanding of children within specific groups which may be identified through gender, social class, attainment or ethnicity (Petty, 2009). An understanding of legislation, including the Equality Act 2010, will support the teacher to develop their practice by planning for the diverse range of learners in their class, as well as making learning accessible through the strategies they employ (Petty, 2009). Robinson et al. (2013) provide a very useful reference to teaching inclusively.

Child protection

A critical and integral part of practice and a key priority for all teachers is the subject of child protection. This encompasses several areas including keeping up to date with safeguarding training. Government guidance stresses that this should take place at least every three years. It is a statutory requirement for teachers to update their knowledge of legislation and guidance and to take action if they have concerns about the safety and welfare of children (DfE, 2014g). Teachers should recognise signs of abuse, including neglect, physical abuse, emotional abuse and sexual abuse. Professional organisations are worth contacting for further guidance and information or for up-to-date support on specific safeguarding issues, such as the National Society for the Prevention of Cruelty to Children (NSPCC). Guidance is also available on government sites accessed through the website www.gov.uk. Every school will have a child protection policy and a Designated Person who is the key person responsible for issues regarding child protection. It is every adult's responsibility to read the policy, to find out who the Designated Person is in a school and to know what steps to take in cases of suspected child abuse.

Child safety and well-being

The Children Act 2004 stipulates the legal responsibilities of schools. It has implications for teachers and this includes having an understanding of keeping children safe. A teacher is deemed to be acting in loco parentis, assuming responsibility for the children in their care as any reasonable parent would. As part of a teacher's duty of care towards children, they must be aware of issues such as bullying and cyber bullying. These are serious issues and must not be regarded as commonplace by teachers (Jaques and Hyland, 2010). It is essential that teachers familiarise themselves with the school policy on bullying and discipline. Other aspects of keeping children safe include developing an awareness of drugs and health and safety as they relate to children and a teacher's own health and safety (the Health and Safety at Work Act 1974). Schools will have a designated member of staff responsible for health and safety. Other key areas for teachers are risk assessments and school trips (University of Bristol, 2014). Teachers often carry out risk assessments for a specific area of the curriculum and this is to be expected as it is the teacher who has specialist knowledge of the children, however they must ensure that they have had appropriate support and training in the principles of risk assessment. Each school will have a policy and a member of staff who will be responsible for this aspect of practice. As well as knowing who in school has the responsibility for child safety, teachers have an individual duty to know how to draw on support and to refer to colleagues for specialist support when required.

We have set out the importance of the national and local contexts and now consider on a personal level how a teacher demonstrates their commitment to Part Two of the Teachers' Standards.

The personal context: values and beliefs

A teacher decides to enter a career in teaching because they value education and believe that every child has a right to an education. Yet this is complex as a teacher's values will influence the kind of education children receive. The values a teacher holds will be evident in their practice, as well as in the way they model this to pupils and in return the pupils will respond to the context they are in (Ewans, 2014). The organisation of learning and the classroom will further demonstrate what the teacher thinks about teaching and learning. A challenge lies in making sure a teacher's values are not imposed on a child. It must be remembered that children will hold their own values about the world and about education. At times, there may be a discrepancy between the values held by children and by the teacher, for example children may have formed their values based on family principles which may lie in contrast to those of the school. In this case, it provides a challenge as the teacher accepts the child's views at the same time as supporting the child to retain ownership of their thinking, whilst encouraging them to question their views and helping them to form their own world view (Taylor and Woolley, 2013). The teacher must learn to respect the fact that others, adults and children, may hold a different view to them and show acceptance of this. Values and beliefs of what education should be are evident in policies and statutory frameworks. Policy is instrumental and has to be considered by schools and this is addressed in the National Curriculum (DfEE, 1999) where a list of values is set out, although not an exhaustive list, that was agreed by a National Forum for Values in Education and the Community. It is suggested that if teachers and schools follow these principles, then they will have the support of the general public:

> Schools and teachers can have confidence that there is general agreement in society on these values. They can therefore expect the support and encouragement of society if they base their teaching and the school ethos on these values. (DEE, 1999, p. 147)

These values are identified in four key areas:

1. *The self:* we value ourselves as unique human beings capable of spiritual, moral, intellectual and physical growth and development.
2. *Relationships:* we value others for themselves, not only for what they have or what they can do for us. We value relationships as fundamental to the development and fulfilment of ourselves and others and to the good of the community.

3. *Society:* we value truth, freedom, justice, human rights, the rule of law and collective effort for the common good. In particular, we value families as sources of love and support for all their members and as the basis of a society in which people care for others.

4. *The environment:* we value the environment, both natural and shaped by humanity, as the basis of life and a source of wonder and inspiration.

As you consider the values set out by the DEE (1999), you will be able to assess how fundamental the values are and how links can be made between education and society. Teachers are in a position of great responsibility, are under scrutiny of government bodies, are accountable to parents/carers and governors and have a duty of care for the children they teach.

Le Métais (as cited in Arthur and Cremin, 2004) states how values are considered as beliefs which define the school and classroom organisation, which in turn can be seen in the curriculum, the teaching and the assessment procedures within the setting. Meanwhile, Woolley (2010) provides a gentle reminder of the way that we think about education and states that teachers need to reflect on their values so that they can demonstrate and model the 'fairness and acceptance we engender in our learners' (p. 21). Our philosophy will be influenced by the range of values that we hold. How have you reached your decisions on classroom organisation, the curriculum, teaching methods and strategies? These will all be selected based on your core values and beliefs and on your personal perspectives. Carr (2006) identifies principled dispositions in which the teacher places importance on values that run deep and are evident in the very character of a person.

The way a teacher's values and beliefs underpin their practice will be evident in observable traits – through their feelings, their behaviours and the outcome or impact which will be seen in a teacher's practice (Figure 9.2). As we consider this model of working, let us visit the idea by exploring the value of independence. A teacher who places importance on supporting children to become independent learners will value a range of feelings of empowerment. This may include opportunities for children to make decisions and choices for themselves, where feelings of being confident are recognised. The result of this may be raised self-esteem, where every child feels their contribution is valued and respected and there is a feeling of trust where children are less dependent on others. The kind of behaviour the teacher demonstrates in the classroom would be evidenced by encouraging children to make their own choices, perhaps through using the language of choice as a behaviour management strategy, where a child would be given two options to decide between. It could be by giving children class responsibilities where they are in charge of registering themselves, getting their own resources or self-assessment. It can be seen daily in practice as teachers encourage children to ask questions and adopt investigative, enquiry-based teaching and learning strategies. Feelings, behaviour and the impact or outcome of these are inextricably linked. Consider how this model will look in a classroom where the teacher values inclusion, pupil voice, collaborative working, real contexts for learning and outdoor learning, to name a few. Built into such a model of working is a recognition that teachers assume responsibility for the classroom ethos, which is dependent on the importance a teacher places on identified values. This rather suggests that a teacher has autonomy over their practice, but in reality it may be bound up with values imposed by society and government or school policies.

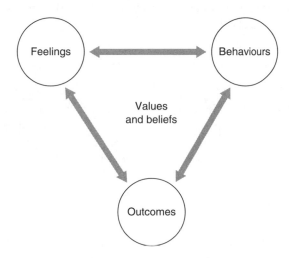

Figure 9.2   Values and Beliefs

It is important not to lose sight of the reason for wanting to enter the field of education and teaching. Through consideration of your motivation for wanting to be a teacher, you will identify your personal values. It is worth taking some time to reflect on what your own motivation is. This may be the desire to make a difference to the lives of others or to contribute to raising achievement so that every child can reach their potential. Teachers impact on the lives of their learners and make a difference to the children in their care.

Now we reach an aporia, a stop point, in which we reflect on how you have recognised the kind of teacher you want to be, based on the values you hold. Effective teachers understand the importance and impact of their behaviour. What does this look like in the classroom? In your practice? Consider the *Top Tips* and practice examples to help you think about your own practice, to learn from what you do and then consider further learning and development. Is your development linked to ideas about your personal growth or intrinsic motivation (Dinham and Scott, 1998, 2000), based on wanting to make a difference in the world of education (cited in Robinson et al., 2013)? The way you manage teaching and learning will be based on a combination of the context you are working in, your knowledge and skills and your underpinning values. Values are an important driver. As Petty (2009) recognises, 'they often decide your strategies, your tactics and ultimately your behaviour' (p. 507).

The Teachers' Standards emphasise competency for professional accountability and quality assurance. As well as teachers using the standards to support external legislation, there is an opportunity to reflect on norms and values and professional development needs. There is a chance to consider how the standards are used by teachers and what they look like in practice. By looking closely at the values you hold, you can start to explore the links between these and the British values set out in Part Two of the Teachers' Standards.

British values

In June 2014, Michael Gove, the Secretary of State for Education at that time, stated that it would be compulsory for schools to promote British values from September 2014. The Education (Independent School Standards) (England) (Amendment) Regulations 2014 for the new social, moral, spiritual and cultural (SMSC) standard came into force on 29 September 2014 (DfE, 2014h).

Part Two of the Teachers' Standards states that teachers uphold trust by: 'not undermining fundamental British values, including democracy, the rule of law, individual liberty and mutual respect, and tolerance of those with different faiths and beliefs.'

The government defines what is meant by British values and these are explicitly outlined in the statement above. Through promotion of these values, schools can demonstrate how they are meeting the requirements of section 78 of the Education Act 2002, in their provision of spiritual, moral, social and cultural (SMSC) aspects (DfE, 2014h). However, within schools teachers need to hold a shared understanding of what is understood by British values to ensure a wider awareness of practice in relation to the promotion of such values. For many schools, a consideration of values is nothing new and they already engage in supporting children to work together within their communities. The values held by the school will be evident in the way that the school is managed, through its ethos and embedded in its mission statement. In some school policies, the rights and responsibilities of the school community will be set out and this may be evident in procedures such as school and class rules.

The curriculum in schools in England is a vehicle through which the values of democracy, individual liberty, mutual respect and tolerance of different faiths can be accessed. Through practice, teachers can actively promote these values and this may be through challenging opposing views held by children or adults in school that conflict with fundamental British values (DfE, 2014h). It has been highlighted how the Teachers' Standards state that teachers should uphold public trust in the profession and maintain high standards of ethics and behaviour, within and outside school. This includes the augmentation of British values. Expanding on this, it is necessary to place our understanding within a wider context which links to society and community.

Government-led ideology has driven forward a programme which recognises possible tensions in some communities and through education attempts have been made to provide coherence in societies and 'to formulate and promote a set of values that would underpin a harmonious and diverse society' (Ewans, 2014, p. 162). Cooper (2014) recognises that some teachers may feel uncomfortable with this political stance, which has its roots in counter terrorism and 'which has arisen as a result of the Home Office Prevent strategy for counter terrorism' (Elton-Chalcraft et al., 2013, cited in Cooper, 2014, p. 249). The suggestion is that there may be a bias and a possible mis-interpretation of Islam. This serves to reinforce what a complex issue it is to determine a shared understanding of fundamental British values. Teachers need to be able to consider how their own values, alongside legislation, inform practice. It is hard not to accept the values as set out in Part Two and surely these are at the heart of all communities, regardless of race or religion.

Values in education: evidencing through practice

Values are embedded in the daily practice of teachers, in the interactions between parents, staff and children and they are evident in school policies. Every school is different and the values of each school will shape the character of the setting. Although Part Two does not require you to evidence the values, it is important to understand what they look like in practice and how you contribute to a shared understanding alongside colleagues in school. To do this, we look through the lens of the school curriculum, classroom practice and teaching strategies. Some schools follow a values-based education. This is where different values are the focus of how the children, learn, behave and treat each other within and beyond the school environment. The teachers and children model the values in their daily practice and this is planned into the curriculum. (Further reading which may be helpful can be accessed at www.valuesbasededucation.com/vbe.html.) It can be difficult for children to understand about values and schools address this in different ways. Some schools include a whole-school policy with a focus on values education which is integral to each and every class within the school. Other schools make their values explicit through their mission statement. Each school will evidence its values through its everyday rules and routines, the influence of which will be seen in the daily practice of adults and children within the setting. Schools include the pupil voice in values education through such forums as school councils where children are elected by their peers to sit on a board and give the view of their classmates so that every class is represented in decision making.

A meaningful importance is placed on specific elements, such as those listed below:

- *Teaching and learning:* being ready for learning, being well prepared and having the right equipment, being punctual and having good attendance, being an active member of the school.

- *Property:* looking after our own property through being tidy and keeping things in the correct place, looking after other people's property and not taking something that does not belong to us, taking care of the environment inside and outside.
- *School resources:* putting things back in the place where they belong, looking after school equipment.
- *Behaviours:* treating others with respect and consideration, having zero tolerance to bullying, managing feelings and emotions, being helpful and polite to others, trying our best.
- *The environment:* not dropping litter, staying on the paths, not using the grassy areas when it is muddy, taking care of the different areas in school, such as the dining room, our classroom and the playground and field.

An obvious question to ask is, why have you chosen to teach at a specific school? Why that place and not a different setting? This sense of connectedness will be based on your personal values and beliefs. You will have gained a sense of the ethos and character of the school to which you can relate and in which you feel comfortable. It is in this setting that you can contribute to the school's aims and vision through your own behaviours, in the way you speak and relate to other adults and children, in your planning and teaching and in this way you portray to the general public what it means to be a professional.

What do values look like in classroom practice?

Values form an integral part of the classroom environment and are used to support children to appreciate and understand how to participate as an active member of the school community. Table 9.1 offers some ideas of values but should not be taken as an exhaustive list.

Table 9.1   Overview of care values

Respect	Courage	Appreciation	Co-operation
Fairness	Responsibility	Tolerance	Honesty
Friendship	Cooperation	Democracy	Trust
Care	Happiness	Determination	Patience

Values support children to develop a love of learning, being active rather than passive in the learning process and to have respect for themselves and others. Although values can be taught in all lessons and are evident through such opportunities as discussions, debates, having a view and making decisions, they filter through every aspect of school life. Teaching strategies and activities offer chances to clarify and explore values and the position of others, where children can talk and listen to each other within a safe environment. The teacher's role is important as a facilitator and the teacher can be a positive role model. The following case studies are examples of values evident in everyday practice.

Ben: a Year 2 teacher

Ben places importance on supporting the children in his Year 2 class to be autonomous, independent learners. The value of building relationships with his class which are rooted in mutual respect is evident in his classroom practice where he starts with planning. Ben plans opportunities within the curriculum which enable the children to make choices and decisions for themselves. He listens to their ideas and views and considers these thoughts when designing the curriculum. One way he does this is through the planning of a geography unit of work on the school grounds. He uses an enquiry approach which is investigative. The children come up with their own questions about an identified place and then collect data to find the answers. They interpret the data and then decide on the course of action that should be taken. Ben always ensures the children are able to disseminate their findings to other members of staff and other classes. Consequently, the children develop confidence in using this approach which results in them feeling empowered and showing respect as they listen to each other's ideas and take into account the opinions of their peers. Ben's role is pivotal in supporting the children to make decisions about their learning and behaviour and to consider how they can show respect towards each other in their work. This approach helps the children to take ownership of their learning, feel fully engaged and able to ask questions to find the answers for themselves. Ben understands the value of using this approach to build positive working relationships.

Jo: a Reception class teacher

For the last two years, Jo has been involved with a local university in which she has worked alongside tutors to support teaching sessions. This has involved Jo taking her class along to work with the trainee teachers at the university. Jo is an experienced teacher who understands the importance of having a professional regard for the ethos, policies and practices of the school in which she teaches. This is evident to the trainee teachers who notice that the way she treats the children with respect follows that school's philosophy of a values-based education. From the outset, the children made choices such as making a judgement about what they thought of the activity the trainees had planned and it was skilfully managed as Jo encouraged the children to use their thumb to show whether the activity was good (thumb up), OK in parts (thumb in the middle) or not really enjoyable (thumb down). As the children made their choices, they were encouraged to think for themselves, not copy the person next to them and then justify why they had made that decision. Jo also encouraged the children to say thank you individually to the adults who they had worked with, making this a meaningful exercise, rooted in respect, as opposed to an en-masse thank you which did not carry much meaning.

Ultimately, the teaching of values encourages children to develop through the emotional, social, moral and cultural aspects of learning. This contributes to raising standards in school through supporting children to become empowered and take responsibility for their learning.

Links between the Teachers' Standards and Part Two

Since April 2012, the National College for Teaching and Leadership has been able to use Part Two of the Teachers' Standards when hearing cases of serious misconduct. The emphasis of Part Two is on both personal and professional conduct and it is stated that teachers uphold public trust in the profession and maintain high standards of ethics and behaviour, within and outside school. Given that Part Two is addressed as a separate section of the Teachers' Standards, it may appear as disconnected to TS 1–8. Yet this is far from true. Part Two sits in partnership with all of the other standards and acts as the foundation on which to set the other standards in context. The link between the Teachers' Standards and Part Two can be evidenced through teachers' behaviour and professionalism, both throughout the school and in daily classroom practice. Table 9.2 sets out the correlations between each of the Teachers' Standards and Part Two.

Table 9.2 The Teachers' Standards and links to Part Two

Teachers' Standard	Relationship to Part Two through:
Teachers' Standard 1 Set high expectations which inspire, motivate and challenge pupils	<ul><li>treating pupils with dignity</li><li>building relationships rooted in mutual respect</li><li>setting clear boundaries appropriate to a teacher's professional position</li><li>being a good role model for children, parents and colleagues</li><li>ensuring that personal beliefs are not expressed in ways which exploit pupils' vulnerability or might lead them to break the law</li></ul>
Teachers' Standard 2 Promote good progress and outcomes by pupils	<ul><li>ensuring that personal beliefs are not expressed in ways which exploit pupils' vulnerability or might lead them to break the law</li></ul>
Teachers' Standard 3 Demonstrate good subject and curriculum knowledge	<ul><li>not undermining fundamental British values, including democracy, the rule of law, individual liberty and mutual respect, and tolerance of those with different faiths and beliefs</li></ul>
Teachers' Standard 4 Plan and teach well structured lessons	<ul><li>showing tolerance of and respect for the rights of others</li><li>not undermining fundamental British values, including democracy, the rule of law, individual liberty and mutual respect, and tolerance of those with different faiths and beliefs</li></ul>

(Continued)

(Continued)

Teachers' Standard	Relationship to Part Two through:
Teachers' Standard 5 Adapt teaching to respond to the strengths and needs of all pupils	• showing tolerance of and respect for the rights of others not undermining fundamental British values, including democracy, the rule of law, individual liberty and mutual respect, and tolerance of those with different faiths and beliefs • showing tolerance of and respect for the rights of others
Teachers' Standard 6 Make accurate and productive use of assessment	• Teachers must have proper and professional regard for the ethos, policies and practices of the school in which they teach
Teachers' Standard 7 Manage behaviour effectively to ensure a good and safe learning environment	• showing tolerance of and respect for the rights of others • ensuring that personal beliefs are not expressed in ways which exploit pupils' vulnerability or might lead them to break the law
Teachers' Standard 8 Fulfil wider professional responsibilities	• teacher conduct demonstrates a highly professional approach to teaching. understanding and demonstrating that their own conduct is appropriate at all times • Teachers must have an understanding of, and always act within, the statutory frameworks which set out their professional duties and responsibilities • Teachers must have proper and professional regard for the ethos, policies and practices of the school in which they teach • having regard for the need to safeguard pupils' well-being, in accordance with statutory provisions

At times, teachers may find their values and beliefs sit in conflict with the values and beliefs of others. Whilst sticking to core beliefs, it is worth considering how to show respect for those who hold a different view, how to show and demonstrate acceptance and support learners to develop their own values. Reading through school policies can be helpful in exploring what the guidelines are for the school and how these sit in relation to other aspects of the curriculum. It is each teacher's duty to take the initiative in order to gain clarity about how the policies relate to daily practice, so that workplace expectations can be managed with confidence.

Chapter summary

Throughout this chapter, the professional and personal behaviours of teachers have been discussed. In practice, the majority of decisions about teaching and learning are based on the values and beliefs of the school community. What it means to be a professional and a teacher belonging to a profession have been considered in relation to the views held by the public. We must remember what an important and vital job teaching is. In fact, it is held in such high esteem by the general public that it places teaching in the top two most respected professions, alongside medicine (DfES, 2002). Teachers demonstrate their values by maintaining high standards of behaviour on a personal and professional level. This holds when they are both in and outside school.

All teachers are assessed against the Teachers' Standards through the school's appraisal process, providing a platform for professional development. The links between professional development and school improvement have been identified and acknowledged as important, as teachers can identify areas of strength and areas for development. It has been shown that in schools that place CPD at the heart of schools' planning for improvement and that integrate performance management, self-review and CPD into a coherent cycle, teaching and learning improve and standards are raised (Ofsted, 2006). As well as recognising the value of professional development, teachers are aware of the needs of others. By upholding school policies that support school practice, they implement them in teaching, learning and the wider aspects of school life. Further information and reading can be found on the following helpful websites:

www.parliament.uk/education/teaching-resources-lesson-plans
www.teachingtimes.com/articles/what-is-britishness-gove-british-values-in-schools.htm
www.unicef.org.uk/rights-respecting-schools/

CHAPTER 10

KEEPING THE 'L' PLATES: LIFE-LONG LEARNER

What is this all about?

It's that 'stepping into the telephone box moment', where you commence the transition from trainee to teacher and transform, with the speed of a superhero, into an alternative version of yourself, complete with costume, super-teacher powers and well-rehearsed mission statement. Recognising the importance of transition from trainee to teacher and allowing the time and space for this transformation are a vital part of professional development. Sadly, a telephone box is not provided with your certificate of QTS, but perhaps more should be made of the moment when you pat yourself on the back and shout from the rooftops, 'I did it!', for becoming a teacher is no mean feat and your hard work is about the pay-off.

Building on existing subject knowledge in all aspects of national curricula appropriate to the age range of pupils within your setting, coupled with a secure grounding of the requirements and demands of the teaching profession, are essential prerequisites for a newly qualified teacher (NQT) embarking on their induction period.

In addition, knowledge of how to progress in the teaching profession, the supportive mechanisms available to teachers and the importance of continued professional reflection and development, warrant careful consideration.

Chapter overview

As the NQT induction period is often daunting and busy for those new to the profession, Chapter 10 will discuss the transition from trainee to teacher and consider the continuing development of the professional, in relation to the Teachers' Standards (DfE, 2013a, 2014f). The chapter will outline expectations for the NQT induction period, with a focus on continued development through reflective practice; identify key staging posts, roles and responsibilities; and consider evidence for progress reports and practical advice on how to ensure the Teachers' Standards are met, in time for the successful completion of NQT induction. This will include the value and importance of continuing professional development (CPD) and exemplar case studies. The chapter will also explore how to embed the Teachers' Standards in professional practice as a recently qualified teacher (RQT), in preparation for a developing career, performance management and subsequent teacher 'threshold' assessments. In addition, the chapter will consider how to make the most of these crucial preliminary stages in career development, prepare trainees for the rigour involved in teaching and develop excellent habits for future, research-informed practice. Further details and guidance can be found in the Department for Education's Induction for Newly Qualified Teachers (England) document (DfE, 2014d). We will draw on this document, in addition to a range of research, as a theoretical underpinning for the sections that follow.

Crossing the bridge: transition from trainee to teacher

On successful completion of your training and having secured your first teaching appointment, now is the time to reflect on the blood, sweat and tears that went into gaining your teaching qualification. The time to make a difference is here, finally.

For many newly qualified teachers (NQTs), the prospect of embarking on your career, without the 'safety net' of the training provider, can be a daunting experience. In order to reassure you, however, there is support available to you from many different sources and it is important to be able to identify the support that is on offer during the early stages of your career.

Your employer will be your primary source of support and schools often have very comprehensive and structured induction programmes to help NQTs during their early careers. This will be discussed in greater depth later in this chapter. In addition, many training providers maintain high levels of optional support for NQTs, including alumni events; support forums; contact with the training team; and support blogs or online engagement. If you choose to be part of a teaching union, this is another valuable source of support. The Department for Education has developed clear statutory guidance for NQT induction (DfE, 2014d). Whilst settings may vary slightly in approaches and guidelines, this is an entitlement for NQTs and an excellent tool to support your development: statutory induction is the bridge between initial teacher training and a career in teaching. It combines a personalised programme of development, support and professional dialogue with monitoring and an assessment of performance against the relevant standards. The programme should support the newly qualified teacher (NQT) in demonstrating that their performance against the relevant standards is satisfactory by the end of the period and equip them with the tools to be an effective and successful teacher (DfE, 2014d, p. 7). Remember, your employer has chosen you out of many potential candidates during rigorous selection and recruitment processes and therefore, you have demonstrated the skills, knowledge, understanding and attributes required to be an effective teacher. This should boost your self-esteem and promote an 'I can' attitude. As a teacher, you have already made a commitment to life-long learning. When we are learning, we make mistakes and in turn, we learn from these in order to be the best we can be for the children we teach. As an NQT, you are still learning and it is expected that your practice will require refinement, over time.

When approaching your induction period, however, as Beadle (2010, p. 1) reminds us, it is important to maintain a realistic outlook:

> Make no mistake. Your first year as a teacher is tough; nothing like the permanently uplifting stroll you may have been sold by glossy government adverts and brochures. Your days can be confusing, spirit crushing, depressing, frightening even, but you will also have moments of profound joy, in which you see why some regard it as being the best job in the world; moments where you feel 'part of the solution'. (These will last exactly until the next lesson when you are immediately and summarily turned over by Year 4/5/6, and spat out shuddering.)

Whilst this provides a somewhat 'tongue-in-cheek' perspective, it is important to recognise that the journey to success requires continued effort on your part and the development of self-esteem through this. As Dweck (2013, p. 4) asserts:

> Self-esteem is not something we give to people by telling them about their high intelligence. It is something we equip them to get for themselves – by teaching them to value learning over the appearance of smartness, to relish challenge and effort, and to use errors as routes to mastery.

As an NQT, you would be forgiven for expressing the desire to ditch those 'L' plates and be respected as a fully qualified, competent and enthusiastic new addition to any teaching team. It is not unreasonable to want to fast-track along those 'routes to mastery' and be the best, now. There is nothing wrong with having high expectations and striving to be a great teacher, but remember that you are still on your own learning journey and that being 'the best' can take time, patience, support and perseverance. Don't be afraid to 'keep the "L" plates' and recognise the importance of life-long learning. A balanced approach to your induction period, whereby you engage in reflective practice in order to develop, over time, is a reasonable expectation. Be sure to allow yourself this when preparing for your new career. In addition to the support that is available to you, it is essential to be prepared before commencing your induction period, in order to begin to pave the way to successful completion and the best outcome for the pupils in your care.

The three 'Rs': getting a head start through reconnaissance, resources and reflection

In this section, we will examine ways in which you can begin to prepare, followed by examples from practice in order to support your transition. Before you begin, you may wish to consider the following question: What is it really like to have responsibility for a class and supporting adults, on a day-to-day basis and to be accountable for pupil progress and well-being?

It is important to find the answer as quickly as possible on engagement with a teaching post in order to best prepare for your new career and approach it with a realistic outlook. Up until this point, your school experiences have provided an important part of the whole picture and the opportunity for you to grow and develop within the safety of a training situation. Becoming a teacher and taking responsibility for your own group of pupils could be likened to the stabilisers being removed from a push bike: the expectation is not for you to ride, un-aided and without support, straight away, but rather to engage with the support that stabilisers provide and remove them when you feel ready and over time.

Visits to settings

It is a good idea to try to visit the setting in which you will be teaching as much as possible, with the permission of the leadership team. Visits can provide you with a wealth of information in order to inform your future practice, in addition to being a conduit through which you can begin to 'get a feel' for your workplace, colleagues and pupils. Visits enable you to begin to gather resources and ideas and subsequent reflections facilitate forward planning. This is an important step in transition and through observation and discussion, it is an excellent opportunity to build on your evidence of meeting the Teachers' Standards.

Table 10.1 is intended as a useful tool in supporting first steps, which we would encourage you to develop and tailor to your own developing needs. As a starting

Table 10.1 Examples from the Teachers' Standards to support your first steps

Teachers' Standard	How can I achieve this?
2b: Be aware of pupils' capabilities and their prior knowledge, and plan teaching to build on these.	Get to know the pupils through liaison with the teaching team and, where possible, observation. Ask about teacher record keeping and pupil progress records – these will give you an important overview of pupil strengths and developmental needs. Use this information to begin to plan ahead.
3a: Have a secure knowledge of the relevant subject(s) and curriculum areas, foster and maintain pupils' interest in the subject, and address misunderstandings.	Improve your subject knowledge to teach further, specific to the age phase in which you will be teaching, through observation of teaching and liaison with teachers, TAs and other adults. Get to know the pupils (if possible) and speak to them about their interests.
5c: Demonstrate an awareness of the physical, social and intellectual development of children, and know how to adapt teaching to support pupils' education at different stages of development; and 5d: Have a clear understanding of the needs of all pupils, including those with special educational needs; those of high ability; those with English as an additional language; those with disabilities; and be able to use and evaluate distinctive teaching approaches to engage and support them.	If it is possible to engage with the pupils with whom you will be working, you will begin to develop an overview of their capabilities and needs. It will be essential to triangulate your observations and interactions with teacher data and, if applicable, records of interventions from external agencies. Upon analysis, a picture will begin to emerge and will provide you with an excellent grounding to enable you to better cater for pupil needs, ahead of the academic year. By engaging with pupils, you have the important opportunity to talk to them about what engages them and what they feel they are good at.
6a: Know and understand how to assess the relevant subject and curriculum areas, including statutory assessment requirements.	If you are able to conduct observations of teaching, you will see 'live assessment' and this can be enriched through evaluative discussions with the teaching team and formal recorded assessments.
7a: Have clear rules and routines for behaviour in classrooms, and take responsibility for promoting good and courteous behaviour both in classrooms and around the school, in accordance with the school's behaviour policy.	This opportunity is two-fold: it allows the chance to see school policies in action, in addition to giving you the chance to demonstrate your own capabilities in this area. It is important to establish excellent practice in behaviour management, with non-negotiable high expectations at all times, for all pupils.
8a: Make a positive contribution to the wider life and ethos of the school.	What do you have to offer? Perhaps this is an opportunity to discuss this with the head teacher and mentor and reflect on the needs of the setting.
8b: Develop effective professional relationships with colleagues, knowing how and when to draw on advice and specialist support.	View visit opportunities as an extension of the interview process. How you conduct yourself during these visits and the efforts you make to develop professional relationships will be under scrutiny – first impressions count.

point, we have selected examples from the Teachers' Standards and suggested ways in which you can use 'reconnaissance' in supporting your preparation.

Getting your head in the game

In the interests of starting your career with success, it is important to ensure that you are well prepared for the challenges ahead. Here are some *Top Tips* to help you 'get your head in the game'.

 Top Tips:

1. Get a diary and plan your time carefully.
2. Pre-consider how you will achieve a work–life balance. Examine your teaching timetable, allowing time for assessments, meetings, etc. and plan your social and domestic circumstances to complement this.
3. Be aware of 'hot spots' in the academic year. A prior knowledge of this will be helpful in avoiding some of those last-minute panics.
4. Plan for some 'me time'. The role of a teacher can be very demanding and it is important that you make time for yourself.
5. Talk. Talk to colleagues, peers, family and friends about your transition and your developing needs. Ask questions and consider the answers. Gain perspective from the insights of others and develop self-belief and confidence.
6. Dedicate time to prepare for your first term and explore every possible avenue in ensuring that you 'hit the ground running'.
7. Reflect on your training and your engagement with theory. Consider how this will translate into everyday practice.

Making the most of your time: three simple exercises

Between successful completion of your training and your first appointment, you may have the gift of 'time'. It is a good idea to begin to prepare for the new academic year and it can be an exciting time as you ready and refine your resources in time for your first day:

1. If you are commencing post at the start of an academic year, you may wish to begin to plan your learning environment. Refer to previous chapters for excellent ideas to get you started. This may involve the preparation of display items, engaging resources or simply ways in which you intend to facilitate independent learning and transition.

> 💡 *Top Tip*: Find an old shoe box and odds and ends of paper and card. Envisage the box as your learning environment and begin to plan the layout by cutting and pasting items of furniture, resources, etc. Play around with layouts until you feel comfortable and do not be afraid to come back to this at a later stage: classroom environments are flexible and should be adapted, throughout the year, to meet the changing needs of your pupils.

2. You may also have the opportunity to discuss curriculum planning with colleagues. It is good practice to research curriculum content ahead of time and to use this knowledge to enhance your planning and future teaching. Where meeting in person is not feasible, e-links could be made with colleagues; you can then begin to get a feel for how planning is addressed in your new setting and can apply your experiences from initial teacher training in order to begin to develop a curriculum overview.

> 💡 *Top Tip*: Take a large piece of paper and mind-map your curriculum. Use the opportunity to note key ideas and themes, but also to identify areas where cross-curricular links can be made. The mind map may also help you to better understand your own subject knowledge development needs to aid your research and preparation.

3. Reflect on your training and organise useful resources, activities and curriculum ideas into an induction support pack, on which you can draw at a later stage. It is useful to create a repertoire of ad-hoc activities and resources that may come in useful when wishing to expand on topics or promote independent learning and discovery, or for those times when you need a quick activity. You can add to this useful resource, over time.

> 💡 *Top Tip*: Teachers often accumulate a great deal of paper: worksheets, plans, resources, etc. Begin your career by organising the ideas you have already collected into a practical, user-friendly folder. Sections may be by subject, theme or simply alphabetical, but as the repertoire of ideas increases, so too will your bank of ideas. This activity may involve pulling apart folders from your training period and re-organising them so that the ideas are accessible and ready to hand. A little time spent on this organisation early on could pay dividends later.

Expectations for NQT induction and key staging posts

We will now examine the various stages an NQT can reasonably expect to engage with during their induction period. First, it is important to note that we use the term 'induction period' rather than 'NQT year'. The justification for this is that, for some, the induction period may extend beyond an academic year, such as with part-time teaching posts. It is also recognition of the fact that some NQTs do not begin their induction period at the start of an academic year, depending on when they are appointed.

How will my induction be organised and by whom?

As stated by the DfE (2014d), the Teachers' Standards will be used to assess an NQT's performance at the end of their induction period. The decision about whether an NQT's performance against the relevant standards is satisfactory on completion of induction should take into account the NQT's work context and must be made on the basis of what can be reasonably expected of an NQT by the end of their induction period within the framework set out by the standards. Judgements should reflect the expectation that NQTs have effectively consolidated their initial teacher training (ITT) and demonstrated their ability to meet the relevant standards consistently over a sustained period in their practice (p. 8). During the induction period, NQTs will be expected to evidence how they are meeting the Teachers' Standards in relation to their professional practice and the 'appropriate body' (DfE, 2014d) will be the quality assurers, overseeing the institution in which induction takes place.

It is important to remember that NQT induction is a partnership between the NQT, the institution and the appropriate body and that each has clearly defined roles and responsibilities, as outlined in the aforementioned guidance. Some important facts to note from the DfE (2014d) guidelines are as follows:

- An NQT can only complete one statutory induction period. If an NQT fails induction, they may not repeat the process.
- Employers are required to conduct pre-employment check to ascertain whether or not an NQT holds 'QTS' and is therefore eligible to commence induction.
- NQTs are entitled to a reduced timetable in order to complete their induction period.
- It is the responsibility of the Head Teacher to notify the 'appropriate body' prior to an NQT commencing post.
- The NQT induction period is determined by the 'appropriate body' and usually equates to the equivalent of one academic year.
- A personalised monitoring and support plan should be put in place by the institution in which the induction period is taking place. An induction tutor will be appointed by the Head Teacher in order to support this process and this may include:

    i.   Support and guidance from a designated induction tutor who holds QTS and has the time and experience to carry out the role effectively;

    ii. Observation of the NQT's teaching and follow-up discussion;

    iii. Regular professional reviews of progress;

    iv. NQT's observation of experienced teachers, either in the NQT's own institution or in another institution where effective practice has been identified. (DfE, 2014d, p. 17)

- NQTs are required to keep evidence of practice to support their development against the Teachers' Standards.
- Formal assessment 'staging posts' are agreed between the setting and the NQT. Usually, these occur once per term, or equivalent. Formal assessment reports are submitted to the 'appropriate body' and copies provided to the NQT for comments and signature. The process is considered to be 'transparent'.
- Upon successful completion of induction period, the institution notifies the appropriate body of their recommendation, who in turn notify the National College for Teaching and Leadership (NCTL). If the NQT has successfully passed the induction period, they may teach without restrictions.
- Close monitoring of the NQT during induction by the induction tutor. Where difficulties arise, there are clear roles, responsibilities and procedures involved. Please consult the guidelines for further details.

The importance of evidence-based development

Meeting the Teachers' Standards and completing a successful induction period is all about providing the evidence to support your claims. We recommend that you keep a 'reflective portfolio' during your induction period. Segmented into the Teachers' Standards and sub-sets, this useful resource can build into an evidence-based reflection of your teaching journey. There are many ways in which you could approach this, but, whether hard-copy or electronically constructed, the portfolio should be a collection of critical reflections and evidence to show that you are effectively meeting the Teachers' Standards. Ideally, this should build on any reflective documentation used as evidence during your period of training, as this will show development, over time. Refer to the practice examples at the end of this chapter to see instances of this. A reflective portfolio of evidence can be used in progress meetings with your induction tutor and can include a range of items, such as assessments, planning examples, etc. in order to add weight to your critical reflections against the Teachers' Standards.

    Critical reflection, as discussed in previous chapters, is an essential part of professional practice. As Beere (2014) suggests: 'Evaluate your everyday practice in a non-judgemental way by asking: "What did I learn from that?" and "What amendments can I make to get a better result?"' (p. 23). Through engagement with reflective processes, you enhance your own practice and can use this to impact positively on the pupils in your care.

In addition to engaging with reflective practice, it is essential to combine this with professional discourse with colleagues, particularly after observations and to link back to educational theory. In essence, this is professional 'synthesis' for improvement and as Loughran (2010) reminds us: 'Synthesising is an important method of bringing the pieces of a topic together and joining them in learning so that each of the elements interacts in such a way as to build on one another. In doing so, richer understandings of the particular content can be developed' (p. 125).

From NQT to RQT: What kind of a teacher do you want to be?

Once you have successfully completed your NQT induction, this is a time for reflection, consolidation and continuation of professional development. Your professional identity as a teacher will have started to develop and it is important that you continue to develop, in order to be the best you can be. The next steps you take will depend on the route you would like to explore. This may be subject leadership, management, higher education or training to further specialise in a specific area, such as special educational needs and disability. Further details of opportunities for teachers can be found here (correct at time of press): https://getintoteaching.education.gov.uk/why-teach/your-future-is-in-your-hands. Whichever route you choose to explore, you will be subject to regular monitoring by the senior leadership team in your setting, as will all teachers, as part of the appraisal and performance management policies of the setting.

Performance monitoring, appraisals and threshold assessments

Teacher monitoring cycles vary dependent on the setting and staffing structure. Most settings engage teachers in a range of professional development opportunities, such as peer learning through observation and discussion or senior leadership 'learning walks'. It is usual for discussions to take place post-observation and for strengths and areas for development to be identified as part of a discussion. The outcomes of these discussions are monitored at a later stage and often used alongside other attainment targets, as a performance management measure. Performance management or appraisal procedures vary from setting to setting but usually consist of some or all of the following, as an example:

- A meeting at the start of the academic year to review the previous year's achievements and targets and set new targets;
- Formal and informal observations of teaching;
- Informal learning walks, to include a scrutiny of pupil work and conversations with pupils;
- A mid-point meeting;

- Pupil progress meetings with the senior leadership team;
- A meeting at the end of the academic year to review targets and achievements.

The teaching profession is now subject to performance-related pay, which means that pay progression is specifically linked to a teacher's performance. There are several factors that will be taken into consideration, such as impact on pupil progress and wider contributions to school improvements. It is important to become familiar with the guidelines published for schools and further details can be found here (correct at time of press): www.gov.uk/government/news/new-advice-to-help-schools-set-performance-related-pay

Teachers who wish to progress further may choose to apply for 'threshold assessments'. This usually occurs when a teacher has reached the top of the main pay spine and wishes to progress onto the upper-pay spine, or has been identified by a performance manager as eligible for upper-pay spine fast-tracking. Applicants are expected to demonstrate that they are highly competent in meeting the Teachers' Standards and do so through the setting's appraisal cycle, against the criteria for success. Again, this is very much evidence-based and decided in consultation with a teacher's performance manager and senior leadership team. Further details of threshold assessments can be found here (correct at time of press): www.gov.uk/teachers-upper-pay-range-how-to-apply

---

Q *Top Tip*: Get a piece of paper or electronic device and record all of the things you think make a great teacher. Now, take each item in turn and relate these to your own professional practice. Place them under three separate headings: 'I do this'; 'I have started to think about this'; 'I need to do this'. Now, identify the ways in which you could build on those things you do or have started to think about and how you could engage with those things you need to do. Use this as the basis for discussion with your induction tutor or a colleague and identify the next steps in your professional practice.

Enrichment and extension: being the best you can be

As a teacher, it is important to continue to develop and strive for better practice. Many of the experiences you will encounter during your induction period will enrich your professional practice and development as an effective teacher. Enrichment and extension activities are one way in which teachers can monitor their development and ensure that they are engaging in activities that encourage deep thinking and consequently, learning and development. In order to frame this process, we refer now to an example of a model from practice, developed by Alexander (2016). The example in Figure 10.1 incorporates the 'cognitive skills' of Bloom et al. (1956) and embraces the earlier example of good classroom practice shared in Figure 4.2, as a tool for teachers enriching and extending their professional practice, against the Teachers' Standards.

Development of higher order skills: use these as an indicator of your professional development and progress

Cognitive Skills (Bloom et al. 1956) / Teachers' Standards (DfE, 2014)	Enrichment and Extension Activities for Teachers						
	This enrichment and extension grid is a supportive mechanism to encourage you to develop and extend your professional practice and critical reflection skills.						
	Knowing	Understanding	Applying	Analysing	Creating	Evaluating	Your own idea — Please indicate cognitive skills:
1. Set high expectations which inspire, motivate and challenge pupils	'Show how you know.' Record what strategies you employ to find out about your pupils' strengths, needs and individualism	How do other teachers engage with pupil challenge? Reflect upon two examples from your professional observations of practice to show your understanding	Describe three interventions you have applied that have motivated and inspired pupils to learn and have provided additional challenge	Reflect upon a time when you inspired pupils. How did it impact on pupil engagement, progress and future practice?	Create a new and innovative way to motivate pupils to learn. Align this with the policies of your current setting	Evaluate the effectiveness of the challenges you set with your pupils. What is working well and what changes will you make, in light of the 'pupil voice'?	
2. Promote good progress and outcomes by pupils	Record 3 ways in which you know your pupils have made progress	Write a paragraph for another trainee that defines pupil progress	Apply your strategies for promoting pupil progress with a different group of pupils e.g. out of phase, or different class	Write a detailed progress report for parents/carers on the progress of a pupil in your class	Create a pupil progress display in your classroom, involving the pupils	Reflect upon a pupil who did not make expected progress. Evaluate why this may have occurred and work on next steps with the pupil	

3. Demonstrate good subject and curriculum knowledge	Identify an area in each curriculum subject about which you would like to know more and identify how you intend to achieve this	Identify common pupil misconceptions in a curriculum area of your choice and how you will address these in your lessons	Apply a new learning and teaching initiative in your specialist subject	Critically analyse a journal article or academic text relating to a subject of your choice	Design a brief overview for a medium term plan in a subject of your choice	Evaluate the success of a series of lessons in a curriculum area of your choice and indicate the impact upon pupil progress
4. Plan and teach well structured lessons	'Show how you know.' Reflect upon a lesson of your choice. How do you know that pupils have understood?	Identify an area in which your understanding has developed through engagement with theory and professional practice	'Try and apply': 3 new teaching strategies you have observed or read about and review their effectiveness	Engage in a critical analysis of two learning theories in relation to your own professional practice	Demonstrate how you have designed and provided an engaging curriculum for the pupils you teach	Critically evaluate the effectiveness of a lesson plan format you have to plan. Develop your own planning pro-forma based upon this evaluation
5. Adapt teaching to respond to the strengths and needs of all pupils	Write 3 strategies that you know work that others can apply in their daily practice	Write 3 ways in which you identify and act upon pupil strengths	Plan and teach an intervention that builds on pupil strengths in a subject of your choice	Identify strategies for assessment in your lessons and critically reflect on how and why you used these	Create an 'I am brilliant at...' display with your pupils	Critically evaluate your adaptation strategies. Create an evidence-based list of helpful teacher strategies
6. Make accurate and productive use of assessment	'Show how you know.' What learning and teaching strategies work well for your pupils?	How many different types of assessment do you use and what are they used for?	Apply an assessment technique that you haven't yet tried. Reflect on the impact on your own practice and pupil progress	Observe a colleague teaching. Analyse the assessment strategies used and how this will impact on your own practice and pupil progress	Develop your own assessment technique and try it out with your class. Reflect on the effectiveness of this technique	Critically evaluate the success of an assessment that you have planned

(Continued)

Figure 10.1 (Continued)

7. Manage behaviour effectively to ensure a good and safe learning environment	Write a paragraph to summarize how you manage behaviour and encourage a safe learning environment in your setting. Identify how this aligns with the policies of the setting	Write a list of top 10 'safe and effective' learning environment must-haves	Apply a new and original behaviour management strategy or system that you have developed	Reflect on a time when a behaviour strategy didn't work as well as you would have liked. Analyse why this may have been and devise clear next steps	Create a new and exciting behaviour tool to use in your setting, e.g. game, reward system etc.	Reflect upon a challenging behaviour exhibited by a pupil. Critically evaluate the effectiveness of the strategies used to address this and promote learning
8. Fulfil wider professional responsibilities	Find out about safeguarding in your setting	What is your understanding of values? How does this relate to your developing practice?	Identify and apply ways in which you can demonstrate your professionalism in the wider context, including the highest standards of ethics and behaviour	Explore research regarding professional identity. Analyse what elements support your professional development in this area	Create your own extra curricular programme with which pupils can engage e.g. after school club, additional opportunity etc.	Think of a colleague you admire for their professional conduct, values and commitment to learning and teaching. Identify and critically evaluate those aspects you feel contribute to their success
Preparation for transition, induction and continuing professional development	Find out about NQT induction in your setting	Reflect upon your understanding of continuing professional development and how you will plan for this in your career	'Try and apply': Plan, apply and review 3 ways in which you will prepare for your first term as a teacher, as a pilot for your induction period	Analyse your areas for development throughout your training and devise an action plan for the period of transition between training and your first post	Create an NQT reflective professional journal in readiness for induction	Critically evaluate your main successes during teacher training. Create a list of practice you will build on during NQT induction, based upon your critical evaluation

Figure 10.1   Enrichment and extension grid

The rationale for the grid is to provide teachers with a set of professional practice enhancement activities which link to the hierarchical structure of the cognitive skills presented by Bloom et al. (1956) and amalgamate them with the Teachers' Standards. There are many ways in which the grid can be used, but it is intended as a tool to enrich, extend and develop professional practice and critical thinking skills. Teachers are encouraged to choose activities with which to engage from the grid and record evidence of the activity by reflecting critically. Teachers may opt to select one activity from each of the 'cognitive areas' or engage with all, over time. The grid can be used to enhance an NQT's reflective portfolio and to contribute to evidence against the Teachers' Standards.

Consider ways in which you could use the grid in order to support your own professional development. Select activities that allow you to progress along the hierarchy of cognitive skills (Bloom et al., 1956) in order to enrich your practice. Use the activities as a springboard for critical reflection. Once you have engaged with the enrichment and extension activities and reflected critically, use these experiences to contribute to discussions with your mentor or colleagues.

The value of research-informed, critically reflective practice from the outset: continuing professional development (CPD)

As stated in previous chapters, research-informed teaching is practice that is grounded in theory and is evidence of a reflective practitioner. Critically reflective practice aims to synthesise theory with critically reflective evidence-based practice and to use this as a tool for improved practice. As Ghaye and Ghaye (1998) summarise:

> Teaching is value-laden practice. Values help teachers to make decisions on how to proceed. Evidence helps teachers make wise and principled decisions. Confident and competent teaching requires teachers to reflect systematically and rigorously on evidence derived from practice. Reflective teaching and learning then is evidence-based. (p. 9)

Throughout this book, we have considered many ways in which evidence can be used as a tool to support teacher development through active reflection. Early in this chapter, we referred to teachers having a life-long learning ethos. Of course, as

Nottingham (2013) states: 'Lifelong learning depends on learning how to learn and being willing to learn' (p. 57). This 'willingness', we would argue, is a prerequisite to becoming an effective teacher. Teaching is a time-consuming profession, however, it is important that time is set aside for developing practice by engaging in professional development activities. Often called 'continuing professional development' (CPD), there are many opportunities available to teachers. These can range from professional externally hosted courses, internal service training (INSET) and postgraduate academic qualifications, to engagement with research and wider reading. Schools recognise the importance of research-informed teaching and in particular, the sharing of excellent practice. Seize these opportunities and critically reflect on their value and the impact they have on your teaching and pupil learning. What they should not be influenced by, however, as described by Richmond and Greenfield (2015), is the 'Bandwagon Effect': a phenomenon that results in an upsurge of training initiatives following any change in government thinking or political imperative in education (p. 64). Unfortunately, these agendas often dictate the availability of professional opportunities for teachers and as a result, it can be easy to lose sight of personal developmental needs. Whilst these opportunities may have a place in your training and development, use critical reflection as your tool towards self-efficacy.

Using research-informed teaching and professional development opportunities as conduits through which you can learn and develop as an individual is an essential milestone in your professional journey. Biggs (2003) suggests that: 'Wise and effective teaching is not, however, simply a matter of applying general principles of teaching according to rule; those principles need adapting to your own personal strengths and to your teaching context' (p. 6).

Teaching (and learning), we would argue, is contextual and your ability to build on your existing knowledge, understanding, skills and developing values and adapt to apply them to varying contexts, is an integral skill of the effective teacher. It is not, however, a simple case of engaging with the work of others in developing practice, but of developing a grounded understanding of the context in which the work sits, rooted in rigorous examination of supporting theories and personal, critical reflection. Wilson (2009: 23) suggests: 'When we read experts' work, we ought to be aware of the theoretical perspectives informing their viewpoint and appreciate the methods used to collect the evidence, interpret findings and draw conclusions.'

In short, the professional development activities with which teachers must engage themselves, have value to the individual and in turn, to the setting, colleagues and pupils with whom the individual engages. Research-informed, critically reflective practice is all about impact. As an NQT, think beyond your own developmental needs and apply your thinking to the context in which you are working (and learning). The impact and therefore, the benefits will be greater.

Final thoughts

During your NQT induction period, keep the following at the forefront of your mind:

Preparation: it is your responsibility to be prepared and to explore ways in which you can evolve as a developing professional. Use pre-NQT induction time carefully and ensure that you are well prepared for your induction.

Support: be aware of the support mechanisms around you and make the choice to utilise them. Engage in constructive dialogue with colleagues and take a critically reflective attitude to professional development.

Accountability: pupil progress and well-being are your responsibility, from the out-set. Take this responsibility seriously and ensure that you remain impact-focused throughout your induction period and beyond.

Life-long learning: having a commitment to professional development, through engagement with professional and theoretical processes, is an integral part of the erudite teacher. Make time to engage with and then reflect critically on learning experiences, in order to develop further and be the best you can be.

 Practice examples

HOPE

Hope is a trainee who has just secured her first teaching post. Although she has yet to gain her teaching qualification, she is beginning to use her experiences on her final school placement in order to help her prepare for her new teaching post, which is due to commence at the start of the academic year. Hope has created a 'reflective portfolio' which she is choosing to keep electronically, on a tablet. In order to mark the successes and areas for development against the Teachers' Standards, Hope has split the e-portfolio into the following sections:

- An introduction and rationale for the e-portfolio;
- Strengths and areas for development identified at the end of her training;
- An action plan in order to meet set targets;

(Continued)

(Continued)

- Nine sections of Teachers' Standards and sub-sets, including Part Two of the Teachers' Standards. Each section allows e-comments from her induction tutor or links (electronically recorded notes, scans, photos, audio recordings, etc.) to comments from others, such as parents/carers and pupils, in order to support the evidence;
- Additional information.

Hope plans to store evidence in a range of formats, from photographs of pupil work, pupil engagement, audio and video recordings, to links to other electronic documentation, such as planning. She plans to share the e-portfolio with her induction mentor. If successful, Hope intends to continue to use the e-portfolio throughout her practice in order to capture 'snapshots' of her developing progress, as evidence for performance management and appraisal.

JACKSON

Jackson was unable to secure a teaching post for the start of the academic year. In order to consolidate his good practice and remain committed to the teaching profession, Jackson engaged in supply teaching via an agency and ad hoc voluntary support in his local school. As a foundation stage practitioner, Jackson was keen to build on his existing skills and used each opportunity to engage in reflective practice in order to develop further. When he finally secured an interview, he discussed this evidence with the interview panel and displayed a commitment to teaching. Jackson secured a teaching post in a Reception class and felt confident that his excellent training, combined with his additional experiences in working with children in the foundation stage, had provided him with a good grounding for his induction period.

 In relation to Teachers' Standards and transitional practice, consider the following key questions:

- How do you intend to stay current with regard to subject knowledge after your training?
- In what ways can you ensure that you collect evidence in order to demonstrate that you are meeting the Teachers' Standards?

(Continued)

(Continued)

- How will you develop ways to embed theory with professional practice as an NQT?
- How will you identify your developmental needs and communicate these to your induction mentor?
- What career aspirations do you have and how can you facilitate these?
- How can your professional development impact on others?
- In what ways will you prepare for your induction period and engage with support?
- What is your strategy for becoming a life-long learner?

Chapter summary: There isn't an 'I' in NQT

The journey from trainee to teacher is one which should be embraced as an essential part of your professional development. Draw on the experience of colleagues with whom you have come into contact and reflect on your training and school experience. Identify ways in which you can build on your developing practice and feel proud of your significant achievements. Enter your induction period with confidence, commitment and positivity, yet remain humble and self-reflective. Learn from others and resist the temptation to be quick to judge – experience can teach many things. Engage in professional development activities and seek to build on your existing knowledge and skills. Think carefully. 'Make no mistake: the way you think makes you the teacher that you are' (Beere, 2014, p. 7). Ask questions and listen to others, but stay true to your values and develop your own teacher identity. Be inspirational and let this inspiration have an impact: 'What is it that inspirational teachers do? In short, they plan for their pupils to be inspirational' (Ryan, 2011, p. 5). Gilbert (2014: 231) poses the question: 'Why do I need a teacher when I've got Google?' and summarises the answer as follows: 'Poor teachers do damage as they fail in the job they are being paid to do. But the good ones, they change everything. What's more, the future of the world depends on them. That's why I need a teacher when I've got Google' (p. 231).

In summary, as you engage in the transition from trainee to teacher and beyond, remember that learning and teaching create a 'domino effect': your learning impacts on your teaching; your teaching impacts on the learning and progress of the pupils with whom you engage and once again, on your own learning. As a learner and a teacher, you should strive to promote the best outcomes for all. We would argue, therefore, that there are lots of 'Is' in NQT: it is all about identifying, investigating, investing, inspiring and perhaps most importantly, having an impact.

REFERENCES

Adams, K. (2011) 'Managing behaviour for learning', in A. Hansen (ed.) *Primary Professional Studies*. Exeter: Learning Matters.

Alexander, G.N. (2011) *Miss, who is going to make us sing? A singing evolution*. Sarbukken: Lambert Academic Publishing.

Anderson, L.W. and Krathwohl, D. (eds) (2001) *A Taxonomy for Learning, Teaching, and Assessing: A revision of Bloom's taxonomy of educational objectives*. New York: Longman.

Assessment Reform Group (ARG) (2002) *Assessment for Learning: 10 principles*. Available at: www.aaia.org.uk/content/uploads/2010/06/Assessment-for-Learning-10-principles.pdf [accessed 27 August 2015].

Association for Teachers and Lecturers (ATL) (2013) *Ready, Steady, Teach! Our guide for new teachers*. London: ATL. Available at: www.atl.org.uk/Images/atl-ready-steady-teach-jan-2015.pdf [accessed 27 August 2015].

Baker, C. (2006) *Foundations of Bilingual Education and Bilingualism*. Clevedon, OH: Multilingual Matters.

Barton, G. (2015) *The Essentials of Teaching: What you need to know to be a great teacher*. London: Routledge.

Beadle, P. (2010) *How to Teach*. Carmarthen: Crown House Publishing.

Beard, R. (2011) *Outstanding Lessons Made Simple*. Available at: www.outstanding-lessons-made-simple.co.uk/hinge-point-questions [accessed 18 May 2015].

Beere, J. (2012) *The Perfect Ofsted Lesson*. Carmarthen: Crown House Publishing.

Beere, J. (2014) *The Practically Perfect Teacher*. Carmarthen: Independent Thinking Press.

Bennett, W.J. (1996) *The Book of Virtues*. London: Simon & Schuster.

Bentley-Davies, C. (2010) *How to be an Amazing Teacher*. Carmarthen: Crown House Publishing.

Biggs, J. (2003) *Teaching for Quality Learning at University*. Maidenhead: Open University Press.

Black, P., Harrison, C., Lee, C., Marshall, B. and Wiliam, D. (2003) *Assessment for Learning: Putting it into practice*. Maidenhead: Open University Press.

Black, P. and Wiliam, D. (1998) *Inside the Black Box: Raising standards through classroom assessment*. London: GL Assessment.

Blandford, S. (2013) 'Developing a global system of teacher education for a global economy: Is there a role for a Royal College ?' *Education Today,* 63(1): 18–23.

Blatchford, P., Russell, A. and Webster, R. (2012) *Reassessing the Impact of Teaching Assistants*. Abingdon: Routledge.

Bloom, B.S., Engelhart, M.D., Furst, E.J., Hill, W.H. and Krathwohl, D.R. (1956) *Taxonomy of Educational Objectives: The classification of educational goals. Handbook I: Cognitive domain*. New York: David McKay.

Brandom, A.-M., Carmichael, P. and Marshall, B. (2005) 'Learning about assessment for learning: A framework for discourse about classroom practice', *Teacher Development*, 9(2): 201–18.

Briggs, M., Woodfield, A., Martin, C. and Swatton, P. (2009) *Assessment for Learning and Teaching in Primary School*, 2nd edition. Exeter: Learning Matters.

Brighouse, T. (2008) 'Continuous professional development is the key to school success', *Professional Development Today*, 11(2): 52–4.

Brookfield, S.D. (1995) *Becoming a Critically Reflective Teacher*. San Francisco: Jossey-Bass.

Brophy, J. (1981) 'Teacher praise: A functional analysis', *Review of Educational Research*, 51: 5–32.

Buckler, S. and Castle, P. (2014) *Psychology for Teachers*. London: Sage.

Bulman, K. (2006) *BTEC First Children's Care, Learning and Development Student Book: Children's care, learning and development*. London: Heinemann.

Carr, D. (2006) 'Professional and personal values and virtues in education and teaching', *Oxford Review of Education,* 32(2): 171–83.

Carroll, L. (1865 [1982]) *The Complete Illustrated Works of Lewis Carroll*. London: Chancellor Press.

Castle, P. and Buckler, S. (2009) *How to be a Successful Teacher*. London: Sage.

Chandler, C.L. and Connell, J.P. (1987) 'Children's intrinsic, extrinsic and internalized motivation: A developmental study of children's reasons for liked and disliked behaviours', *British Journal of Developmental Psychology*, 5: 357–65.

Chaplain, R. (2003) *Teaching without Disruption in the Primary School: A model for managing pupil behaviour*. London: Routledge.

Clements, D.H. and Sarama, J. (2014) *Learning and Teaching Early Math: The learning trajectories approach*. Abingdon: Routledge.

Cooper, H. (2014) *Professional Studies in Primary Education*, 2nd edition. London: Sage.

Cotton, T. (2010) *Understanding and Teaching Primary Mathematics*. Harlow: Pearson.

Council for Subject Associations (CfSA) (2008) *Physical Education: Supporting gifted and talented children*. Available at: www.learntogether.org.uk/Resources/Documents/Primary subjects_2[1].pdf [accessed 26 June 2015].

Cowley, S. (2014) *Getting the Buggers to Behave*. London: Bloomsbury.

Cremin, T. and Arthur, J. (2014) *Learning to Teach in the Primary School*, 3rd edition. London: Routledge.

Crook, D. (2008) 'Some historical perspectives on professionalism', in B. Cunningham (ed.) *Exploring Professionalism*. London: Bedford Way Papers.

Cullingford, C. (2010) *The Art of Teaching*. Abingdon: Routledge.

Cummins, J. (1980) 'The cross-lingual dimensions of language proficiency: Implications for bilingual education and the optimal age issue', *Tesol Quarterly*, 14(2): 175–87.

Cummins, J. (1984) *Bilingualism and Special Education*. Clevedon, OH: Multilingual Matters.

Cunningham, B. (Ed) (2008) *Exploring Professionalism*. London: Bedford Way Papers.

Dale, E. (1969) *Audiovisual Methods in Teaching*, 3rd edition. New York: Dryden Press/Holt, Rinehart & Winston.

Daniels, H. (ed.) (1993) *Charting the Agenda: Educational activity after Vygotsky*. London: Routledge.

Dave, R.H. (1970) 'Psychomotor levels', in R.J. Armstrong (ed.) *Developing and Writing Behavioral Objectives*. Tucson, AZ: Educational Innovators Press, pp. 20–1.

Davey, R. (2013) *The Professional Identity of Teacher Educators*. Abingdon: Routledge.

Denby, N. (2012) *Training to Teach: A guide for students,* 2nd edition. Thousand Oaks, CA, and London: Sage.

Department for Children, Schools and Families (DCSF) (2008) *2020 Children and Young People's Workforce Strategy*. Nottingham: DCSF. Available at: http://webarchive.nationalarchives.gov.uk/20130401151715/http://www.education.gov.uk/publications/eOrderingDownload/CYP_Workforce-Strategy.pdf [accessed 27 August 2015].

Department for Children, Schools and Families (2009) *Improving Primary Behaviour*. London: Crown.

Department for Education (2011) *Getting the Simple Things Right: Charlie Taylor's behaviour checklists*. London: Crown.

Department for Education (2013a) *Teachers' Standards*. London: Crown.

Department for Education (2013b) *National Curriculum in England: Primary Curriculum*. London: Crown.

Department for Education (2014a) *Reforming Assessment and Accountability for Primary Schools*. London: Crown.

Department for Education (2014b) *Behaviour and Discipline in Schools: Advice for headteachers and school staff*. London: Crown.

Department for Education (2014c) *Statutory Framework for the Early Years Foundation Stage: Setting the standards for learning, development and care for children from birth to five*. London: Crown.

Department for Education (2014d) *Induction for Newly Qualified Teachers (NQTs)*. Available at: www.gov.uk/government/publications/induction-for-newly-qualified-teachers-nqts [accessed 26 June 2015].

Department for Education (2014e) *School Teachers' Pay and Conditions 2014*; and *Guidance on School Teachers' Pay and Conditions*. London: Crown.

Department for Education (2014f) *Teachers' Standards: How should they be used?* Available at: www.gov.uk/government/publications/teachers-standards [accessed 14 June 2015].

Department for Education (2014g) *Keeping Children Safe in Education: Statutory guidance for schools and colleges*. London: Crown.

Department for Education (2014h) *Promoting Fundamental British Values as Part of SMSC in Schools: Departmental advice for maintained schools*. London: Crown.

Department for Education (2014i) *Schools: Statutory guidance for schools and local authorities*. London: Crown.

Department for Education and Employment (1999) *The National Curriculum Handbook for Primary Teachers in England*. London: Crown Copyright.

Department for Education and Skills (2002) *Time for Standards: Reforming the school workforce*. Available at: www.education.gov.uk/consultations/downloadableDocs/200_5.pdf [accessed 4 August 2014].

Department for Education and Skills (2006) *Learning Behaviour Principles and Practice: What works in schools*. The Steer Report. London: Crown.

Dix, P. (2010) *Taking Care of Behaviour*, 2nd edition. London: Pearson.

Douglas Brown, H. (1980) 'The optimal distance model of second language acquisition', *Tesol Quarterly*, 14(2): 157–64.

Dweck, C. (2012) *Mindset*. London: Robinson.

Dweck, C.S. (2013) *Self-Theories: Their role in motivation, personality and development*. Hove: Psychology Press.

Ekins, A. (2012) *The Changing Face of Special Educational Needs: Impact and implications for SENCOs and their schools*. Abingdon: Routledge.

Elliott, A. and Dweck, C. (2005) *Handbook of Competence and Motivation*. London: Guildford Press.

Emeny, W. (2012) *100 Things Awesome Teachers Do!* Charleston, SC: CreateSpace Independent Publishing Platform.

Eraut, M. (1994) *Developing Professional Knowledge and Competence*. London: Falmer Press.

Etzioni, A. (1969) *The Semi-Professions and their Organization: Teachers, nurses, social workers*. New York: Free Press.

Evangelou, M., Sylva, K., Kyriacou, M., Wild, M. and Glenny, G. (2009) *Early Years Learning and Development Literature Review*. Available at: www.foundationyears.org.uk/files/2012/08/DCSF-RR1761.pdf [accessed 26 June 2015].

Evans, L. (2011) 'The "shape" of teacher professionalism in England: Professional standards, performance management, professional development and the changes proposed in the 2010 White Paper', *British Educational Research Journal*, 37(5): 851–70.

Ewans, T. (2014) *Reflective Primary Teaching*. Northwich: Critical Publishing.

Forehand, M. (2012) in M. Orey (2012) *Emerging Perspectives on Learning, Teaching and Technology*. Createspace: Independent Publishing Platform.

Frederickson, N. and Cline, T. (2009) *Special Educational Needs, Inclusion and Diversity*. Maidenhead: Open University Press.

Ghaye, A. and Ghaye, K. (1998) *Teaching and Learning through Critical Reflective Practice*. London: David Fulton.

Ghaye, T. (2011) *Teaching and Learning through Reflective Practice: A practical guide for positive action*. Abingdon: Routledge.

Gibbs, G. (1988) *Learning by Doing: A guide to teaching and learning methods*. Oxford: Further Education Unit, Oxford Brookes University.

Gilbert, I. (2007) *The Little Book of Thunks: 260 questions to make your brain go ouch!* Carmarthen: Crown House Publishing.

Gilbert, I. (2014) *Why do I Need a Teacher when I've Got Google?* Abingdon: Routledge.

Glazzard, J. (2011) 'Including all learners', in A. Hansen (ed.) *Primary Professional Studies*. Exeter: Learning Matters.

Glazzard, J. and Stokoe, J. (2011) *Achieving Outstanding on your Teaching Placement: Early Years and Primary School-based Training*. London: Sage.

Glazzard, J. and Stokoe, J. (2013) *Teaching Systematic Synthetic Phonics and Early English*. Northwich: Critical Publishing.

Gov.UK (2015) www.gov.uk/government/groups/commission-on-assessment-without-levels

Haigh, G. (2001) 'Read this carefully: Dyslexia can make you a better teacher', *Times Educational Supplement*, 12 January. Available at: www.tes.com/article.aspx?storycode=342463 [accessed 31 October 2015].

Hammersley-Fletcher, L. (2008) 'The impact of workforce remodelling on change management and working practices in English primary schools', *School Leadership and Management*, 28(5): 489–503.

Hansen, A. (2011) *Primary Professional Studies*. Exeter: Learning Matters.

Hansen, A. (2012) *Reflective Learning and Teaching in Primary Schools*. London: Sage.

Harlen, W. and James, M. (1997) 'Assessment and learning: Differences and relationships between formative and summative assessment', *Assessment in Education: Principles, Policy & Practice*, 4(3): 365–79.

Harris, K. and Lowe, S. (2014) 'Monitoring, assessment and record keeping', in H. Cooper (ed.) *Professional Studies in Primary Education*, 2nd edition. London: Sage.

Harrow, A. (1972) *A Taxonomy of Psychomotor Domain: A guide for developing behavioral objectives*. New York: David McKay.

Haslam, L., Wilkin, Y. and Kellet, E. (2005) *English as an Additional Language: Meeting the challenge in the classroom*. London: David Fulton.

Hayamizu, T. (1997) 'Between intrinsic and extrinsic motivation: Examination of reasons for academic study based on the theory of internalization', *Japanese Psychological Research*, 39: 98–108.

Hayes, D. (2009) *Learning and Teaching in Primary Schools*. Exeter: Learning Matters.

Herbert, S. (2011) *The Inclusion Toolkit*. London: Sage.

Jackson, A. (2013) *Teaching as a Master Profession*. Available at: www.cumbria.ac.uk/Courses/SubjectAreas/Education/Research/TEAN/TeacherEducatorsStorehouse/MastersRouteTeacherProfessionalism/Home.aspx [accessed 1 June 2015].

Jacques, K. and Hyland, R. (2007) *Professional Studies: Primary and Early Years*. Exeter: Learning Matters.

Jacques, K. and Hyland, R. (2010) *Professional Studies: Primary and Early Years*, 3rd edition. Exeter: Learning Matters.

James, G. (2013) 'Learning and behaviour management: Two sides of the same coin?', *The Guardian*, 2 April. Available at: www.theguardian.com/teacher-network/2013/apr/02/learning-behaviour-management-joined-up-schools [accessed 25 August 2015].

James, M., et al. (2007) *Improving Learning How to Learn*. London: Routledge.

Jordan, A., Carlile, O. and Stack, A. (2008) *Approaches to Learning: A guide for teachers*. Maidenhead: Open University Press.

Kagan, M., Robertson, L. and Kagan, S. (1995) *Cooperative Learning Structures for Classbuilding*. San Clemente, CA: Kagan Publishing.

Keeling, D. (2009) *Rocket Up Your Class! 101 high impact activities to start, break and end lessons*. Carmarthen: Crown House Publishing.

King, P.M. and Kitchener, K.S. (1994) *Developing Reflective Judgment: Understanding and promoting intellectual growth and critical thinking in adolescents and adults*. San Francisco: Jossey-Bass.

Kipling, R. (1902) *Just So Stories for Little Children*. London: Macmillan.

Kolb, D.A. (1984) *Experiential Learning: Experience as the source of learning and development*. Englewood Cliffs, NJ: Prentice-Hall.

Krathwohl, D. (2002) 'A revision of Bloom's Taxonomy: an overview', *Theory into Practice*, 41(4): 212–54. Available at: www.unco.edu/cetl/sir/stating_outcome/documents/Krathwohl.pdf [accessed 18 May 2015].

Le Métais (2004) in J. Arthur and T. Cremin (2010) *Learning to Teach in the Primary School*, 2nd edition. London: Routledge.

Loughran, J. (2010) *What Expert Teachers Do*. Abingdon: Routledge.

McMahon, M., Forde, C. and Martin, M. (2011) *Contemporary Issues in Learning and Teaching*. London: Sage.

McVittie, E. (2012) 'Children as reflective learners', in A. Hansen (ed.) *Reflective Learning and Teaching in Primary Schools*. London: Sage.

Menter, I. (2010) *Teachers: Formation, training and identity – A literature review*. Newcastle upon Tyne: Creativity, Culture and Education.

Milkova, S. (2014) 'Strategies for effective lesson planning', Center for Research and Learning (CRLT), University of Michigan. Available at: www.crlt.umich.edu/gsis/p2_5 [accessed 24 June 2015].

Miller, B. (2010) *Brookfield's Four Lenses: Becoming a critically reflective teacher.* Faculty of Arts Teaching and Learning Committee, University of Sydney. Available at: http://sydney.edu.au/arts/teaching_learning/academic_support/Brookfield_summary.pdf [accessed 24 June 2015].

Millerson, G. (1964) *The Qualifying Associations.* London: Routledge & Kegan Paul Ltd.

Moon, J. (2004) *A Handbook of Reflective and Experiential Learning: Theory and practice.* London: Routledge Falmer.

Morgan, N. (2015) *New Reforms to Raise Standards and Improve Behaviour.* Press release, 16 June. Available at: www.gov.uk/government/news/new-reforms-to-raise-standards-and-improve-behaviour [accessed 3 July 2015].

Moseley, D., Baumfield, V., Elliott, J., Higgins, S., Miller, J., Newton, D.P. and Gregson, M. (2005) *Frameworks for Thinking: A handbook for teaching and learning.* Cambridge: Cambridge University Press.

Mosley, J. (1996) *Quality Circle Time in the Primary Classroom: Your essential guide to enhancing self-esteem, self-discipline and positive relationships.* Whitestone, NY: LDA.

National Association for Language Development in the Curriculum (NALDIC) (2009) in N. Frederickson and T. Cline (eds) *Special Educational Needs, Inclusion and Diversity.* Maidenhead: Open University Press.

National Foundation for Educational Research (NFER) (2007) https://www.nfer.ac.uk [accessed 8 November 2014].

Nottingham, J. (2013) *Encouraging Learning.* Abingdon: Routledge.

O'Brien, T. and Guiney, D. (2001) *Differentiation in Teaching and Learning: Principles and practice.* London: Continuum.

O'Shaughnessy, A. W. E. (1874) 'Ode', in D. J. Elliott (1995) (ed.) *Music Matters – A New Philosophy of Music Education.* Oxford: Oxford University.

Ofsted (2006) *The Logical Chain: Continuing professional development in effective schools.* London: Crown.

Ofsted (2008) *The Deployment, Training and Development of the Wider Workforce.* London: Crown.

Ofsted (2010) *Workforce Reform in Schools: Has it made a difference?* London: Crown.

Ofsted (2011) *How Young Learners Master Maths: Ofsted report on best practice in early arithmetic.* London: Crown.

Ofsted (2012) in J. Glazzard and J. Stokoe, (2013) *Teaching Systematic Synthetic Phonics and Early English.* Northwich: Critical Publishing.

Ofsted (2014) *The Framework for School Inspection.* London: Crown.

Ofsted (2015) *Guidance. Ofsted Inspections: Clarification for schools.* London: Crown.

Prashnig, B. (1998) *The Power of Diversity.* London: Continuum.

Petty, G. (2009) *Teaching Today: A practical guide,* 4th edition. Cheltenham: Nelson Thornes.

Pritchard, A. (2014) *Ways of Learning,* 3rd edition. London: Routledge.

Richmond, K. and Greenfield, R. (2015) *The Primary Teacher's Career Handbook.* Abingdon: Routledge.

Roberts, H. (2012) *Oops! Helping children learn accidentally.* Carmarthen: Crown House Publishing.

Robins, G. (2012) *Praise, Motivation and the Child.* Abingdon: Routledge.

Robinson, C., Bingle, B. and Howard, C. (2013) *Primary School Placements: A critical guide to outstanding teaching.* Northwich: Critical Publishing.

Rogers, B. (2011a) *Behaviour Management: A whole-school approach.* London: Sage.

Rogers, B. (2011b) *Classroom Behaviour,* 3rd edition. London: Sage.

RSA Animate (2010) *Changing Education Paradigms*. Available at: www.youtube.com/watch?v=zDZFcDGpL4U [accessed 26 June 2015].

Rubie-Davies, C. (2015) *Becoming a High Expectation Teacher: Raising the Bar*. London: Routledge.

Ryan, R.M. and Deci, E.L. (2000) 'Intrinsic and extrinsic motivations: Classic definitions and new directions', *Contemporary Educational Psychology*, 25: 54–67.

Ryan, W. (with Gilbert, I., ed.) (2011) *Inspirational Teachers Inspirational Learners: A book of hope for creativity and the curriculum in the twenty-first century*. Carmarthen: Crown House Publishing.

Sachs, J. (2003) *The Activist Teaching Profession*. Buckingham: Open University Press.

Saunders, L. (2013) 'What can be learned about a Royal College of Teaching from the experience of the General Teaching Council for England?', *Education Today*, 63(1): 13–17.

Schön, D.A. (1983) *The Reflective Practitioner: How professionals think in action*. London: Temple Smith.

Smith, J. (2014) *The Lazy Teacher's Handbook: How your students learn more when you teach less*. Bancyfelin: Crown House.

Sotto, E. (1994) *When Teaching Becomes Learning*. London: Cassell.

Standards and Testing Agency (2015) *Interim Teacher Assessment Frameworks at the End of Key Stage*. Crown copyright and Crown information 2015.

Taylor, K. and Woolley, R. (2013) *Values and Vision in Primary Education*. Maidenhead: Open University Press and McGraw-Hill Education.

Training and Development Agency (TDA) (2007) *Role and Context for Teaching Assistant Trainers*. TDA: London. Available at: http://webarchive.nationalarchives.gov.uk [accessed 8 August 2014].

Tucker, K. (2010) *Mathematics through Play in the Early Years*. London: Sage.

United Nations Educational, Scientific and Cultural Organization (UNESCO) (1994) *The UNESCO Salamanca Statement and Framework for Action on Special Needs Education*. Paris: UNESCO.

University of Bristol (2014) *Handbook for Education Professionals: The Bristol guide 2014*. Available at: www.bristol.ac.uk/media-library/sites/education/migrated/documents/bgpreview.pdf [accessed 29 Novemer 2014].

University of Worcester (2015) *Meeting the Teachers' Standards (Autumn Term) 2014–15*. Available at: http://www.worcester.ac.uk/discover-education-partnership-documentation2.html [accessed 24 January 2016].

Walker, M., Jeffes, J., Hart, R., Lord, P. and Kinder, K. (2011) *Making the links between teachers' professional standards, induction, performance management and continuing professional development*. Research Report DFE-RR075. Slough: National Foundation for Educational Research (NFER), Development for Education (DFE).

Watt, N. (2014) 'Labour plans to license teachers in new move to raise standards.' *The Guardian*. [Online] Available at: http://www.theguardian.com/politics/2014/jan/11/labour-license-teachers-raise-standards [accessed 14th February 2014].

Whitehead, M. (2010) *Language and Literacy in the Early Years 0–7*. London: Sage.

Wilkins, R. (2013) 'A road map to teacher professionalisation in the UK', *Education Today*, 63(1): 10–12.

Williams, B. (2008) *Review of Mathematics Teaching in Early Years Settings and Primary Schools*. Interim Report. Available at: www.education.gov.uk/consultations/downloadableDocs/Interim%20Report%20Williams%20Maths%20Review%20vfinal%20(2).doc [accessed 24 June 2015].

Wilson, E. (2009) *School-Based Research: A guide for education students.* London: Sage.

Woolley, R. (2010) *Tackling Controversial Issues in the Primary School: Facing life's challenges with your learners.* London: Routledge.

Useful websites

Assessment Reform Group (ARG) – www.aaia.org.uk/afl/assessment-reform-group

Association for Achievement and Improvement through Assessment (AAIA) – www.aaia.org.uk/

Health and Safety at Work Act 1974 – www.legislation.gov.uk

National Foundation for Educational Research – www.nfer.ac.uk

Beyond Levels: alternative assessment approaches developed by teaching schools – www.psqm.org.uk/docs/beyond-levels-alternative-assessment-approaches-developed-by-teaching-schools.pdf

The Key for School Governors – https://schoolgovernors.thekeysupport.com/sample-articles/promoting-british-values-in-schools

INDEX